ANTIQUITIES

OF

LONG ISLAND

BY GABRIEL FURMAN

TO WHICH IS ADDED

A BIBLIOGRAPHY BY HENRY ONDERDONK, JR.

EDITED BY FRANK MOORE

NEW YORK
J. W. BOUTON, PUBLISHER
1874

John F. Trow & Son,
Printers and Bookbinders,
205-213 *East 12th St.*,
NEW YORK.

INTRODUCTION.

THIS volume contains the notes of Mr. Gabriel Furman, on "Long Island Antiquities and Early History; with the Manners and Customs of its Inhabitants;" "Notes Geographical and Historical, relating to the Town of Brooklyn, in Kings County, on Long Island," by the same laborious and enthusiastic collector, and a Bibliography of Long Island, by Henry Onderdonk, Jr., of Jamaica, New York.

Of the preparation of the Antiquities, with which the volume is opened, Mr. Furman has left no account. The manuscript from which it is printed is fragmentary, and seems to have been put together at odd times during the period embraced within the years 1824 and 1838. It was discovered by the editor, among the gatherings of a quaint and popular dealer in old books, pictures and *bric-à-brac* on University Place, in this city, and was thought valuable enough to merit multiplication. A few errors of date, but none of judgment, have been corrected, and some obscurities made plain. Otherwise the work is given as it was left by its industrious author.

The notes relating to the Town of Brooklyn, by the same author, which necessarily contain some slight repetitions of material found in the Antiquities, are republished from the edition issued in 1824. The extreme scarcity of this little volume causes its reproduction here.

The Bibliography of Mr. Onderdonk, to whom I am indebted for permission to publish, is printed from a manuscript, prepared by that historical scholar and gentleman in 1866, and presented to the New York Historical Society.

FRANK MOORE.

NEW YORK, *October*, 1874.

CONTENTS.

LONG ISLAND ANTIQUITIES.

Although Indian history in our day seems to have lost many of its charms, by reason of the numerous other more highly interesting subjects which the advance of science and the recent increase of knowledge have presented to our minds, we cannot, in treating of the antiquities and early history of this Island, avoid giving some account of the aboriginal tribes which formerly lived upon it, intimately connected as they were with that period in the history of our own race. We shall, however, as far as possible, avoid giving mere dry historical details, which at the same time afford but little information in the case of an uncivilized people, and fatigue the mind of the reader. And, also, so far as we can do it, we will endeavor to strike out a somewhat new path, by giving sketches of their history, and points of their general character, which seem to promise a more accurate idea of them as a race, in preference to following in the usual beaten track.

1*

Governor De Witt Clinton, who devoted much time to the aboriginal history of this continent, and especially of the State of New York, in his anniversary discourse delivered before the New York Historical Society in December, 1812, when speaking of the Indian tribes on the Atlantic coast of New York and Connecticut, including, of course, those upon Long Island, observes: "In 1774 the Government of Connecticut, in an official statement to the British Secretary of State, represented the original title to the lands of Connecticut as in the Pequot Nation of Indians, who were numerous and warlike; that their great sachem, *Sassacus*, had under him twenty-six sachems, and that their territory extended from Narragansett to Hudson's River, and over all Long Island."

Samuel Jones, Esq., of Oyster Bay, South, upon Long Island, a gentleman of much learning, in some criticisms on this discourse, which he addressed to John Pintard, Esq., Secretary of the New York Historical Society, and which are printed in the third volume of the collections of that society, thinks the statement, thus cited by Governor Clinton, erroneous, and he remarks: "This must be a mistake, unless the Long Island Indians were part of the Pequot Nation; for it is certain, that when the Europeans first began their settlements on the island, the Indians on the western part of it were tributary to the Mohawks."

As happens in many other cases of historical and literary controversy, in this instance the dispute is more imaginary than real, and there is really no difference between the two gentlemen, except what is caused by the use of a name only. The Indians upon the mainland of Connecticut, and to the Hudson River, and also upon Long Island, were of one people or nation, the great Mohegan Nation; which was divided into several tribes, who were sometimes, but erroneously, called by the whites, nations; and these several tribes had a species of union among themselves, recognizing a common descent, and arising from that cause. It was this circumstance that caused so much apprehension among the inhabitants of this colony, during King Philip's celebrated Indian war with the United Colonies of New England, lest the Indians upon Long Island, who were then both numerous and powerful, might not, from being of the same blood and nation, feel themselves bound to take part in that contest. The Pequots were one of the largest and most powerful of the Mohegan tribes, and their name has been erroneously used in this instance for that of the whole people; both writers considering and admitting the aborigines upon Long Island, to be of the same race with those upon the mainland of Connecticut.

The writers on the Indian history of this country, and especially that of the tribes formerly upon our Atlantic coast, previous to the last thirty years, have fallen into many errors from this same cause to which we have just before adverted.

Charles Thomson, Esq., late Secretary to Congress, and also Samuel Jones, Esq., believed the *Lenni Lenapi*, called the *Loups* by the French, and the *Delawares* by the English, occupied Manhattan Island, Staten Island, and that part of New York and Connecticut which lies between the Hudson and Connecticut Rivers, from the Highlands down to the Sound. But Governor De Witt Clinton thinks the statement of Smith, the historian of New York, that all the Indians within the territory thus described were tributary to the Five Nations, or the Iroquois, when the Dutch commenced their settlement of this colony, inconsistent with the view thus taken by Mr. Thomson, and subsequently by Mr. Jones.

This difference in opinion, like that before referred to, has but little real basis in the history of those Indian nations. The course of aboriginal emigration was directly the reverse of that of the white man, being from west to east; and the *Mohegans* and *Lenni Lenapi* were of the same origin, their ancestors forming the first Indian emigration to the Atlantic coast; where, afterwards, in consequence of their great increase in population, being in a fertile region where their necessary wants were more than supplied by slight labor, both from the earth and the ocean, they became divided into two nations, retaining the evidences of their common origin, not only in their traditions, but also in their language, habits, manners and customs. Thus divided, they became permanently seated on this coast, the Mohegans occupying the country east of the Hudson River, including Manhattan Island, Staten Island, and Long Island, and the Lenapi holding the country west of that river.

The Iroquois, or Five Nations, were an entirely different race of people, and a subsequent migration to the east; and the same spirit which brought them to the banks of the Hudson River, and there seated one of their tribes, the Mohawks, a little to the south of the present city of Albany, also induced them to extend their incursions down that noble stream, the Hudson, and also to the east of it, until they had rendered the Mohegan tribes below them, and upon Long Island, their tributaries.

The ease with which the white men fell into the error of applying the name of a single tribe to a whole people is shown in the case of the *Mohawks*, a single tribe of the Iroquois; but which for very many years was the name by which the whole five nations was known to the white population of this country, and also to Europeans. And the tenacity with which the Indian tribes held on to the history of their common origin, and the extent to which they not only recognized it, but also acted upon it, is shown in the union effected between the Five Nations of this State and the Tuscaroras of North Carolina. These Tuscaroras originally formed part of the same people with the Five Nations, and in their first emigration from west to east, they separated from the others on the great prairies of the West, and migrated down farther south until they eventually seated themselves in North Carolina, where they were found by the first European settlers; while their other brethren turned their course towards the north, and fought their way through the previous occupants of the lands, in some instances exterminating whole nations, as is the traditionary history of the Eries, until they bebecame seated in the western part of New York, and along the fertile valley of the Mohawk River. Although so far removed from the descendants of their common ancestors, by intervening forests of hundreds of miles and numerous hostile tribes, the remembrance of their being of the same blood was sedulously preserved, and our records afford frequent evidence of the Five Nations sending assistance to the Tuscaroras in the prosecution of their wars. And at last when the Iroquois feared they were too much reduced by their frequent wars for their safety, as well as the maintenance of their predominance among the surrounding Indian tribes, they invited the Tuscaroras to remove to western New York and to settle with them; which invitation was accepted, and in the early part of the last century the Tuscaroras migrated to that portion of this State where they now are located, and thus was formed the *Six Nations* of Indians; this being the last of those aboriginal migrations which had continued upon this continent for very many ages, and bringing it within the period of our colonial history.

There were many tribes of Indians on this island, who were seated at the following places, as far as can be ascertained at this distant day:

IN KINGS COUNTY.—In this county the most powerful and extensive tribe was the Canarse, who were the first inhabitants of the New World to welcome the arrival of Hendrick Hudson, the European, who first discovered and explored the fine river now justly bearing his name. The account which he gives in his journal of this welcome, and the appearance which the western extremity of this island presented to his men upon their first landing, is truly beautiful, and as it affords us a much better idea of these Indians, and of their mode of living, than anything we can obtain from any other source, we shall substantially give the description which he has left us.

When Hudson came to anchor in Gravesend Bay on the fourth day of September in the year 1609, the Canarse Indians visited him and came on board his vessel, apparently without any apprehension, and, as Hudson says, seemed very glad of their (the Europeans) coming. They brought with them green tobacco, and exchanged it for knives and beads. They were clad in deerskins, *well dressed*, and desired clothing, a rather unusual request for the aborigines to make on their first intercourse with white men, and exhibiting an advance in the arts of life which we have not been accustomed to attribute to the Indians of Long Island; and they were "very civil." When they visited him on the ensuing day, Hudson says, some of them were dressed in "*mantles of feathers*," and some in skins "*of divers sorts of good furs*." He also states that they had *yel-*

low copper, *red copper*, *tobacco pipes*, and ornaments of copper about their necks; it was the abundance of instruments of this *yellow copper* that first attracted the attention of the Spaniards when they originally landed upon the coast of Mexico; and which they, believing to be gold, purchased in great numbers.

Does this show an intercourse between these Indians of Long Island, and the more civilized race found by the Spaniards in Mexico; or did the Canarse Indians understand the art of manufacturing these different kinds of copper?

The solution of these inquiries affords matter not only of curious, but also of a highly interesting nature; and which, singular as it may appear, seems never to have attracted the notice of a solitary writer on Indian history, or on the Antiquities of America.

Hudson also represents these Long Island Indians as having *great store of maize*, or Indian corn, "whereof they make good bread," and currants, some of which, dried, his men brought to him from the land on the second day, and which, he says, were "sweet and good." Some of the Indian women also brought him *hemp*, which they must have known the use of, and highly valued, or they would not have thought of bringing it as a present.

Some of his men landed upon this island in what is now the town of Gravesend, and they there saw "great store of men, women and children," who gave them tobacco upon their landing; they also described the country to Hudson, as being full of great, tall oaks, and "the lands were as pleasant with grass, and flowers, and goodly trees as ever they had seen, and very sweet smells came from them."

Unfortunately this pleasant and peaceful intercourse between the Indians and their European visitors was not long preserved. On the third day a party of Hudson's crew again landed at the same place. Among them was John Colman, an Englishman; and although nothing is said in Hudson's journal about any provocation to the Indians, yet it is certain some must have been given, and most probably not of a trivial character, or the people who had welcomed their arrival in such a friendly manner would not have become so immediately changed as to attack this party of the crew on this occasion. The result of this contest was, that John Colman was killed by an arrow shot into his throat, he probably being the principal offender in this instance, as the Indians shoot no chance shot, but invariably aim at a particular object; and two others were wounded. Colman was buried upon the point of

Coney Island, which Hudson from that circumstance named *Colman's Point.*

This serious occurrence terminated Hudson's intercourse with the shore of this island, although the aborigines came and visited him the next day, as he says, in the same manner as if nothing had happened; they evidently regarding Colman's death in no other light than as a just punishment for some offence he had committed; and the next day Hudson pursued his course up the river.

The old Dutch inhabitants of King's county have a tradition that the Canarse tribe was subject to the Mohawks, as all the Iroquois were formerly called, and paid them an annual tribute of dried clams and wampum. When the Dutch settled in this county they persuaded the Canarses to keep back the tribute; in consequence of which a party of the Mohawks came down and killed their tributaries wherever they met them. The Canarse Indians are at this time totally extinct; not a single member of that ill-fated race is now in existence.

We have still preserved in the records of the Dutch Government of this colony historical evidence of the truth of this tradition, and some account of this extraordinary incursion of the Iroquois or the Five Nations of Indians upon Long

Island. They seemed to have regarded all the Indians of the great Mohegan family, in the southern part of this colony, as their tributaries; and they probably were so long anterior to the Dutch settlement of this country. After the Dutch colonization the Indians upon Long Island appear to have discontinued the payment of the usual tribute to the Iroquois, or to the Mohawks, as they were generally called, that being the Iroquois tribe most contiguous to the European settlements, being located then a little south of Albany, upon the west side of the Hudson River, and thus for a long period with the European colonists the name of Mohawk was used to designate the whole Iroquois Confederacy; and the Long Island Indians did this probably from the belief that the Iroquois would not dare come down and attack them among the European settlements. But in this they were greatly mistaken. For in the year 1655, with the view of chastising all their former tributaries in the southern part of this colony, a large body of these northern Indians descended the Hudson River and made a landing upon Staten Island, where they massacred sixty-seven persons—a very great number, considering the state of the colony at that period; whether they were white people or Indians who were thus slain is not stated, but probably a large portion of them were in the first class, and were killed in attempting to prevent the landing of this hostile force. After this, this Indian army crossed to Long Island, and invested the town of Gravesend, which they threatened to destroy; but which was relieved by a detachment of Dutch soldiers sent from New Amsterdam (New York). Upon their abandoning the siege of Gravesend, the Dutch records give no further account of them, than to mention that all this was done when those northern Indians were upon their way to wage war against the Indians upon the east end of Long Island. It was undoubtedly directly after leaving Gravesend that they fell upon and destroyed the Canarse tribe, and afterwards proceeded down through the island with that terrible foray of murder the account of which has been preserved in tradition to this day; and to prevent a repetition of which the Consistory of the Dutch Church at Albany undertook to be the agents to see that the required tribute was regularly paid by the Long Island Indians to the Five Nations. So great was the dread of the Iroquois among the Indians of this island, arising from the tradition preserved of this terrible incursion, that a very aged lady, who was a small girl of eight or nine years before the commencement of the Revolutionary war, tells us that five or six Indians of the Iroquois Nation were for some offence brought to New York and sent to Jamaica, upon Long Island; and that, although they were prisoners, not one of the Long Island Indians could be induced to look, with his person exposed, upon one of these terrible "Mohawks," as they called them; but very many of them would be continually peeping around corners, and from behind other people, to get a sight at those northern Indians; at the same time expressing the utmost fear and dread of them.

Mrs. Remsen, the widow of Anthony Remsen, deceased, formerly of Brooklyn, on Long Island, says that, soon after she was married, they moved to Canarse on that island, now (1832) about forty years since, where she made the shroud in which to bury the last individual of the remnant of the Canarse tribe of Indians. This last member of that tribe also told her the tradition before mentioned, of the destruction of the greater portion of the Canarse tribe by the Mohawks, in consequence of their failure to pay the required tribute. This Indian told her that three or four families of them, having become alarmed by the shrieks and groans of their murdered friends, fled for the shore of the bay, got into their canoes, and paddled off to Barren Island, forming part of the great south beach, whither the Mohawks could not, or did not, follow them. They returned late on the following day, and soon ascertained that they constituted the only living representatives of their entire tribe, who had the night previous laid them down to rest in apparent security; and that no trace was to be discovered of their vindictive and barbarous enemies. It was some days, however, before they ventured to return permanently to their old residences, and not before they became entirely satisfied that the Mohawks had returned to their homes.

This Indian incursion caused the Dutch Government to feel much apprehension on the subject of Indian attacks upon the towns of the western part of this island for a long time subsequent. The inhabitants of Flatbush were ordered by Governor Stuyvesant, in 1656, a short time after that foray, to enclose their village with palisadoes, to protect them from the Indians.

And again, to prevent the incursions of Indians, the Governor, in 1660, ordered the inhabitants of Brooklyn to put their town in a state of defence, and also commanded the farmers to remove within the fortifications under the penalty of forfeiting their estates.

The Dutch colonists seem to have lived in almost continued apprehension of the Iroquois. On the 26th of June, 1663, Governor Stuyvesant informed the church of Brooklyn that the Esopus Indians, who were then in league with the Iroquois, had on the 7th of that month attacked and burnt the town of Esopus (Kingston), "killing and wounding a number of the inhabitants, and taking many prisoners; burning the new town, and desolating the place." July 4, 1663, was observed as a day of thanksgiving on account of a treaty of peace with the Indians, the release of the prisoners, and the defeat of the English attempt to take the whole of Long Island.

And good reason the Dutch had for their fears of the Iroquois, for a more enterprising and vindictive nation never existed among the aborigines of this continent. Immense extents of wild, unsettled country seem to have afforded no protection against their incursions. They not only made regular expeditions to the southern part of this colony, and even to its utmost extremity; they not only invaded Canada and subjugated all the region north of Lake Erie, and between lakes Ontario and Huron, and nearly exterminated its former population, but they also made frequent incursions through what is now the State of Kentucky, and claim to have acquired that country by right of conquest, and also upon the back settlements of South Carolina. In the *South Carolina Gazette* of April 11, 1753, we have the evidence of one of their expeditions to that region, in a proclamation of the Governor, and a vote of the Assembly of that Province, offering a reward of one hundred pounds currency to any person who should kill or take alive any one of the body of northern Indians that had lately come into that province, and "committed sundry robberies and other acts of violence."

The Iroquois preserved their power and influence upon this continent by the union of five small tribes, which but for this confederacy would have been destroyed or obliged to merge themselves into their more powerful neighbors. Strange as it may seem, it is to them we owe our present form of government in the United States. Their chiefs had for years observed that the French in Canada, although not the one-tenth of the English colonies in either power or resources, owed their success mainly to a want of union in the colonies; and that the only colonies that offered them any effectual resistance were the United Colonies of New England, and they urged upon the Governor of New York, and the British commanders of the forces, the necessity of a union. Their suggestion was sent to England, approved there, and resulted in the congress held at Albany in 1754, at which the Privy Council of England directed the chiefs should be invited, and their advice taken. This policy of a strict confederation was adhered to by the Iroquois throughout their history; and when, about the commencement of the eighteenth century, they found themselves by their frequent wars reduced below the number they regarded necessary for their safety and preponderance among their Indian neighbors, they invited the Tuscaroras from North Carolina to remove to the western part of New York, and become a member of their league; which invitation was accepted, and the Tuscaroras gradually moved up to their present location, and became the sixth nation of the Iroquois confederacy, which afterwards was known as the *Six* instead of the *Five Nations.* The Tuscaroras retained their lands in North Carolina, on which they were formerly settled, until within the last ten or twelve years, when they sold the same and divided the proceeds among their tribe. This does not look very much like that robbing Indians of their lands, of which we hear so much from the English press. So late as 1820 the Seneca and other tribes forming the Six Nations in this State, assumed the power of trying and punishing, and in some cases capitally, members of their respective tribes for crimes by them committed within the Indian reservations. The question of conflict between this assumed jurisdiction, and that claimed by the State over them in common with all others its inhabitants, was brought up by the case of Soo-non-gize, otherwise called Tommy Jemmy, an Indian of the Seneca tribe, who in 1821 was indicted for the murder of an Indian woman of the same tribe committed within the Seneca reservation near Buffalo, in this State. On the trial the defence set up was, that the alleged murder was committed by authority derived from the councils of the chiefs, sachems, and warriors of that tribe, who were an independent nation, and had full power and jurisdiction in the premises, and were competent to grant the authority upon which the alleged act was committed. The Court of Oyer and Terminer, at which, we think, Chief-Justice Spencer presided, refused to entertain this defence, and held that the Indians of this tribe, as well as all others within this State, were subject to the laws of this State; and the Indian was thereupon convicted of the murder, and sentenced to be executed. The court, however, under the peculiar circumstances, commended his case to the favorable notice of the Governor, and the Governor communicated it to the Legislature, upon which the Legislature, on the 12th of April, 1822, passed "An Act declaring the jurisdiction of the courts of this State, and pardoning Soo-non-gize, otherwise called Tommy Jemmy." That act, after reciting the claim of the Indians to jurisdiction, proceeds to declare: "And whereas the sole and exclusive cognizance of all crimes and offences committed within this State belongs of right to the courts holden under the constitution and laws thereof, as a necessary attribute of sovereignty, except only crimes and offences cognizable in the courts deriving jurisdiction under the constitution and laws of the United States; and whereas it has become necessary as well to protect the said Indian tribes as to assert and maintain the jurisdiction of the courts of this State, that provision should be made in the premises"—they then enact that the sole jurisdiction is in the State courts, with the exception above mentioned; and that Soo-non-gize, otherwise called Tommy Jemmy, is "fully and absolutely pardoned of said felony." And thus terminated the last effort on the part of the Six Nations to maintain their standing as an independent government; a measure that would have been very injurious to them as a people if they had been successful, as it would have left them without the protection of the State government.

The Rev. Dr. John Bassett, the minister of the Dutch Reformed Church in Bushwick, on this island, and who was formerly a minister of the same Church in Albany, states that the Montauk Indians upon the east end of Long Island for a long period paid a tribute to the Six Nations of Indians (the Five Nations of Colden, the Iroquois); and that the consistory of the Dutch Reformed Church in Albany were the agents for receiving and paying over this tribute.

We recollect to have heard, about ten years ago, that, fifteen or twenty years previous to that time, it was usual for the farmers coming to the city of New York from the east end of Long Island, in the fall of the year, to bring with them to the city a quantity of wampum (Indian money), which was to be sent to Albany. What its ultimate destination was we were not then informed, but we now have little doubt that it formed in part, if not entirely, the tribute in question to be paid to the Six Nations of Indians.

It is not a little strange that, after all we have on this subject in our public records and histories, and also the fact that the consistory of the Dutch Reformed Church at Albany were for many years the agents for the receipt of this tribute from the Montauks and other Indians on the eastern part of Long Island and its transmission to the Iroquois, Samuel Jones, Esq., of Oyster Bay, South, should have expressed it as his belief, in 1817, that there was no evidence that the Indians on Long Island, eastward of about thirty miles from New York, were tributary to the Five Nations. And he makes the further extraordinary statement, directly opposed to the evidence afforded us by the extracts from the Dutch records which we have previously cited, that "we have no reason to believe that the Five Nations had any war with the Indians on Long Island after it was settled by Europeans" (New York Hist. Society's Collections, vol. iii., page 324).

In these statements Mr. Jones is evidently giving us the results of his own thoughts, without having examined the original documents, which should alone determine such a question, or otherwise he would soon have found evidence enough of their incursions upon this island after the Dutch settlement.

A small tribe of Nyack Indians was settled at Nyack, on Long Island, in 1646; and they are mentioned in the records of the Dutch Colonial Government of the New Netherlands (now New York) of that year.

It is said there is a tradition that a small tribe of Indians formerly inhabited the valley between the Brooklyn, Jamaica, and Flatbush Turnpike road, and the Gowanus mill-ponds in the town of Brooklyn. On the arrival and settlement of the Europeans here a quarrel ensued between them and this tribe, in which one of the settlers was killed. In order to avoid the vengeance of the whites, the little tribe moved to the Jersey shore not far from Communipaw, where they had scarcely seated themselves before the whites attacked them in the night and slaughtered them all. (This tradition I had from Mr. Jacob Hicks, æt. 58.) The tradition, however, we do not put much faith in. There were undoubtedly several small tribes scattered over different parts of the island of which we know little or nothing at present.

At the first settlement of the white inhabitants there was a very numerous Indian population on this island, as is evident from the large portion which Daniel Denton, in his description of New York, printed at London in 1670 (the first work on this colony in the English language, and he an inhabitant of this island), devotes of his work to describing their manners and customs. We have also preserved the names of fourteen of their tribes who were formerly located upon Long Island.

Every few years some discoveries are made in various parts of this island of the remains of these aborigines. On digging a few feet below the surface recently at the Narrows, in Kings County, more than a wagon-load of Indian stone arrow-heads were found lying together, under circumstances calculated to induce the belief that a large manufactory of those articles once existed at this place; they were of all sizes, from one to six inches long, some perfect, others partly finished. There were also a number of blocks of the same kind of stone found in the rough state, as when brought from the quarry; they had the appearance of ordinary flint, and were nearly as hard; not only arrow-heads, but axes and other articles of domestic use were made from these stones.

In Queens County.—In this county the Rockaway, Merrikoke, and Marsapeague tribes of Indians were settled on the south side; and the Matinecoc tribe on the north side. The middle of the island seems to have been by common consent the acknowledged boundary between the tribes on the north and south sides. In this county, about the year 1654, a battle was fought between the English, under Captain John Underhill, and the Marsapeague Indians. This is the only contest of any importance between the English and Indians on Long Island, of which we have any account. The Indians were defeated with considerable loss.

In Suffolk County.—In this county were the Nissaquage, Setauket, Corchaug, Secataug, Patch-

'ogue, Shinecoc and Montauk tribes of Indians. The Manhanset tribe was on Shelter Island, Ram Island, and Hog Island. Tradition asserts they could bring 500 warriors into the field. Most of the tribes of Indians have totally disappeared like

"The baseless fabric of a vision."

The Montauk, which occupied Montauk Point and Gardiner's Island, is the only tribe which has any number in it, except the Shinecoc tribe.

In this decrease of the Indian tribes the white population has not had the extensive agency which many persons in our day seem to imagine; and a minute inquiry into the circumstances of the case could scarcely fail to satisfy them that, even where the utmost exertions were honestly used to prevent it, this decrease could not be stayed or retarded, much less arrested in its progress. The Dutch Government believed in the possibility of converting the Indians, and also of forming them into civilized communities, and with that view were very rigid in their enactments against all courses and practices which they thought would interfere with the attainment of that end. Thus it was that Governor Stuyvesant, in 1647, prohibited the sale of strong drink to the Indians, under the heavy penalty of five hundred Carolus guilders "and the further responsibility for all the misdemeanors that may result therefrom;" a law which was strictly enforced. In addition to this he directed that in all cases justice should be done to the aborigines; that their lands should not be taken without a fair compensation, and that the inhabitants should pay them for any work which the Indians should do for them; under "the penalty of such a fine as according to the occasion shall be deemed right."

These regulations were substantially continued by the English Government for many years after they came into possession of the colony. Many exertions were used both by the Dutch and English Colonial Governments to Christianize the Indians upon this island, but with little success; the restraints which religion imposed were not suited to their feelings or dispositions. The attempt, however, was not abandoned. In the year 1741, the Rev. Azariah Horton was the missionary to the Long Island Indians, a duty which he assumed in the month of August of that year. He states that then at the east end of the island there were two small towns of the Indians, and lesser companies settled at a few miles distance from one another, for the length of above one hundred miles between the extremities of the island. At his first coming he was well received by most of them, and heartily welcomed by some; the Indians at the east end especially gave diligent and serious attention to his instructions, and a general reformation of manners was soon observable among them. Up to the close of the year 1743, he had baptized thirty-five adults and forty-four children. "He took pains with them to teach them to read, and some of them have made considerable proficiency." But notwithstanding all this, Mr. Horton, in the early part of 1744, complains of a great defection of some of these Indians from their first reformation, caused by "a relapse into their darling vice of drunkenness; a vice to which the Indians are everywhere so greatly addicted, and so vehemently disposed, that nothing but the power of Divine grace can restrain that impetuous lust, when they have an opportunity of gratifying it." Under these discouraging circumstances the mission was still continued; and we are under the impression that it was not abandoned until after the commencement of the Revolutionary war, which broke up most of the churches in this colony.

To show how extremely difficult it was to prevent the Indians from drinking, notwithstanding all the restrictions imposed by the Government, we refer to the case of the Rev. Samson Occom, the celebrated Mohegan minister, and a man who the Rev. Dr. Buell, in a letter of May 9, 1761, characterizes as a "preacher of the Gospel who seems always to have in view the end of the ministry, the glory of God, and the salvation of man," and who he also speaks of as "the glory of the Indian nation." Yet this Indian clergyman, learned and good as he undoubtedly was, could not avoid the curse of his race, and in a letter which he addressed to the Presbytery of Long Island on the 9th of June, 1764, confesses himself "to have been shamefully overtaken by strong drink, by which (he says) I have greatly wounded the cause of God, blemished the pure religion of Jesus Christ, blackened my own character, and hurt my own soul."

This Indian avidity for strong drink is thus portrayed by a chief of the Six Nations, in a speech he made to the Commissioners of the United States at Fort Stanwix in the year 1788. He observed: "The avidity of the white people for land, and the thirst of the Indians for spirituous liquors were equally insatiable; that the white men had seen and fixed their eyes upon the Indian's good land and the Indians had seen and fixed their eyes upon the white men's keg of rum. And nothing could divert either of them from their desired object; and therefore there was no remedy, but the white men must have the land and the Indians the keg of rum."

This speech affords a correct view of the case. The Indians could not be prevented from drinking, although great exertions were used to accomplish that end; nothing human could effect it; it was alone (to use the words of the Rev. Mr. Horton, in 1744) the power of Divine Grace that could restrain this impetuous lust.

This account of the Rev. Mr. Horton's mission in 1744 was unfortunately the history of every attempt to ameliorate the condition of these poor tribes. So long as they were in the course of instruction, and everything was done for them, or they were assisted in doing matters in order to teach them, things went on tolerably well; but the moment they were left to themselves to put in practice the instructions they had received, in governing their own towns, in conducting their own church service, teaching their own schools, and in cultivating their own fields, they began to retrograde; the benefits which they had received were not communicated by them to their children, and of course the next generation was almost as much of savages as were their fathers before the advantages of civilization were introduced among them. Notwithstanding these discouraging circumstances, oft-repeated attempts were made to induce the remnants of these aborigines to adopt the habits and practices of civilized life, but with very limited and partial success, and laws were enacted by the State Legislature to facilitate these benevolent efforts, and to prevent trespasses upon the lands of the Indians, in order to induce them to resort to its cultivation for their support. It seems to have been impossible to satisfy the aboriginal inhabitants of this island as to the value of education, or to convince them that it was not a disadvantage for them to possess it. This trait, however, is not peculiar to the Indians of this island; it is now found in full operation in the minds of great numbers of the aborigines west of the Mississippi, and is a most serious bar to their advancement in the arts of civilized life. They esteem their own education (if it may be so called) as immensely superior to that which we offer them, for the life which they lead, and which they desire to continue in; and they look upon the learning and knowledge which we tender to them as only calculated to be of use alone to the white men. Nothing effectual can be done towards civilizing and instructing the Indians until this idea is removed from their minds, and until they become cultivators of the soil for a subsistence,—until they look to the grain which they raise, and to the cattle and stock which they rear for a living, in place of seeking it by the chase, and in fishing upon the lakes and rivers. The moment they become truly fixed to the soil (and that will probably not be until one generation of cultivators shall have passed away), they will see and feel the necessity of knowledge, and they will then of their own motion seek for it; until that time arrives all efforts to impart education to them are thrown away, they place no value on it, but, on the contrary, regard it as an impediment to the course of life on which they depend as a means of existence.

There has always been a very great and serious difficulty which we have had to contend with in all attempts to Christianize the aborigines, to which sufficient attention has not been paid. We refer to their religious belief. They believe in one God, whom they call the Great Spirit; and who they believe controls and orders all things. They also recognize the existence of an evil spirit, and have their system of future rewards and punishments. It, therefore, often becomes extremely difficult for the missionary to convince them that he is preaching a new religious faith. To their untutored minds the variances, so marked and palpable to us, do not present themselves; and often has the sincere teacher of the Gospel been obliged to confess that his prospect of success would be very much better with a people who were the avowed worshippers of idols, stocks, and stones, than with the North American Indians, and arising from the circumstances before referred to. It is true our Indians believed in a plurality of gods, but they were all subordinate to the Great Spirit, and could not be distinguished by them from the angelic host of the Christian faith; for their subordinate gods were the ministering spirits of their superior god. The religious faith of the Long Island Indians is described by the Rev. Samson Occom, an educated Mohegan Indian minister, as follows: "They believe in a plurality of gods, and in one great and good Being, *who controls all the rest.* They likewise believe in an evil spirit, and have their conjurers or pawaws." Occom was perfectly conversant with their old religion, and one who had great influence with them; and when he removed to Western New York with the remnants of some of the New England tribes, a considerable number of the Montauks from this island accompanied him.

In the year 1792, in the hope that it would benefit them, the Legislature of this State conferred upon the Shinecoc Indians upon the east end of this island, the power of electing three trustees from their own tribe to manage and apportion their lands among the members of their tribe, with a view to its improvement. At these elections, each male Indian above twenty-one years of age was a voter; and the elections were to be held annually in Southampton, on the first Tuesday in April, at the place of holding the annual town meeting; and the town clerk of Southampton was required to be present, and to preside at these Indian elections. But the Legislature would not permit these trustees to lease out the lands of the tribe to any one without the consent of three Justices of the Peace residing next to them, and then not for a longer period than three years.

In order to promote friendship and a future good understanding between the Montauk Indians and the white settlers, an agreement, in writing, was entered into between them on the 3d day of March, 1702–3, by which all previous differences were declared settled, and the respective rights of the Indians and the white inhabitants to the lands in that vicinity adjusted. Under this agreement they continued to live in peace with each other, until about the year 1787, when the Indians began to imagine that the white proprietors were in possession of much more land than had been declared to belong to them by the agreement of 1703; and to test this question they turned their cattle into some of the fenced fields of the white people, which caused their impounding. Upon the trial which resulted from this act, it was shown that the white proprietors held the same lands that were awarded them by that agreement and no more. Then the Indians came to regard the agreement itself, under which they had so long lived in peace, as a serious grievance; and in 1807 they petitioned the Legislature of this State for relief in respect to certain grievances which they said had been imposed upon them by the proprietors of the lands on Montauk in reference to the improvement of their lands; and they prayed the interference of the Legislature to procure an alteration of the agreement made by their ancestors with those proprietors. The Legislature saw that these poor Indians could not be referred to the courts of law to test the validity of their agreement, as would have been the course if that petition had emanated from any other of the inhabitants of this State, and they therefore appointed Ezra L'Hommedieu, John Smith and Nicoll Floyd, Esq., of Suffolk County, commissioners to inquire into the grievances complained of by those Indians; and authorized them, with the consent of the proprietors and the Indians, to make such arrangement as they might judge equitable, for the future improvement of the land at Montauk by the Indians, notwithstanding the agreement made by their ancestors; and to report their proceedings to the Legislature at their next meeting.

These commissioners made their report to the New York Legislature on the 30th of January, 1808, from which it clearly appeared that the Indians were in error in believing their ancestors had not conveyed to the white proprietors all the lands they were then in possession of; and they also appended to their report the original agreement which was made on the 3d of March, 1702–3, which the Legislature ordered to be filed in the office of the Secretary of State. By their report the commissioners state that "the uneasiness of the Indians in respect to their rights to land on Montauk has been occasioned principally by strangers (not inhabitants of this State), who, for a number of years past, have made a practice of visiting them, and have received from them produce and obligations for money for counsel and advice, and their engagements to assist them in respect to their claims to lands on Montauk, other than those now held by the aforesaid agreement." And the commissioners further state, that "the neck of land they (the Indians) live on contains about one thousand acres of the first quality, on which, by the aforesaid agreement, they have a right to plant Indian corn without restriction as to the number of acres, besides improving thirty acres for wheat or grass; to keep two hundred and fifty swine, great and small, and fifty horse, kind and neat cattle, and to get hay to winter them. They now enjoy privileges equal with their ancestors, since the date of the said agreement, although their numbers have greatly diminished;" and the commissioners conclude with expressing it as their opinion that "there is no necessity of any further legislative interference respecting them."

The explanations made by these commissioners appear to have been satisfactory to the Indians, and we hear nothing further from them until 1816, when they complained to the Governor and the Legislature of some trespasses committed upon their lands by the white people, which complaint was answered by the appointment of another commission to inquire into their condition, and to remedy the evils of which they complained, which is hereafter mentioned.

A considerable number of the Montauk Indians appear to have emigrated in 1783, together with some other fragments of the great Mohegan nation, of which they formed a part, into the western part of this State under the direction of the

Rev. Samson Occom, where they all together merged into one tribe and became known as the *Brothertown Indians.* They were also sometimes called the New England Indians, and consisted of the following tribes—the Mohegan (embracing all whose particular tribe was unknown, and therefore the general national name was applied to them), the Montocks (or Montauks), the Stonington and Narragansett Indians, the Pequots of Groton, and the Nehanticks of Farmington.

The Legislature of this State, in 1813, confirmed to these Indians the land previously set apart for their use, and declared that it should remain to them and their posterity, without the power of alienation, and that the said tract should be called *Brothertown.* They also provided that a school should be established there for the Indians, to be supported out of the annual sum of $2,160.79, to be paid out of the State treasury, and that after also deducting the salary of their attorney to look after their interests, the balance should be applied to the use of those Indians as should be judged most beneficial to them.

In 1816, Governor Tompkins, at the request of the Montauk Indians, appointed Richard Hubbel and Isaac Keeler, Esqrs., commissioners to inquire into the trespasses committed upon their property, and as far as practicable to have them redressed. In their report the commissioners state: "That about fifty families, consisting of 148 persons, men, women, and children, inhabit said point—that fourteen of the women are widows, and that they all live in about thirty huts, or wigwams, nearly in the same style as Indians have for centuries past." These Indians, at present, obtain their living principally from the sea, although they till some land for raising corn, beans, and potatoes, in small patches or lots. They are in possession of about 500 acres of land of the best quality. They keep cows, swine, poultry, one horse and one pair of oxen. Their land, through bad tillage, is unproductive. Civilization and education appear to be much on the decline, and their house of worship, which was formerly in a flourishing state, is now going to ruin. The elder inhabitants have learning sufficient to read and write, but the children are brought up in a savage state. The Montauk and Shinecoc Indians are the only tribes now remaining on this island. There are a few miserable individuals the remnants of some eastern tribes of this island, but no great number of them.

About the year 1819, Stephen, the king or sachem of the Montauk Indians, died, and was buried by a contribution. This Indian king was only distinguished from others of his tribe by wearing a hat with a yellow ribbon on it (E. S. King, æt. 22, Jan., 1825).

The Sag Harbor newspaper, in 1830, mentions that on the 5th of January of that year, there died at Poospatuck, near Moriches, on Long Island, Elizabeth Job, aged seventy-two years, relict of Ben Job, and queen of the Indians in that place, "leaving but two females of her tribe, both well stricken in years. Thus ends the custom, for many years kept up, of paying a yearly tribute of a handful of *rushes* to their queen."

Notwithstanding the Indians upon the east end of Long Island were so much reduced in numbers, the State Government, in 1831, made another attempt to elevate them in the scale of life, and on the 19th of April of that year, the Legislature passed an act directing the Superintendent of Common Schools annually to pay the additional sum of eighty dollars from the school fund to the treasurer of the county of Suffolk, to support a school among the Shinecoc Indians, for the instruction of their children. And they require the Commissioners of Common Schools in Southampton to include in their annual report "a statement of the length of time that a school has been taught in pursuance of this act; the number of children taught in said school;

the manner in which such moneys have been expended; and whether any and how much remains unexpended, and for what cause."

This law was limited to three years, but by another act passed March 1st, 1845, it was renewed for four years, from April 28th, 1844, "and no longer, unless the same shall be extended by the Legislature."

Thus we see the Indians upon Long Island dwindling away notwithstanding all the exertions used by the Government for their support and advancement. The Indian and the white man, it seems, cannot live together; the former insensibly waste away before the latter, even where they are well and kindly treated, and the utmost care taken for their preservation. At Eastham, on Cape Cod, in 1674, Rev. Mr. Treat, the minister settled there, states that there were four Indian villages under his care. They had teachers and magistrates of their own people, and they were so kindly and affectionately treated by him that they venerated him as their pastor, and loved him as their father. There were then five hundred adult persons in their four villages, all of whom attended public worship. But all these exertions made for their benefit were of no avail, they wasted away by fatal diseases and other causes not easily explained, so that in 1693 they were reduced to only *four individuals.* So it was also on Long Island, as we have learned from the old inhabitants who were born on that island and resided upon it all their lives; here the Indians, although permitted to erect their wigwams where they pleased upon the farms of the proprietors, not in the grain fields, and one family of them passed their whole lives upon the farm of our grandfather, free of rent, and were employed about farming duties, and paid for their services, and treated with kindness, yet they seemed to die away in an unaccountable manner; no flocks of children were to be seen playing about their huts. Their destruction cannot be attributed, as some now imagine, to the introduction of ardent spirits among them by the white men, for old people will tell you that many of them did not indulge that way, and our Pilgrim fathers and Dutch ancestors made many very strict regulations to prevent the sale of those liquors to the Indians. There were indeed numerous cases of inebriation among them, for this seems to be a vice which the Indian cannot well avoid. We must bear in mind that the liquors then in use throughout the country were pure and unadulterated, the people having not then learned the art of making the noxious compounds now vended under those names, so that they would not produce the deleterious effects which we witness in those who now use them. But the real truth of the case is, the Indians had performed their duty, and fulfilled their destiny in this world, and Providence designed that their place should be supplied by a different race and order of men, and had so ordered matters that portions of this continent became gradually no longer fitted for their state of existence, and as a necessary consequence they faded away. If we would accustom ourselves to look upon such things in a different and more extended point of view, and not attempt to explain them from our finite political considerations, we would be more frequently much nearer the truth.

Lewis and Clarke's Travels (8vo, Phila., 1814) shows us that the small-pox, which had then become an epidemic disease in civilized countries, also raged with almost unparalleled malignity on the banks of the Missouri river among the Indian tribes at the commencement of the present century; whole villages and nations were swept away by it.

The following account of its effect upon the nation of the Mahas will exhibit one of the causes in progress for the destruction of the Indian tribes.

"The ancient village of Mahas consisted of three hundred cabins, but was burned about four years ago (in 1800), soon after the small-pox had destroyed four hundred men, and a proportion of women and children. On a hill in the rear of the village are the graves of the nation."

"The accounts we have had of the effects of the small-pox on that nation are most distressing; it is not known in what way it was first communicated to them, though probably by some war party. They had been a military and powerful people; but when these warriors saw their strength wasting before a malady which they could not resist, their frenzy was extreme; they burnt their village, and many of them put to death their wives and children to save them from so cruel an affliction, and that all might go together to some better country."

At various periods of our history the fell pestilence has swept before it whole tribes and nations of the red men from the face of the earth. Thus it was the year before the pilgrims landed in New England, the country had been nearly depopulated by some fell disease among the aborigines. The first white settlers upon landing found nothing but the graves of the previous inhabitants, and their corn-fields with the crop ungathered. It was in this way that Providence opened the country for its settlement by a civilized race, which, in all human probability, would not have been effected by the small number of pilgrims who made their landing at Plymouth, if the native tribes had existed in their pristine strength. And again, within our own time, about twenty-five years since, the small-pox made its appearance amongst the Marden Indians, one of the most numerous, and the most civilized, as well as the most powerful tribe west of the Mississippi river, and entirely destroyed them. Their manners, habits and customs are preserved to us by the sketches of George Catlin, Esq., who visited their villages, and remained with them some months, about two years previous to their destruction.

A singular natural phenomenon appears when the Indian blood is mixed with that of the white man; it scarcely ever lasts beyond the second generation; and is very rarely met with beyond the third generation, but gradually wastes away, so that it is a common remark that the half-breeds soon run out. All these things melt away the Indian tribes from before the face of the white man; and yet, notwithstanding all this, the Europeans, and especially the English, are often reading us homilies on our treatment of the Indians, in which they only exhibit their ignorance of the entire subject.

A writer in the *Gentleman's Magazine*, London, for December, 1846, under the head of *Extracts from the Portfolio of a Man of the World*, seems to think he has found a panacea for all the evils attending this decrease of the Indian race, in a project which he admits cannot now be tried; it is this:

"Had settlements of the Europeans been made at once in the far West by a set of bachelor soldiers, and the Roman and Sabine *mariages forcés* been effected in a civil way, the two races might have melted into one another unperceived, and spread their civilization backwards to the East, and red men and white men become as little distinguishable as a Sabine from a Roman in the time of Cicero."

Nothing but a want of knowledge could induce such a proposition, otherwise he would have known that this mixed race, so far from spreading civilization over the continent, would have been in every respect a more debased and worthless race, and less likely to communicate any of the benefits they had received from their European fathers than even the pure Indian race.

And who is there accustomed to take enlarged and extended views upon such subjects, that when he looks upon the Indian race and the mode practised by them in obtaining their food, can help but be struck with the idea, that Providence is by this means preparing the way for the extinction of that race of men, and for having their place supplied by one of an entirely different character. Nothing in our judgment shows this more clearly than the common Indian practice of setting fire to the prairie, and even to the forest, in order to drive to them their game. Sir *Francis Head*, in his *Emigrant*, on this point observes, that the aborigines for many years have been and still are in the habit of burning tracts of wood so immense, that, from very high and scientific authority, he was informed that the amount of land thus burned has exceeded many millions of acres, and that it has been and still is materially changing the climate of North America. But besides this effect it is simultaneously working out another great object of nature. This improvident mode of obtaining game, by the destruction it brings upon all the small game and the young of the larger variety, while it for a short time affords the Indian an abundance, eventually afflicts with famine and destitution all engaged in it, to the utter destruction of the Indian tribes; an instance of which is given in the Beaver Indians of Canada, who forty years ago were a numerous and powerful tribe, and are now reduced to less than one hundred men, who can scarcely find wild animals enough to keep themselves alive. The red population all over this continent have, from the period of its first discovery to the present day, been diminishing in the same ratio as the destruction of the moose and the buffalo, upon which they and their forefathers have subsisted; and thus it is that we see, under a dispensation of Providence, by the agency of the aboriginal race, this continent is gradually undergoing a process which, with other causes, will assimilate its climate to that of Europe, and that the *Indians themselves* are clearing and preparing their own country for the reception of another and different race, who will in subsequent ages gaze upon the remains of the elk, the bear, the buffalo, and the beaver, with the same feeling of astonishment with which similar vestiges are now regarded in portions of Europe, the monuments of a state of existence that has passed away. What, let us ask, has the civilized race in America to do with this certain and unerring cause of extinction operating upon the nations of the aborigines on this continent? It is indeed curious and worthy of note, that English writers, in treating of Canada, can both readily see and recognize the operation and effect of this great law of Providence; but when they turn their eyes to the United States and observe the same effects produced and operating upon our

Indian tribes, they insist upon their being the result of *our policy* towards the aborigines, and that we are driving them before us out of existence. So little qualified are the English, as a people, to judge correctly in matters affecting other nations, and especially if they are pleased to regard them in any light as rivals.

TRADITIONS.

THE DEVIL'S STEPPING STONES.—It is said that, at a certain time, doubtless some ages ago, the devil set up a claim against the Indians to Connecticut as his peculiar domain; but they being in possession, were determined, of course, to try to hold it. The surfaces of Connecticut and Long Island were at that time the reverse of what they are at present. Long Island was covered with rocks, and Connecticut was free from them. The Indians refused to quit on so short a notice, and accordingly both parties prepared for the contest. His satanic majesty crossed to Connecticut, to enforce his claim by dispossessing the Indians; but he was disappointed, the Indians were too much for him, and forced him to retreat to

Throg's Point. The tide being low and the passage not very wide, the demon secured his retreat by stepping from rock to rock until he reached Long Island. After having seated himself in the middle of the island at Coram and brooding over his defeat in a sullen humor, he suddenly roused himself, and collecting together all the rocks he could conveniently get at on the island, he deposited them in heaps at Cold Spring, where he amused himself with hurling them across the sound on the fertile plains of Connecticut. The Indians who last remained in that part of the country, not only undertook to show the spot where he stood, but also insisted that they could discern the prints of his feet.

RONKONKAMA POND.—This piece of water, from its lonely and secluded situation, was often the theme of Indian story. Among the many traditions respecting this interesting little lake, the following is all that I have been able to obtain at this distant day. The aborigines appear to have regarded it with a sort of awful veneration. They considered its depths as unfathomable, and believed that the fish were specially placed there by the Great Spirit. Under this impression, at the time of the first settlement, they refused to eat them, regarding them as superior beings.

JOHN BULL'S TALK TO THE INDIANS.—King Ben,

who styled himself one of the last of the Indian chiefs on Long Island, often resided on Whale's Neck, Queen's County. He used to relate many wonderful stories about the first settlers, and often told the story of John Bull speaking to the Indians, which was as follows: The English had a large cannon which they told the natives was John Bull, and that on a certain day he would make a talk to them. Accordingly, on the day appointed, the poor Indians were placed in a line fronting the mouth of the gun, which being shotted was fired off to their destruction. King Ben says that the wrath of the Great Spirit, by reason of this outrage, was so great that at the season of the year when this foul murder was committed, no grass will grow upon that accursed spot, which still bears the stain of human blood. The fact is, that the place where this wicked deed is alleged to have been committed is a ridge of red gravelly soil, on which in the dry season nothing can grow for want of moisture.

MONGOTUCKSEE.—Canoe place, on the south side of Long Island, derives its name from the fact, that more than two centuries ago, a canal was made there by the Indians, for the purpose of passing their canoes from one bay to the other, that is, across the island from Mecox bay to Peconic bay. Although the trench has been in a great measure filled up, yet its remains are still visible and partly flowed at high water. It was constructed by *Mongotucksee* (or Long Knife), who then reigned over the nation of Montauk.

Although that nation has now dwindled to a few miserable remnants of a powerful race, who still linger on the lands which were once the seat of their proud dominion, yet their traditional history is replete with all those tragical incidents which usually accompany the fall of power. It informs us that their chief was of gigantic form, proud and despotic in peace, and terrible in war. But although a tyrant of his people, yet he protected them from their enemies and commanded their respect for his savage virtues. The praises of *Mongotucksee* are still chanted in aboriginal verse to the winds that howl around the eastern extremity of this island. The Narragansetts and the Mohocks yielded to his prowess, and the ancestors of the last of the Mohicans trembled at the expression of his anger. He sustained his power not less by the resources of his mind than by the vigor of his arm. An ever watchful policy guided his counsels. Prepared for every exigency, not even aboriginal sagacity could surprise his caution. To facilitate communication around the seat of his dominion for the purpose not only of defence but of annoyance, he constructed this canal, which remains a monument of his genius, while other traces of his skill and prowess are lost in oblivion, and even the nation whose valor he led may soon furnish for our country a topic in contemplating the fallen greatness of the last of the Montauks. After his death the Montauks were subjugated by the Iroquois or Five Nations, and became their tributaries, as did all the tribes on this island. The strong attachment and veneration which the Montauk Indians entertained for their chief is evidenced by the following fact: Within a short distance of Sag Harbor, in the forest by the roadside, is a shallow excavation, which the Indians were formerly very particular in keeping clean; each on passing stopped to clean it out. The reason they gave for their so doing, was, that a long time ago a Montauk chief having died at Shinecoc, the Indians brought him from that place to Ammagansett to be interred in the usual burying-place, and during their journey they stopped to rest, and placed the body of their dead chieftain in that excavation during the meanwhile; in consequence of which the spot had with them acquired a species of sacred character.

About forty years ago, there were upwards of 130 families of Indians on Montauk; now (1827) they have dwindled to four or five families.

Some of their squaws are very handsome women. The royal family of the Montauks were distinguished among the English by the name of Faro. The last of the family, a female, died a year or two ago. The authority or pre-eminence of the Montauk chieftain, as the head of the Mohegan family on this island, appears not only to have been claimed by them, but also to have been acknowledged by the other tribes, and his assent seems to have been required to any treaty or conveyance made by any of the tribes upon Long Island with or to the white men. In the deed of confirmation given to the white settlers of Hempstead on the 4th of July, 1647, by the Massapeage, Merioke, and Rockaway tribes of Indians, they mention the fact of the Montauk Sachem "being present at the confirmation." And again, in another deed of May 11th, 1658, by which the Indians acknowledge to have received full payment of the balance due for the lands purchased by the settlers of Hempstead, the payments being made by instalments, at the bottom, after signatures of all the chiefs of the tribes, it is said, "Subscribed by Wacombound, Montauk Sachem, after the death of his father, this 14th of February, 1660, being a general town meeting at Hempstead." His allowance or confirmation of the deed appearing to be esteemed necessary to its validity. The Montauk chief was also styled the Grand Sachem of Paumanacke, or Long Island; no inconsiderable dignity in that day.

MANETTA HILL.—About thirty miles from Brooklyn, and midway between the north and south sides of this island, is a hill known by the name of *Manet*, or *Manetta Hill*. This, however, is a corruption of the true name, which was *Manitou Hill*, or the Hill of the Great Spirit; which appellation is founded on the tradition, that many ages since, the aborigines residing in those parts suffered extremely from the want of water. Under their suffering they offered up prayers to the Great Spirit for relief. That in reply to their supplications, the Good Spirit directed that their principal chieftain should shoot his arrow into the air, and on the spot where it fell they should dig, and would assuredly discover the element they so much desired. They pursued the direction, dug, and found water. There is now a well situated on this rising ground, which is not deep, and the tradition continues to say that this well is on the very spot indicated by the Good Spirit. This hill was undoubtedly used in ancient times as the place of general offering to the Great Spirit in the name and behalf of all surrounding people; and was of the character of the hill-altars so common among the early nations. It is from this circumstance that the name was most probably derived.

This is another of our Long Island Indian traditions, all of which are now fast fading from the recollections of our oldest inhabitants, and which, most generally, are not deemed of sufficient importance by the younger portion of the community to be preserved in memory. This is the reason why we have sought to preserve those of which we have heard, in our plain and homely language.

The Long Island Indians possessed all that peculiar eloquence which has so long distinguished the aborigines of the West; and it was mainly from them that the Europeans first obtained their ideas of Indian oratory, and of the strong and bold imagery which characterize the Indian speeches. The aborigines of this island had all that singular tact, which still marks the Indian, of discovering at once, in their intercourse with white men, who are really the men of power and consequence, and who are not; and to the former they pay their respects, taking no notice of the others. The following official account of an interview which took place at Flatlands, upon Long Island, between Governor Sloughter and a Long Island Indian Sachem and his sons, will afford an instance of their eloquence and their sagacity—they saw that Leisler, however powerful he might have been only a few weeks previous, was then a fallen man, without power, and at the mercy of his inveterate enemies.

This extraordinary interview took place on the 2d of April, 1691, between the Governor of New York and a Sachem of Long Island, attended by two of his sons and twenty other Indians. The Sachem, on being introduced, congratulated Governor Sloughter in an eloquent manner upon his arrival, and solicited his friendship and protection for himself and his people; observing that he had in his own mind fancied his Excellency was a *mighty tall tree, with wide-spreading branches*, and therefore he prayed leave *to stoop under the shadow thereof.* Of old (said he) the Indians were a great and mighty people, but now they were reduced to a mere handful. He concluded his visit by presenting the Governor with thirty fathoms of wampum, which he graciously accepted, and desired the Sachem to visit him again in the afternoon. On taking their leave, the youngest son of the Sachem handed a bundle of brooms to the officer in attendance, saying, at the same time, that, "as Leisler and his party had left the house very foul, he brought the brooms with him for the purpose of making it clean again."

In the afternoon the Sachem and his party again visited the Governor, who made a speech to them, and on receiving a few presents they departed. Some of the Indians upon this island have evinced considerable talent in other respects as well as in oratory. The Rev. Samson Occom, the celebrated Mohegan minister, was for a considerable time a missionary among the Indian tribes on this island. Some of his sermons and other pieces, which have been printed, are well written, and exhibit an educated mind, to such an extent as would unquestionably surprise those who have not thought much upon the subject of these people.

Paul Cuffee was also an Indian minister, a native of the Shinecoc tribe, and a man of considerable powers of mind, with some eloquence, who formerly labored among the Indians of Montauk and his native tribe; and although not possessing much education, he was a useful and respectable man. He was buried about a mile west of Canoe place, where the Indian church then stood, and over his grave a neat marble slab has been placed, having upon it the following inscription: "Erected by the Missionary Society of New York, in memory of the Rev. Paul Cuffee, an Indian of the Shinecoc tribe, who was employed by that society for the last thirteen years of his life on the eastern part of Long Island, where he labored with fidelity and success. Humble, pious and indefatigable in testifying the Gospel of the Grace of God, he finished his course with joy on the 7th day of March, 1812, aged 55 years and 3 days."

In the early period of the settlement of this colony under the Dutch Government, the Indians upon Long Island were far from preserving uniformly peaceful relations with the colonists, and the latter suffered from their incursions upon their settlements, and were not unfrequently under serious apprehensions from attacks by the Indians.

This fact is abundantly shown by a reference to the minutes of the proceedings of the Dutch Colonial Government, still preserved in the office of our Secretary of State, at Albany. The Council minutes of March 25, 1643, has the following entry, narrating a previous state of hostility, and the concluding of a peace between the Long Island Indians and the Dutch Government.

"Whereas, in some time past, several misunderstandings have taken place between the savages of Long Island and our nation, by which, from both sides, blood has streamed upon the land, the houses have been robbed and burned, with the killing of the stock and carrying off the corn by the Indians, so it is, that between us and them who already follow the banner of their great chief, *Pennowits*, a solid peace has been established, so that all injuries, from whatsoever side, are hereby forgiven and forgotten."

The hostile spirit manifested by the Indians in what is now Kings County, in the year 1644, was such that the Dutch government stationed soldiers in the town of New Utrecht to defend the inhabitants from the aborigines. The "English soldiers" mentioned in the following official document, describing an Indian attack upon New Utrecht, in which their conduct is complained of, were not foreign soldiers brought into the colony, but were the inhabitants of the adjoining *English town* of Gravesend, who had been enrolled by the Dutch authorities in this emergency.

"March 9th, 1644, appeared before the Secretary, Cornelis Cornelissen, from Utrecht, twenty-two years old, and declares that being a sentinel at night before the house of Jochem Pietersen; being about two o'clock, near the cow-rick, about fifty paces from the barn, he saw approaching a burning pile * (an arrow), the

* The Indians are still in the habit of shooting arrows having tow, hemp or other inflammable substance on fire against buildings, so as to destroy them, in their wars.

flames as blue as the flame of brimstone, about twenty paces from the house, between the dunghill and cherry-tree door, which pile or arrow fell on the reeden cover of the house, which was soon in full flame by the violence of the wind. A little after he heard the firing of a gun from the same spot from which the arrow came. The English soldiers would not leave the cellar where they slept, wherefore obtaining no assistance the house was consumed.

"Jacob Lambertsen, aged twenty, declares that going at night, about two o'clock, on patrol, around the house of Jochem Pietersen, he saw a flaming arrow, the flame resembling much the color of brimstone, etc. When the house was in full flame he heard the report of a gun, which they suspected was fired by the Indians whom they heard yet the next morning hallooing and firing. During the fire the English soldiers did not stir from the cellar where they slept.

"John Hagaman, Peter Jansen, and Dirk Gerritsen also declared that the English soldiers offered not the least assistance."

The Dutch government seem to have considered this Indian attack, and the circumstances attending it, a very important matter, and had the same under advisement, and were collecting testimony about it late in the month of May following. On the 19th of May, 1644, Cornelis Cornelissen was again examined, and he "certifies that some time before the house was burned he asked Jochem leave to go to the Manhattan, etc."

The only battle which the English settlers upon Long Island had with the Indians was in 1653, in the storming of the Indian fort upon Fort Neck, in Queens County. The Indians had for some little time previous shown a very unfriendly disposition towards the English settlers in that part of the island; at last they garrisoned this fort upon Fort Neck, from which they at times issued forth in parties, destroying the crops of the colonists and driving off their cattle and horses, and eventually killed some two or three of the settlers. The colonists at once assembled, and all of them being armed, they put themselves under the command of Capt. John Underhill; who at once stormed the Indian fort, and in doing which destroyed so many of their people that the Indians were very peaceful towards the English colonists on Long Island ever after.

The following extraordinary circumstance connected with the battle is related by Samuel Jones, Esq., in his communication addressed to John Pintard, Esq., Secretary of the New York Historical Society, and printed in the third volume of the collections of that Society.

"After the battle at Fort Neck, the weather being very cold, and the wind northwest, Capt. Underhill and his men collected the bodies of the Indians, and threw them in a heap on the brow of the hill, and then sat down on the leeward side of the heap to eat their breakfast.

"When this part of the country came to be settled, the highway across the Neck passed directly over the spot where it was said the heap of Indians lay, and the earth in that spot was remarkably different from the ground around it, being strongly tinged with a reddish cast, which the old people said was occasioned by the blood of the Indians."

Mr. Jones, speaking of this tradition, observes: "This appearance was formerly very conspicuous. Having heard the story above sixty years ago (that is before the year 1752), I frequently viewed and remarked the spot with astonishment. But by digging down the hill for repairing the highway the appearance is now entirely gone."

The ancient Indian name of Long Island is said to have been *Mattenwake;* and that this word is compounded of the word *Mattai*, which in the Delaware or Lenape language signifies an island (see Heckewelder), and the word *wake* marking its peculiar characteristic. All the Indian names of places, so far as we know them, derive their origin from local circumstances; are peculiarly and graphically characteristic of the places to which they were applied, and were therefore composed of two or more words.

It is, however, a difficult matter to ascertain at the present day, what the true Indian name of this island was. In the early settlement of the eastern part of the island, the Montauk chieftain in his deed to the settlers, styles himself Sachem of "*Paumanacke*, or *Long Island*." Hubbard, in his History of New England, says: "That at the time of the grant to the Earl of Stirling in 1635, it was called by the Indians *Mattanwake*."

In Beauchamp's "Description of the Province of New Albion," etc., London, 1648, this island is called by the Indian name of *Pamunke;* and in the patent of Charles II. to his brother the Duke of York in 1664, it is called *Meitowax*, as being its Indian name. It is probable that the name as given by Hubbard is the true one. In the Narragansett language, *Mattan* was a term used to signify anything fine or good, and *duke*, or *ake*, meant land or earth, thus the whole word would mean the good or pleasant land, which was certainly highly characteristic of Long Island, even at the period of its early settlement, as abundantly appears from the description of it by Vanderdonck, Denton, and other writers.

The celebrated Indian war in New England, called "King Philip's War," caused much excitement and apprehension in this city and colony, from the fear lest the Indians upon Long Island and near New York, being of the same great Mohegan family with the Pequots and Narragansetts, might be induced to join Philip's league against the English, as they knew he had sent his envoys among them for that purpose.

Under this view of the case the Court of Assizes of this Colony, then being the legislative power, at their term held in New York on the 13th day of October, 1675, "ordered, that in case there should happen a war with the Indians in this Government (which God forbid), for the better carrying on of the same, one or more rates shall be levied, according as there shall be occasion, an account whereof to be given to the following Court of Assizes." To take away all excuse for any such war on the part of the Indians within this colony, they also ordered:

"That in all cases the magistrates through the whole government are required to do justice to the Indians as well as Christians."

At the same session this Court of Assizes, to prevent if possible all excitement among the Long Island Indians, ordered, "That the law be observed which prohibits selling strong liquors to the Indians in Yorkshire, upon Long Island and Dependencies."

"And that, pursuant to the law, the constables of the several towns take care no powder or lead be sold to the Indians, but by them as directed, or by their consent."

It then became a question of the utmost moment how these two great branches of the Mohegan family should be separated, and the branch upon Long Island kept from uniting with that in New England, and the Court of Assizes at this session adopted the following regulations:

"Upon a proposal whether it will not be convenient at this juncture of time of the Indians' disturbance to the eastward, to bring all the canoes on the north side of Long Island to this place, or to have them all destroyed, to prevent any intercourse with the Indians on the main and our Indians; or that these canoes be brought to the next towns and secured by the officers: It is resolved that all canoes whatsoever belonging to Christians or Indians on the north side of Long Island to the east of Hell Gate, shall, within three days after the publication hereof, be brought to the next town and delivered into the constables' custody, to be laid up and secured by them near their block houses; and that whatever canoe shall be found upon the sound after that time be destroyed."

The enforcing of these regulations prevented the apprehended Indian war in this colony, and secured the neutrality of the Long Island Indians during the Indian war of King Philip in New England.

CHANGES IN THE ASPECT OF THE COUNTRY.

That the greater part, if not all, of this island on the south side of the range of hills called the Backbone of Long Island, is that kind of soil called alluvial, and has been formed from the ocean's bed, must be apparent to attentive observers of the face of the country, and its geological formation.

Several years since, in digging a well on some of the highest ground in Brooklyn, a hemlock board was found at the depth of thirty feet; and again at the depth of seventy-three feet oyster and clam shells were met with, which crumbled on being exposed to the air.

It is believed that Governor's Island and Red Hook Point, on this island, were connected together. It is said to be an established fact that many years since cattle were driven from Red Hook to Governor's Island, which places at that time were only separated by a very narrow channel, which is called Buttermilk Channel, and is now wide and deep enough to admit the passage of merchant vessels of the largest size. Mr. Charles Doughty, formerly a very respectable inhabitant of the town of Brooklyn, who has been dead about twenty-five years, and was about eighty-five years of age when he died, used to say that when he was a young man he had been told by old people that they recollected when an Indian squaw waded from Governor's Island to Long Island with her papoose.

This is rendered the more probable from a statement we received from a gentleman in the close of the year 1846, now residing in the city of New York, who informed us, the summer of 1821 he crossed from the extensive flats south of Cornell's Red Mills, and between those Mills and Red Hook in Brooklyn, to Governor's Island, and back again, and that he walked the whole distance except about twenty-five feet, which he was obliged to swim. He says he is certain it was not over twenty-five feet, and he thinks it was less.

Gravesend, in Kings County, was at its first settlement laid out in streets crossing each other at right angles and intended for a city, and had a bold shore with a good depth of water. Old Mr. Barry, an inhabitant of New Utrecht, now (1822) eighty-nine years of age, says that he perfectly recollects of old people telling him when he was young, that they remembered when the sea broke against the land at Gravesend, which now breaks upwards of a mile distant; the beach having been formed since that time, as well as the meadow between the beach and the main land. Mr. Rutgert Van Brunt, who is now about sixty years of age, says that the beach is decreasing, and he doubts not but the time will arrive when both the beach and meadow will be washed away, and the sea again break on the land.

In the township of Flatbush (which is very level), in sinking a well on the place of William I. Furman, Esq., distant about five miles from the Jamaica Bay, at the depth of one hundred feet two petrified clams were found, one of which appears to be of the species called sand clams, and is in the cabinet of Judge Furman of Newtown. The other is of the species called the mud clam, and is in the possession of the compiler.

Hempstead Plains is composed of small pebble stones, such as are found on the seashore, and there is not a stone larger than your fist, if so large, to be found in all Hempstead. All their building stone is brought from the ridge of hills before referred to as the Backbone of Long Island.

There is a tradition (whether correct or not, I

am unable to say) that Blue Point Bay was formerly a swamp, in which wild allspice grew in large quantities; and it is said that the oystermen frequently draw up with their rakes decayed pieces of that wood. This bay was formerly famous for its very large and very fine oysters.

The people on this island have a curious account of the disappearance of these oysters. They say, that the poor people from all the country round used to support themselves in a great measure by the oysters which they took here for their own consumption and to sell. The town of Brookhaven, in which the bay is situated, at last determined they would derive a revenue from these oysters, and passed a law, in town meeting, that no one should take them without a license, for which they should pay a certain sum. This was resisted for some time, but at last the town raised a body of armed men and fitted out two or three armed boats, and drove off the poor people: and that as soon as this was consummated, not an oyster was taken, the rakes brought up nothing but empty shells. And this continued to be the case until, about 1839, when the whole bottom of the bay, for some feet in thickness, was found to be covered with young oysters about the size of a dollar, which the poor now take up in great quantities. A similar circumstance also occurred in

Southampton Bay. The town there laid a tax on the taking of oysters by the poor people, and the oysters which were before very abundant at once disappeared. And the people, to this day, in both instances, say that God killed the oysters because they would not let the poor have them.

The town of Southampton seems to have been anxious to secure that and similar powers to themselves beyond the possibility of dispute, and although they claimed to exercise them as a corporation, under their charter from Governor Dongan in 1686, yet they sought a confirmation of them under an act of the State Legislature, declaring the powers and duties of "the trustees of the freeholders and commonalty of the town of Southampton," passed April 25, 1831, which act declares that they "are and shall continue to be a corporation," to be elected at the annual town meeting. And it further provides that, "the said trustees shall have the sole control over all the fisheries, fowling, seaweed, waters and productions of the waters, within said town, not the property of individuals, and all the property, commodities, privileges and franchises granted to them by the charter of Governor Dongan in 1686, except so far as abrogated, changed and altered by the laws of this State, passed in conformity to the Constitution, and not now belonging to individuals nor to the proprietors, by virtue of an act entitled 'an act relative to the common and undivided lands and marshes in Southampton, in the County of Suffolk,' passed April 15, 1818;" and also gives them authority to make rules and bye-laws in the premises, under penalties not to exceed fifty dollars for any one offence, to be sued for and recovered by said trustees. We never before saw a charter so loosely referred to in an act or public document; not even its date, or the full name of the Governor, is given; we should think from this that the charter itself is not in existence.

Mr. John Velsor, who lives about two miles southwest of Cold Spring Harbor in Oyster Bay, in digging a well some years since, at the depth of one hundred and ten feet, found part of a tree about four feet in length and several inches in diameter, entire, with the usual marks distinct, but which soon decayed on its being exposed to the open air.—*See Wood's Geography of Huntington.*

The shores of Long Island have undergone frequent, and at times very rapid, changes. This arises from their consisting of a loose sand-beach exposed to the action of the waves of the ocean. In the case of Nicoll *vs.* the Trustees of Huntington, tried in the Court of Chancery of this State, in 1814, the following testimony was given: Jacob Seaman says that about fifty years ago the ocean broke through the beach, between Fire Island Gut and Gilgo Gut, with great violence, and formed what was called Cedar Island Gut, but which in a few years was filled up and gone. Isaac Thompson speaks also, but loosely, of a gut called Huntington Gut, between Cedar and Oak Islands, now disappeared; and he says that within his memory the water has several times broke through the beach, and that the inlets afterwards closed up. John Arthur says he has always understood from a boy (he said this in 1770, and was then seventy-four years old) that Fire Island inlet broke through after Nicoll settled there (which was in 1688), and that it used to be called the New Gut.

Richard Udall says that old Mr. Willis told him that he had been informed by his ancestors that Fire Island Gut broke through in the winter of 1690 or 1691, in a storm. The Chancellor said that this Gut was a passage for the privateers during the Revolutionary war.

About a century ago, the father of Samuel Jones, the late Chancellor of this State, accompanied some old people, he being then a boy, to the south side of this island, to view a new inlet which had then just broke through the beach during a very heavy storm. This inlet was afterwards known as "Jones inlet," and was in Oyster Bay south. When they came to the spot it was low water, and where the sand was washed away they discovered a meadow soil very many feet below high-water mark, and which had, apparently, been covered by the beach sands for many ages. The most extraordinary fact connected with it was, that on this meadow soil they found the tracks of cloven-footed animals, which it was impossible could have been made after the inlet was washed through, for they could not by any means get there, and which they supposed at the time were buffaloes' tracks, there having been no neat cattle on this island at the period when they thought those tracks must have been made. At which period the large expanse of water between the outer beach, through which the inlet was formed, and the mainland must have been an extensive meadow, exhibiting a most extraordinary change.

This inlet is now nearly closed, and it is probable that in a few years it will again be a sand beach. For a long time after it was thus opened it was navigable for small schooners. On the north side of this island, in the town of Oyster Bay, Queens County, about one and a half miles from the upland, is a small island of salt-meadow called *Squaw's Island.* There is now between it and the main meadow a channel which is navigable for the small schooners which usually navigate the bays and inlets of Long Island, and which at the lowest water is too deep for a man to wade across. The tradition is, that it acquired its name from the fact that when the Indians inhabited this part of the country, the squaws were accustomed to wade across this channel, which was then very shallow, with their papooses on their backs, to this small island, for the purpose of taking clams on the flats and sand bars which were around it.

There are a great number of shell banks on this main meadow, on the banks of the creeks, many of which shell banks are from five to six rods in length. They are formed principally of clam shells, many of which, from the great length of time they have lain there, are broken up quite fine. They form an excellent manure for land, and from these beds have been carted many thousands of wagon-loads for that purpose, and they still continue to use them.

The largest of the shell banks in this county are situated in a southerly direction below Merrick, on a creek in Hempstead Township. The inhabitants have been digging for very many years from these banks, and say they have never as yet come to the bottom of them. Thousands and thousands of loads have been taken away, and still remains a sufficient quantity for many generations.

The best wampum is formed of the heart of the clam shell, and even at this day wampum is manufactured on this island to be sent to the Indians in the Western States and Territories for the purposes both of a circulating medium and of conventions and treaties. In the summer of 1831, several bushels of wampum were brought from Babylon, on this island, and the person who had them stated that he had procured them for an Indian trader, and that he was in the habit of supplying them. This wampum was bored, but not strung.

Extraordinary changes—extraordinary in their extent and character—are frequently occurring upon Long Island; and especially upon that part of it known as the *Great South Beach*, extending from Southampton to Sandy Hook. At that part known as *Fire Island*, one of these changes has happened within the last few years, and is still in progress. This island, at the southerly end, where the channel of the inlet is, is continually washing away, and the channel continually progressing slowly to the northward; while the beach on the opposite side of the inlet is as continually receiving additions to it, the effect of which has been such that, where forty years ago there was depth of water sufficient to navigate one of the coasting schooners that trade along the south side of Long Island, is now a solid sand beach, in some places elevated from twenty to twenty-five feet above the ordinary wash of the ocean.

The northern extremity of Fire Island has within that period received an addition of between forty and fifty acres; and what is still more curious is, that this new-made ground, which, forty years ago, was under the waves of the ocean, is now covered with a scrubby white oak tree, and there are no trees of the kind at any other place within many miles of that spot. How did they come there? Some will say the seed was carried there by birds. But if that be so, why do we not find some other trees and plants there; the birds do not live alone upon the seed of the scrub white oak, and the soil is quite as well adapted for the growth of several other kinds of plants as it is for that species of tree? But that is not the explanation of that phenomenon. The earth is filled, even under the sea, and at very great depths, with the seeds of numerous trees and plants, which will retain their germinating properties for an indefinite period of time; and it may even be from a period anterior to the great deluge; and they require only to be brought up to within a certain depth of the surface to have the vivifying principles of the sun and air to operate upon them to develop those germinating properties.

This continual progressing of the beach and inlets from south to north affords the opportunities, at long intervals of time, of the land becoming submerged by the ocean, with all its seeds of trees and plants in it, and of being cast up again to reproduce them.

That seeds will retain their power of germinating when not subjected to the action of heat, is within the knowledge of great numbers of people, who often see it without thinking at all about it. Not to refer to the instance of the Egyptian wheat, which after being buried with a mummy in air-tight enclosure, for a period of three thousand years, was found to germinate and grow well, and is now cultivated in many parts of Europe, and also in this country; you may dig down a hill of mere sand, fifty or an hundred feet, and the year subsequent to the exposure of this new surface to the action of the atmosphere, it will be covered with a growth of plants and grasses peculiar to itself. Some years since, Israel Carll, Esq., of Suffolk County, having a large number of young cattle, which he kept in an extensive pasture by themselves, finding it very inconvenient to his herdsmen to drive them some distance for water, determining to sink a well on that pasture lot, near its centre, did so. They obtained water sufficient at the depth of about forty feet; but several feet before obtaining that depth, they passed through nothing but gravel; this gravel was spread out in a circle around the well at a regular declination from it on every side. The summer of the second season, after digging that well, the circle thus covered with that gravel stood as thick with a luxuriant crop of white clover as possible, and not a blade of that grass could be seen in any other part of that field. We have heard Mr. Carll say, that he could stand at his well and point out the circle in which that gravel was strewn by the circle formed by that white clover, none of it being seen beyond the line of the gravel. He was a man of sound sense and much observation, and at once explained this phenomenon by stating, that the seeds of the white clover had been buried in the earth among this gravel to the depth of between thirty and forty feet; and that when the gravel was thus cast up and spread, the germinating principle of the seeds was brought into activity, which had before been dormant for a long and an indefinite period of time.

This Fire Island is a place of great resort in the pleasant season of the year, both for the sportsman, the pleasure seeker and the valetudinarian. The latter go there in search of relief from the healthful breezes of the ocean; and those affected with rheumatic complaints to enjoy the benefit of the sand-bath. The patient if able to help himself walks, otherwise he is carried down to the beach just as the water is falling; and four or five feet above the water-line, a hole is excavated large enough to bury him, all but the head, and the right arm if that is not affected is left out. He then strips his clothes and gets into the hole and is covered over with the sand. Very soon he is in a profuse perspiration, and continues so as long as he remains thus covered; they are advised not to continue in this bath longer than fifteen minutes, the action is so violent; but very few would be willing to continue even that time, unless it was deemed necessary, the heat is so great, and the pricking sensation through the limbs so intense. There is no instance, I believe, where it has been used without effecting a cure. It is necessary to be very careful and to go warmly clad for a day or two after taking this sand-bath, because the pores of the body are so open, and the whole system so relaxed, that they would be very liable to take a severe cold, and to be again laid up with their old complaint much worse than they had it before.

We heard a gentleman about sixty years old say, that he had been much troubled with rheumatism so that he could scarcely move. He went down to Fire Island and tried this sand-bath, and was at once relieved. But that was not all: he said the next day he felt in such spirits and so light, that he was continually wanting to jump and skip like a boy.

A very striking alteration in the coast since the first settlement of the country, is mentioned in Smith's History of New Jersey (see page 58). But as this does not refer particularly to Long Island, we only mention it.

The State Legislature found it necessary, very soon after the close of the Revolutionary contest, to make provision for the preservation of the Great South Beach of Long Island. And on the 24th of April, 1784, they passed an act to prevent feeding the grass, or burning it, or cutting the timber, "on any of the beaches or islands lying between a certain gut or inlet, called Mastick Gut, to the eastward, and another certain gut or inlet called Huntington West Gut, to the westward," under the penalty of five pounds to any one who would sue for it, to their own proper use. The reason of this enactment was, that the sand forming those beaches and islands is so loose, and the particles have so little adhesion to each other, that if the grass is removed, either by cattle eating it, or by burning it, or the timber is cut off so that the surface is exposed to the action of the terrible gales of wind which often blow there, the beach or island would soon blow away to near the water-level, and then very soon after be washed away by the sea in a storm.

With the same view the State Legislature again, on the 21st of April, 1831, passed "An act respecting the Great South Beach of Long Island," by which they authorize any three or more persons owning, or thereafter to own, "that part of the Great South Beach on the south side of Long Island, in the County of Suffolk, lying between the South Bay on the north and the Atlantic Ocean on the south, and extending from the United States line near the light-house at Fire Island, on the west, easterly to Horsefoot Creek," to maintain suits at law or in equity in their own names, in behalf of themselves and all other joint owners and tenants in common of the premises, for any injury done thereto, or for the protection of the rights of the owners thereof. But this act provides that nothing in it "shall authorize any suit to be brought, as herein provided, against any person or persons who shall come or remain upon the premises aforesaid for the purpose of rendering assistance to any vessels driven ashore, or wrecked, or to any persons or property in such vessels, or to secure any property driven ashore."

Again, on the 8th of April, 1834, they found it necessary to pass another "Act to preserve the grass on part of the South Beach in the County of Suffolk," which part they defined to be that lying between *Horsefoot Creek*, otherwise called *Long Cove*, on the west, and Smith's inlet on the east. The object of this act was to protect the grass on a still greater extent of the South Beach, and on a part not included in the act of April 21, 1831; the proprietors having experienced the beneficial effects of that act upon that portion comprised within its operation. Timber is not protected by this last act, because there is none upon this last mentioned extent of the South Beach.

Under this head, referring more particularly to the natural history of Long Island than any other, we have thought it best to introduce the following interesting facts connected with the early history of this island:

In the year 1762, no rain fell on this island or in the city of New York from early in the month of May until November; and this is recorded as the most remarkable drought ever known in this country. It of course caused great distress not only upon this island but throughout the province of New York, as Long Island then produced more of the means of human sustenance than all the rest of the province put together; and it was this unlooked-for event which probably gave birth to the first association established in this colony for improving its agriculture. A society mainly for that purpose, but also embracing within its scope the encouragement of domestic industry and manufactures, was formed in the city of New York the following year, 1763, embracing the most talented and distinguished men of the colony. We have now before us the circular issued by that association upon its organization, signed in their proper handwriting, by William Smith, the historian of New York; John Morin Scott, afterwards major-general in the Continental Army; James Duane, the celebrated banker, and others. At a meeting of this society held in the city of New York on the 21st of December, 1767, ten pounds premium was awarded to Thomas Young of Oyster Bay, on Long Island, for a nursery of 27,123 apple trees. And at the same meeting the fact was established to the satisfaction of the society that

Joshua Clark and Francis Furnier, both of Suffolk County, had been very successful in setting out the grape, and making it grow in the eastern part of this island; that from the year 1762, to the first day of April, 1767, Clark had set out three thousand two hundred grape vines, and Furnier had set out fifteen hundred and fifty-one grape vines—the description of these grapes is not stated. The society had not offered any premium for raising the grape, no one then believing it possible to do so with any success, they having already forgotten that their Dutch ancestors in and about New York had, at the early settlement of the colony, been very successful in their attempt to introduce the vine; and having no discretionary premium at their command, they did the next best thing in their power—they gave Messrs. Clark and Furnier certificates of the fact, commending them to the favorable notice of a similar association then existing in England, at London, which had among their more extended list of premiums, offered one or more for the cultivation of the grape.

That the vine was cultivated in New Netherland, we have the evidence of Vanderdonck, in his history, who tells us that several persons in this colony had vineyards and "wine hills" under cultivation; and also that "Providence blessed their labours with success, by affording fruit according to the most favorable expectation." They introduced foreign grape stocks, and induced men to come over from Heidelberg, who were vine-dressers, for the purpose of attending to the cultivation of the vineyards and the manufacture of wine.

ANCIENT FORTIFICATIONS AND REMAINS.

The most ancient fortification on this island is one on Fort Neck, which was garrisoned by the Indians in 1653, and taken from them by the English, under the command of Captain John Underhill, during that year. The storming of this fort was the only battle between the English and Indians on this island.

On the subject of this fortification, or rather these fortifications, for there were more than one of them, Samuel Jones, Esq., of Oyster Bay South, on this island, addresses a letter to John Pintard, Esq., Secretary of the New York Historical Society, enclosing the following memoranda, written by him in the year 1812 (see Collections of New York Hist. Society, vol. 3).

"When this part of Long Island was first settled by the Europeans they found two fortifications in this neighborhood, upon a neck of land ever since called, from that circumstance, Fort Neck. One of them, the remains of which are yet very conspicuous, is on the southernmost point of land on the neck, adjoining the salt meadow. It is nearly, if not exactly a square, each side of which is about thirty yards in length. The breastwork or parapet is of earth; and there is a ditch on the outside which appears to have been about six feet wide. The other was on the southernmost point of the Salt Meadow, adjoining the Bay, and consisted of palisadoes set in the meadow. The tide has worn away the meadow where the fort stood, and the place is now part of the bay and covered with water; but my father has often told me, that in his memory, part of the palisadoes were standing."

This last described work was a true Indian fort, as is shown by all the plates and sketches of such works accompanying Smith's *History of Virginia*, De Bry's *Voyages*, and all the early works on this country; but no instance has ever been shown of the North American Indians having, either in ancient or modern times, erected for the purposes of defence, or for any other purpose, a four-square fort of earth, with regular walls and ditch, or such a work of such materials in any other form. When the ancient fortifications, and other erections of this character, scattered over our country, first attracted public attention, they were, without any examination, or much thought, attributed to the Indians, and were called *Indian Forts;* for then no idea existed in the minds of any that there had ever been, at any time, any other people upon this continent but the Indians and the modern European settlers. With this belief evidently operating upon his mind, Mr. Jones regards these fortifications upon Fort Neck as a strong proof that the extensive and systematic works of the West (some of which Carver, himself a military officer, in his travels, characterizes as evincing a skill in engineering that would not have discredited even Vauban) were erected by our aborigines. He seems not to have seen any of these ancient Western works, or his error would have been apparent to him at once; and he would have realized the utter impossibility of keeping together a sufficient number of people, who, like the Indians, subsist by the chase, the length of time that must have been required for the erection of those fortifications. This fact, together with their character and the ability manifested in their construction, have satisfied all who have visited them, and reasoned in the least degree upon the question involved in their existence, that they are the results of the labor of a race of men who were numerous in population, and who subsisted by the cultivation of the soil.

All this view of the case brings us to the conclusion that the two forts upon Fort Neck were constructed at different periods of time, and it may be far remote from each other; that the one first described, regular in its form, and built of earth, was the work of a people entirely different in the modes of living and in other respects from the aboriginal race found here by our forefathers; and the last described work was a true Indian fort, such as they were in the habit of building long before the European settlement of this hemisphere, and which they continued to erect long after that event; and that the two have only been confounded together from the want of the proper knowledge to enable us to discriminate between them.

There are many remains of fortifications erected by the Americans and English during the Revolutionary war; the most of them are in the town of Brooklyn, on the west end of the island. In 1782, a fortification was erected in the centre of the public burying-ground of Huntington, by Colonel Thompson (since Count Rumford), who commanded the British troops there at that time. Throughout the island are scattered relics of the aborigines. At Bergen's Island, in Kings County, an excellent road has been formed of clam-shells and oyster shells. At Maspeth Kills, in Queens County, Indian corn-grinders, axes, and arrow-heads have been frequently ploughed up. In Suffolk County there are numerous shell banks and other remains, as axes, arrow-heads, etc. The shell banks in the western towns of Suffolk County are much larger and more numerous than in the eastern towns, where shell-fish are as abundant, which proves that the western part of the island had been the longest settled, and that the Indian emigration proceeded from west to east.—*See Wood's History.*

Among other ancient remains may be reckoned the two venerable oak-trees at Flushing, in Queens County, under the shade of which the famous George Fox preached in the year 1672. I visited these trees, August 4th, 1825, in company with Messrs. Spooner and Bruce, and assisted Mr. Bruce in measuring them, which we did around the trunk, six feet from the ground. We found one to be thirteen feet in circumference, and the other to be twelve feet four inches in circumference.

In the month of July, 1841, eleven human skeletons were unearthed in excavating the ground to run a road through the Linnæn Garden, at Flushing, in Queens County. The place where they were found has been for fifty years used as a horticultural nursery. They were within a circle of thirty feet, their heads all lay to the east, and some nails and musket-balls were found with them. Conjecture has been foiled in speculating upon the circumstances under which they were inhumed.

In the village of Brooklyn, in Kings County, upon Long Island (1826) is a barren sand hill which exhibits many interesting curiosities to the antiquary as well as the natural philosopher. This hill scarcely affords support for even the coarsest and most hardy kind of grass, but on the top of it are three old Buttonwood or plane trees, and on each side of it the hills are covered with verdure. The surface of this sand hill, which is about seventy feet high, is covered with stones, many of which are completely vitrified, and others nearly decomposed, by the action of fire; and about a foot and a half, and in some places between three and four feet, below the surface is a distinct layer or stratum of ashes and cinders, interspersed with pieces of coarse earthenware and the stone heads of Indian arrows. Among the other articles found here have been the remnants of rough tobacco pipes formed of clay, and we have had in our possession one of these tobacco pipes almost entire, which we found in the sand on this hill. The oldest inhabitants of

Brooklyn have no tradition that there was ever any building erected on this spot. For a long

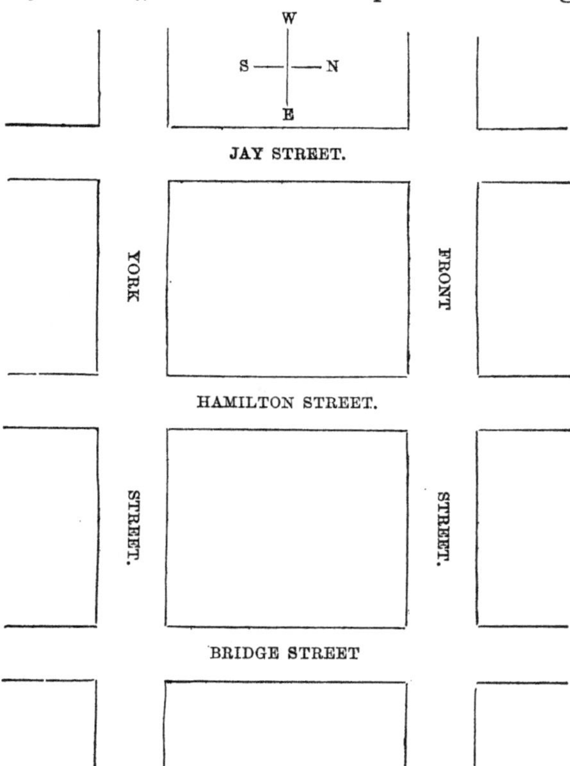

time previous to the American Revolutionary war, it constituted part of the farm of the Ra-palye family.

The preceding diagram will show the situation of this hill with reference to the streets of the village of Brooklyn, as they are laid out upon the village map, and intended hereafter to be opened.

This sand-hill extended beyond and east of Bridge street, which was dug through it nearly at its highest elevation; but the part exhibiting the appearances above described, and containing the articles above-mentioned as having been found, is that bounded by Jay street, Front street, Bridge street and York street. Similar remains may have existed to some extent east of Bridge street, but the examination was not made there.

FOUNDATION OF CHURCHES.

The first church founded on this island was *Congregational* or *Presbyterian*, and was built by the English at Southampton in 1645. In 1680, the salary of the minister of that church (Rev. Joseph Whiting) was £100. Congregational or Presbyterian churches were founded in different parts of this island at the following times. The first church in Hempstead was also raised in 1645, but not completed until 1648. It was a four-square edifice, like some of the early churches in the New England towns. Their first minister was the Rev. Richard Denton, the father of the first historian of New York. Cotton Mather de scribes this Rev. Mr. Denton as "a little man, yet he had a great soul; his well accomplished mind in his lesser body was an Iliad in a nut-shell."

Salary of the minister in 1682 (Jeremiah Hobart), £66, 14s. 0d.

At East Hampton in 1651. Salary of the minister in 1659 (Thomas James), £60.

The church in East Hampton, finished in the year 1717, being the second one built in that town, was, when erected, the largest and handsomest building of the kind on this island, and it is still a noble structure; although more than one hundred and thirty years old, it promises to continue in use for very many years to come. It had, what is not very common, a *second* gallery, and was furnished with a *bell* and a *clock* more than one hundred years ago.

At Jamaica in 1662. Salary of the minister in 1663 (Zachariah Walker), £60.

At Huntington in 1665. The first minister of this church was William Leveridge. These churches were not large buildings, in consequence of the difficulty of obtaining proper materials.

The first Presbyterian Church in the County of Kings dates its foundation no further back than the year 1822. It was established in the village of Brooklyn, and incorporated on the 13th of March, 1822, under the name of the "First Presbyterian Church of Brooklyn," and placed under the government of nine trustees. The corner-stone of the first church edifice was laid on the 15th of April, 1822. The church is of brick, and stands on Cranberry street. When it was erected, a large portion of the ground in the immediate vicinity was vacant lots; Orange, the next street south of Cranberry street, was only opened a short distance; and the ground south of it was in large lots, used for agricultural purposes, surrounded by posts and rail fences. Hicks street was opened up to the northerly line of Clark street, where a fence crossed it. Henry street was partially opened to Orange street. All the other streets south of Orange street, and to Joralemon street, were unopened.

FOUNDATION OF DUTCH REFORMED CHURCHES.

Dutch Reformed churches were founded on this island at the following dates:

The first indication of the establishment of any church of any denomination on the western end of Long Island is an entry in the Dutch Colonial Government Records, now preserved in the office of the Secretary of State at Albany, under the date of October 13th, 1654, that the Rev. Joannes Theodorus Polhemus, a minister of the Dutch Reformed Church, was permitted by the Governor to preach at Midwout (now Flatbush), and Amersfort (now Flatlands). And, subsequently, on the 17th of December, 1654, the Governor ordered a church to be built at Midwout (Flatbush), to be sixty feet in length, twenty-eight in breadth, and fourteen feet in height below the beams.

As this church was designed for the accommodation of the colonists in Brooklyn and Amersfort, as well as those in Midwout, the Governor, on the 9th of February, 1655, ordered the people of Brooklyn and Amersfort to cut timber to aid Midwout in building that church. The cost of it was 4,637 guilders, of which sum 3,437 had been collected in New Amsterdam, Fort Orange, and on Long Island. The Governor added 400 more, and 800 remained to be raised to discharge the debt. The first minister was the Rev. Joannes Theodorus Polhemus.

The year following the erection of this church at Flatbush, it was found not to afford the convenient accommodation anticipated to Brooklyn and the other towns, and on the 15th of March, 1656, the Governor, to accommodate the four villages of Gravesend, Amersfort, Midwout, and

Brooklyn, directed that the Rev. Mr. Polhemus should preach every Sunday morning at Midwout, and Sunday evenings, alternately, at Amersfort and Brooklyn.

The inconveniences attending even this latter arrangement became more apparent every year, until at last, in 1659, the colonists in Brooklyn determined that they would establish a church for themselves; and they petitioned Governor Stuyvesant for leave to call a minister, assigning as a reason for their request, the badness of the road to Flatbush, the difficulty of attending Divine service at New York because of the East River, and the old age and inability of the Rev. Mr. Polhemus to perform his services at Brooklyn. The Governor, upon this petition, sent Nicasius de Sille, Fiscal of New Netherland, and Martin Kregier, Burgomaster, of New Amsterdam (New York), as a committee to Brooklyn to examine into the matter; and upon their favorable report, he granted the desired permission; upon which the inhabitants of this town prepared the necessary call, and sent it to Holland for a minister. The Rev. Henricus Selwyn, or Solinus, was sent out to the New Netherlands pursuant to this request—one of the best scholars ever in this country, and one of the best preachers in his day. He afterwards became the personal friend of the celebrated Cotton Mather of New England; and a Latin poem, of much elegance, written by Selwyn, addressed to Mather, is in the Magnalia Christi Americana. The Rev. Henricus Selwyn, in 1660, was installed as the minister at Brooklyn by order of Governor Stuyvesant, by the Fiscal de Sille and Burgomaster Kregier, at a salary of six hundred guilders a year; three hundred of which were to be paid by the inhabitants of Brooklyn, and three hundred by the fatherland, Holland.

On the 7th day of September, 1660, four days after the installation of the Rev. Mr. Selwyn, a letter was written to the Rev. Mr. Polhemus of the fact, and thanking him for his labors and attention to the congregation. This letter was sent by a "respectable person," to whom the Rev. Mr. Polhemus returned his thanks for the attention which the church of Brooklyn had paid him, and furnished the messenger with a list of the names of the church members in that town, twenty-five in number. The popularity of Mr. Selwyn's preaching soon became such that the Governor was anxious to have him preach at his chapel on his Bowery or plantation (New York), and he offered, on consideration that Mr. Selwyn should preach at the Bowery on Sunday evenings, to pay two hundred and fifty guilders of that part of his salary which was to be paid by the inhabitants of Brooklyn.

The proposition was acceded to, but Mr. Selwyn had preached at the Bowery only a short period before the people of Brooklyn became dissatisfied with the arrangement, and desired to have him to themselves. And on the 25th of May, 1662, the inhabitants of that town petitioned the Governor that Mr. Selwyn should reside permanently with them.

When the first church was erected at Brooklyn in which Mr. Selwyn officiated, it is now impossible to say, no record existing which speaks of it. But the old stone Dutch Church which stood in the middle of the public highway, now Fulton Street, in the City of Brooklyn, just one mile from the old or Fulton Ferry, opposite the present Dutch church burying-ground on the southerly side of that street, was built in the year 1666. It was a square edifice with very thick walls, and small high windows, filled with stained glass, representing large flower-pots at the base of the windows, from which ran up through the panes, to the top of the windows, numerous vines laden with a profusion of brilliant flowers of every imaginable hue. On the top of the church was a short, open steeple, in which hung a small bell brought from Holland, as was also the window glass. The inside of the church was panneled to a great height, and that work, together with the pews and pulpit, were of oak and were either very dark from age or painted some sombre color, probably the former. The effect of which was, in connection with the small windows, that even in midsummer, after four o'clock in the afternoon, it was extremely difficult to see to read in that church; in consequence of which their morning service in the summer was at nine A.M., and their afternoon service at two P.M., and between the first of September and the first of May the morning service was at half past ten o'clock, and there was no afternoon service. This church continued to be used until about 1810; the people seemed reluctant to abandon their ancient edifice; but the incorporation, by the State Legislature, of a company to convert the old highway, filled as it then was with ruts, holes, small ponds of water, immensely large rocks, and tortuous windings to avoid them, rendered the removal of the old church imperatively necessary. So they built a new stone church on Joralemon street, partly on the site of the present edifice; which they continued to use until a few years ago, when, not being suited with its appearance and condition, they erected the present beautiful edifice, in the form of a Grecian temple, on the square of ground formed by Joralemon, Court, and Livingston streets.

The Rev. Mr. Selwyn, on the 23d of July, 1664, took leave of his congregation at Brooklyn, and sailed in the ship *Beaver*, for Holland, from whence he designed never to have returned. After his departure Charles Debevoise, the schoolmaster of the town, and sexton of the church, was ordered to read prayers, and a sermon from an approved author, every Sabbath in the church, for the improvement of the congregation, until another minister was called.

During the ministry of Mr. Selwyn the marriage fees do not seem to have been a perquisite of the minister, as appears by an account rendered by him to the Consistory on the 29th of October, 1662, when he paid over to the Consistory the sum of 78 guilders and 10 stuyvers for fourteen marriage fees received by him.

After the establishment of the English government in this colony, the Dutch congregation in that city remembering Mr. Selwyn's acceptable services in this country, sent him an invitation to come over and take charge of their church in the city of New York, which he declined accepting. Again, in the year 1681, that church sent him another call, with many urgent solicitations that he would accept it; to which he assented, and came to New York in 1682, and continued the pastor of the Dutch Reformed church in that city until his death in 1701.

A catalogue of all the members of the Dutch Reformed church in the city of New York, in the year 1686, with the names of the streets in which they resided, taken from the original manuscript of the Rev. Henricus Selwyn, their pastor, will be found in the first volume of the second series of the Collections of the New York Historical Society. To those who derive their ancestry from the old Dutch burghers of this venerable city, this record will be looked upon with something of the pride and attachment manifested for the roll of Battle Abbey.

At the period of his ministry there were but two Dutch Reformed churches in that city, the South Dutch or Garden street church, and the chapel at Governor Stuyvesant's Bowery (on the site of the present St. Mark's church); the Dutch church in the Fort being considered government property, went with the Fort to the English, and became an Episcopal church. With it there were then five churches in the city, two Episcopal, two Dutch Reformed, and one French Huguenot.

In the month of April, 1708, fifty-seven of the inhabitants of Brooklyn, being probably all the members of the church, entered into an agreement (which is written in Dutch) to call a minister from Holland, to preach in the church of this town. The elders of the church at that time were Daniel Rapalje and Jores Hanse. This connection with the classis of Holland continued long after this period.

Notwithstanding the establishment of the new church in Brooklyn, the church at Flatbush continued to flourish, and the Rev. Mr. Polhemus found full employment for all his services in the ministry.

On the 29th of January, 1658, Midwout petitioned the Governor that the one hundred morgen of land reserved in that town for the public use might be appropriated as follows: Twenty-five morgen to complete the church. Twenty-five morgen for a school. Fifty morgen for the minister's house and other purposes. The first two the Governor granted ; the other he denied, and reserved the land for the benefit of the vicarage.

In every town patented by the Dutch Government in the New Netherlands (now New York and New Jersey), there was one hundred morgen of land reserved for the public use. In some cases, like that above mentioned, the Dutch Colonial Government authorized the disposition of it, but always for some use considered a public use at that time. The English Colonial Government do not seem to have been ever aware of the existence of this public property, and they made no regulations or disposition of it; and the probability is that in very many cases these public lands have by long continued possession become private property.

The church at Flatbush does not appear to have been entirely finished at the time when the new church was established in Brooklyn, although it had been used for three years or over. On the 20th of December, 1659, the Rev. Mr. Polhemus requests of Governor Stuyvesant, that paint may be furnished, at the expense of the Government, to paint the church at Midwout. And, again, in September, 1660, the Rev. Mr. Polhemus and Elder Stryker petition the Governor for glass for a window for the same church. This was undoubtedly stained glass they wished the Governor to send to Holland for, for the principal window of the church; for then all the windows were of glass, unless it might be in the poorest small houses and cottages, set in lead in small diamonds; and "a glass window" for the church meant something different from those in common use; which could be nothing other than stained glass, there being then only those two modes of glazing windows.

In this application for the window they state that they had received 3,437 guilders and 12 stuyvers towards the cost of erecting that church, in New Amsterdam (New York), Fort Orange (Albany), and on Long Island; and that they still wanted 1,200 guilders to discharge the expenses attending the completion of that edifice. Upon which Governor Stuyvesant gave them 400 guilders.—The Rev. Mr. Polhemus died in June, 1676.

The people in Flatbush have a tradition that their second church in that town was erected in the year 1663. This can scarcely have been the fact, unless the first edifice was destroyed by fire, or the elements, which is not said to have been the case; for the first church was still in an unfinished state in the latter part of the year 1660—only two years before. It may be that an addition was made to the church in 1663, but I do not even think that was done, and am rather inclined to the opinion that this first church was not entirely finished and did not get up its stained-glass window until the year 1663, and that the people, many years after, not bearing in mind how long this first church was in building, and what a long period intervened before it was completed, the Government records showing over six years, they, when the date of its completion was referred to, came to believe it the time when a second church was built, and subsequently to speak of it as such.

The Dutch Colonial Government, as a general rule, followed the practice of their home government in the Fatherland in allowing the free exercise of all forms of religion, so long as they did not endanger the public peace. But the excitement in New England against the Quakers had arisen to such a high pitch, and so much had been said and written and printed by the leading men of those colonies against the principles and practices of the Quakers as being highly dangerous to all forms of civilized government, and utterly subversive of Christianity, that it was next to an impossibility that some of their feeling and temper should not manifest itself in the New Netherlands, an adjoining colony, and one with which they had frequent intercourse; it, however, showed itself in a very mild and modified form in this colony. In this spirit Governor Stuyvesant had, in the year 1662, directed a Quaker, by the name of John Bowne, to be transported from the colony to Holland, on account of his religious tenets.

The Dutch West India Company, to whom Governor Stuyvesant was subject, writes thus to the Governor in a letter from Amsterdam, dated in 1663:—"We perceive, from your last letter, that you had exiled and transported hither a certain Quaker named John Bowne. Although it is our anxious desire that similar and other sectarians may not be found among you, yet we doubt extremely the policy of adopting rigorous measures against them. In the youth of your existence, you ought rather to encourage than check the population of the colony. The consciences of men ought to be free and unshackled, so long as they continue moderate, peaceable, inoffensive, and not hostile to the government. Such have been the maxims of prudence and toleration by which the magistrates of this city (Amsterdam) have been governed, and the consequences have been, that the oppressed and persecuted, from every country, have found among us an asylum from distress. Follow in the same steps and you will be blessed."

These are certainly noble sentiments, worthy of being written in letters of gold, and while we cannot but feel high pleasure in awarding the meed of applause to men who could thus think and act worthy of the station in which they were placed, we cannot at the same time avoid lamenting that the same liberality of sentiment had not distinguished the early settlers of the New England Colonies, who, if they fled from persecution, were themselves the first to persecute in this new empire of freedom of conscience, which they claimed to have founded.

This John Bowne the Quaker, thus exiled by Governor Stuyvesant, resided at Flushing, upon Long Island, and his house is now in existence, or was very recently. The tradition is, that when he landed in New York in the spring of 1665, after having remained abroad several years, upon his return from his exile to Holland, he waited upon Governor Stuyvesant, then a private citizen, the colony having passed to the English, who welcomed him back, and expressed his regret for having used so much severity towards him and some others of his particular faith, some of whom he frankly admitted to be among the most valuable citizens of the colony; and assured him that the course of policy which he had theretofore felt it his duty to pursue had been based upon what he had ascertained to be an erroneous representation of the views and intentions of Bowne and his friends, and that he felt it an act of conscientious duty to make such declaration to him.

This, if it be true (which it has always been asserted to be), is highly honorable to Governor Stuyvesant as a man; who must indeed, from the accounts of him, have been very high souled and honorable, one well calculated for the important and dignified office he held.

Great injustice will be done to the memory of Gov. Stuyvesant if he is ranked as a persecutor of the Quakers, and others differing from him in religious sentiments. No ruler was ever more tolerant of the *religious* opinions of others than was Stuyvesant; and if in any case he appeared to deal harshly with any man, or any set of men, differing from the Dutch Established Church, it will be found on examination not to have been from their religious faith, but for the *political use* which they were believed to make of it. And we should bear in mind that very many of the Quakers of his day were a very different kind of people from those of our time, and men who were almost the opposite of George Fox in everything but name. In place of the mild, inoffensive conduct and strict attention to their own business, without intermeddling with the concerns of others, which now characterize them as a sect, and as among the most useful and valuable of our citizens, there were then too many of them who were fond of seeking every opportunity to abuse, in public assemblies, by the most pointed language, the magistracy and laws of the land; representing them not only as anti-Christian, but as originating from the Evil One, and of declaring all the ministers of religion out of their own creed, to be hirelings, wolves in sheep's clothing, base, wicked creatures, who were leading the people astray; and at the same time declaring it their settled intention to resist the laws which they asserted had no controlling force or effect over them, who were governed by a new light which they received from Heaven itself as their guide and law-giver, and which was confined within their own bosoms; and that they actually reduced these principles to practice, by refusing obedience not only to the laws in relation to an uniformity of religious worship, but also to all civil regulations, whether made by the superior government of the colony, or the towns in which they resided; refused the payment of taxes, or the performance of any of the duties of citizens, unless matters were done according to their peculiar notions. All this is lost sight of by those who condemn Gov. Stuyvesant for his proceedings against the Quakers. The error he committed was in noticing them at all; but in the principles and policy of government, he had not then the experience to guide him which we now possess, and it is therefore unjust to judge him not only by the light of the present day, but also by assuming that the Quaker character of his time possessed the same estimable uniformity which marks it in our age, which is very far from being truth.

Governor Stuyvesant's character appears to

have been singularly misunderstood by some modern writers; and which, in our judgment, has mainly arisen from the error of regarding it in the lights and principles of the science of government as understood and practised in our day, rather than in those which were common and received in the age in which he lived. It could alone be from an opinion thus formed that the talented author of Thompson's *History of Long Island* (second edition, vol. i., page 108) charges that Governor Stuyvesant persecuted and discouraged those whose religious tenets differed from his own, and that he exercised his prerogative in a capricious and arbitrary manner. Charges which are certainly scarcely supported by the fact mentioned by the same author, that *the English* who settled the towns of Gravesend, Newtown, Flushing, Jamaica, and Hempstead, and *who reluctantly became Dutch subjects, were allowed to hold their lands*; *to enjoy liberty of conscience, and to employ their own ministers;* rights which they would not have been permitted to enjoy at home in England, and those which they had little reason to expect here, from their reluctance to submit to the Dutch Government, the then undoubted authority of the country, and made so by a treaty between the Commissioners of the United Colonies of New England and the

Dutch Colonial Government. All which affords an evidence of tolerant principles on the part of Governor Stuyvesant, and a forbearance for the views and tenets of others conflicting with his own, not only in religion but also in government, rarely found in any age, and certainly not to be discovered in the proceedings of the most civilized nations of Europe in his time, except it might be in the case of Holland.

This house of Bowne, in Flushing, is built of wood, in the old-fashioned Dutch style, and was said to have been erected in the year 1661, only one year previous to his exile.

Opposite this house, in front of it, are two large old oak trees, under the shadow of which the celebrated George Fox, a preacher of the Society of Friends, or Quakers, in 1672, preached a sermon to the people assembled around them. These trees are still standing. Fox was then on a preaching tour from Yorkshire, in England, and was travelling through the colonies; he was then stopping at Bowne's house.

The case of Bowne the Quaker was the only instance in which the Dutch Colonial Government attempted to exile a man for his religious opinions. But its general course, and particularly the administration under Governor Stuyvesant, was marked by a series of measures calculated to advance the interests of the settlers, and to build up the little insignificant colony on the banks of the Hudson into a city of that character and importance, and a colony of that value as to attract the attention of the English Government, and upon the first opportunity that offered to induce them to fit out an expedition for its capture.

To the encouragement offered by Governor Stuyvesant is to be attributed the first emigration of the French Huguenots to this country, whose descendants now, and for many generations past, have been some of our most respectable and intelligent citizens. It appears from the Council records that on the 24th of January, 1664, M. Van Beeck, a merchant in New Amsterdam, informed the Governor that he had received letters from Rochelle, in France, signifying the wish of several persons professing the Protestant religion to emigrate to New Netherland, as their churches had been burnt, etc. Upon which the Governor and Council resolved to receive them hospitably, and to allow them land gratuitously. They at once came over upon receiving this information, and a considerable number of them received grants of land in what is now Westchester county, and settled a town there, which they named after their old home in France, New Rochelle. This was in accordance with the settled policy of the Dutch West India Company; which evinced a more enlightened view of the advantages to result from the commerce of the Fatherland, from the establishment of a prosperous colonial system, than appear to have been entertained by any other nation of Europe, and it was the success which attended this Dutch commercial policy that led to the celebrated navigation act of England. To the good character which this colony thus obtained abroad, throughout Europe, we may attribute the continuance, in some measure, of the same policy under the English Colonial Government, although a different policy was at the same time pursued in England itself. Thus in 1710, 3,000 Palatines, who had the year previous fled into England from persecution in Germany, emigrated to New York under the guidance of Gov. Robert Hunter; some of them settled in New York City, others on Livingston Manor, and the remainder in Pennsylvania, where their descendants continue to this day.

During the prevalence of the terrible witch mania in New England, great exertions were made to enlist the officers of this government and the clergy of this colony in that horrible persecution of poor infirm old men and women. They, however, refused to entertain the subject in any manner, and were in consequence of that refusal very freely denounced as infidels by the wise leaders in New England, who were, according to their own showing, almost daily receiving and acting upon the evidence of the evil one against their neighbors and fellow-Christians, members of the same church with themselves, and whose walk in life had been consistent with their Christian professions. There was then no Presbyterian church in the City of New York, and the whole population was nominally divided among the Episcopalian, the Dutch Reformed, and the French Protestant Churches—the latter was also under the ecclesiastical government of the Episcopal Church. The clergy in New England, who had been active in the matter of witchcraft, addressed a letter to the Dutch Reformed ministers of this colony, as approaching nearest to them in form of church government, desiring their judgment in reference to spectral evidence, and other matters connected with prosecutions for witchcraft; and the Dutch clergy, in reply, cautioned them against the use of such testimony, as coming from an improper and evil source, and more likely to be available against good than against bad persons of evil lives; it is very strange that this did not occur to them before.

The only trial for witchcraft which ever took

place in this colony was that of Ralph Hall, and Mary his wife, from the eastern part of Long Island, in the court of assizes held in the City of New York, on the 2d of October, 1665. The jury who tried them for this alleged offence, consisted of twelve men, five of whom were selected from this island, and seven from the City of New York ; and they found a special verdict, "acquitting the man, and that there were some suspicions against the woman, but nothing to take away her life." Upon which Hall was discharged, and his wife also, on his giving security for her good behavior, and that she should appear at the next assizes; and at the following term the recognizance was discharged, and this ended the first and only trial for witchcraft in this colony or state.

Although the New York government exhibits but this solitary instance of a trial for witchcraft, yet when some of the eastern towns on this island annexed themselves to the United Colonies of New England, and came under the Government of Connecticut, as a necessary consequence, all the peculiar notions of the inhabitants of the mainland in reference to demonology and witchcraft began to manifest themselves in that part of the island. And in the year 1657, the wife of Joshua Garlick being suspected of witchcraft, was arrested upon that charge in Easthampton, a proceeding which caused great excitement in that town; as usual, in most other cases of a similar character, witnesses were not wanting in this instance who deposed to facts, which, in the minds of an excited and credulous people, fully established the truth of the accusation. But the town court before whom she was brought, being composed of persons not very deeply versed in the science of demonology, and feeling themselves incompetent to decide upon so grave a question, sent the unhappy woman a prisoner to Hartford, in Connecticut, to be tried by the General Court at that place. What became of her is not known, but she was probably subsequently discharged, or her name would appear among those who fell victims to that awful mania.

Prior to the American Revolution, sermons were preached, and also printed, in the Dutch language, in the City of New York. We have seen two sermons which were printed in the Dutch language, in 4to form, at New York, by "Hendricus De Forest, in't Jaar 1752." In Kings County, upon Long Island, sermons in Dutch were preached in the towns of Flatbush, New Utrecht, Gravesend and Bushwick, until about the year 1818. The last Dutch clergyman, or parson, as the English called him, or dominie, as the Dutch styled him, for those towns, was old Dominie Martinus Schoonmaker, who officiated alternately in the churches of those towns until he was nearly, if not quite, ninety years of age; he also used, about the commencement of the present century, occasionally to preach a Dutch sermon in the church at Brooklyn. He was the last connecting link of the chain which had bound together the churches of Flatbush and Gravesend from the year 1654, and which had united the other churches named with that of Flatbush from a period long anterior to the American Revolution; at his death this tie was severed, and ever since the churches have each had their ministers and formed independent congregations.

Before the commencement of the present century, it was very common on the west end of Long Island, in the burying-grounds of the Dutch Reformed congregations, to put Dutch inscriptions on the monumental or grave-stones, both prose and poetical; but this has now ceased to be the practice. Inscriptions in this language on grave-stones, are in the Bushwick burying-ground of as late date as the year 1780.

The Dutch Reformed church of Flatbush, in Kings County, was incorporated July 31, 1784, under a general act of Legislature of the State of

New York, entitled, "An act to enable all the religious denominations in this state to appoint trustees, who shall be a body corporate, for the purpose of taking care of the temporalities of their respective congregations, and for other purposes therein mentioned," passed April 6th, 1784. The first trustees of this church, named in the certificate, were Jeremias Vander Bilt, Joris Martense, Cornelius Wyckoff, Hendrick Suydam, and Peter Lifferts. This was one of the first, if not the first church upon Long Island, incorporated under this general law.

A Dutch Reformed church was erected in Jamaica, on this island, in 1715; in Newtown shortly after; and in the towns of North Hempstead and Oyster Bay about the year 1732. These churches were supplied with ministers from Kings County until about the middle of last century.

Many of the Dutch churches on this island were of a curious style of architecture; either circular, six-square, or eight-square, with high roofs, and a belfry or cupola springing from the top of the six-square or octagon roof, with a small bell in it. The churches at Jamaica, New Utrecht, and Bushwick, were of this character. The latter, which was six-square, was taken down in the year 1827. A few months previous to its destruction, a lady of our acquaintance, who had a fine taste for sketching, at our request made a drawing of this antique church, which we now possess, and prize highly as an accurate representation of those curious old churches which have now all disappeared from our island before the march of modern improvements.

FOUNDATION OF EPISCOPAL CHURCHES.

It is generally supposed, and so stated, that the first attempt to establish the Episcopal Church in this colony was by the act of 1693. This is an error. The code of laws for the government of the colony of New York, known as the *Duke's Laws*, adopted by the convention of deputies at Hempstead, on Long Island, March 1, 1664, evidently contemplated the establishment of that church, as will be seen upon reference to its provisions. This code, after stating that "the public worship of God is much discredited for want of painful and able ministers to instruct the people in the true religion, and for want of convenient places capable to receive any number or assembly of people in a decent manner for celebrating God's holy ordinances," then proceeds to provide that, "in each parish within this government, a church be built in the most convenient part thereof, capable to receive and accommodate two hundred persons."

"That, for the making and proportioning the levies and assessments for building and repairing the churches, provision for the poor, maintenance for the minister, as well as for the more orderly managing of all parochial affairs in other cases expressed, eight of the most able men of each parish be, by the major part of the householders of said parish, chosen to be overseers."

Out of this number of overseers, the constable and the eight overseers were annually to make choice of two to be churchwardens. These churchwardens had very much the same powers possessed by those officers in England; and were required twice in each year to make written presentments to the court of sessions of all offences coming within their knowledge against good morals.

"To prevent scandalous and ignorant pretenders to the ministry from intruding themselves as teachers, no minister shall be admitted to officiate within the government but such as shall produce testimonials to the Governor that he hath received ordination, either from some Protestant bishops or minister within some part of His Majesty's dominions, or the dominions of any foreign Prince of the Reformed Religion; upon which testimony the Governor shall induct the said minister into the parish that shall make presentation of him, and as duly elected by the major part of the inhabitants, householders."

It is not a little curious that this code of laws, which are understood to have received the sanction of the Duke of York, afterwards King James II. of England, and which were framed for the government of a colony of which he was the proprietor, should have so rigidly excluded the Roman Catholic religion, and allowed no ministers from any part of the world to exercise their calling here unless they were Protestants; and not even Protestants who had been ordained in a foreign country under a Roman Catholic monarch; and that, too, when James himself was such a rigid Roman Catholic, and made such extraordinary exertions to introduce that faith into England, where he had the opposition of a powerful and wealthy Establishment to contend with, and eventually lost his crown in the contest; and here, where he had no Establishment to encounter, and might easily have introduced it under the general toleration which was from the establishment of his government here allowed, it is truly strange and wonderful.

The same code declares that: "No person shall be molested, fined, or imprisoned, for differinty in judgment, in matters of religion, who professes Christianity."

The regulations in relation to the ministers, as established by this code, were as follows:

"The minister of every parish shall preach constantly every Sunday, and shall also pray for the King, Queen, Duke of York and the Royal family." "No minister shall refuse the sacrament of baptism to the children of Christian parents, when they shall be tendered, under penalty of loss of preferment." "Ministers are to marry persons after legal publication, or sufficient license. Legal publication shall be so esteemed when the persons to be married are three several days asked in the church, or have a special license."

"No person of scandalous or vicious life shall be admitted to the holy sacrament, who hath not given satisfaction therein to the minister." The court of assizes, which, previous to 1683, formed the legislative authority of the colony under the Duke of York, at their term commencing September 28, 1665, ordered the churches in each parish to be erected within three years after that term, and provided "to which end a town rate may be made to begin this year."

The same authority, the court of assizes, at a term commencing October 2, 1672, ordered "that the laws of the government be duly observed as to parish churches; and that although divers persons may be of different judgments, yet all shall contribute to the minister established and allowed of; which is no way judged to be an infringement of the liberty of conscience to which they may pretend."

Again, this court of assizes, at the term of October 13, 1675, had the establishment of the church under their consideration, and seem particularly desirous that some maintenance for the ministry in each town or parish should be actually realized. The record of their proceedings upon this point is to the following purport:

"The church affairs being taken into consideration, and particularly the maintenance of the ministry, it is ordered, that towards the maintenance of the ministry, besides the usual country rate, there shall be a double rate levied upon all those towns that have not already a sufficient maintenance for a minister."

The Government appears to have been truly anxious that churches should be established, and a minister of the gospel called and settled in each town of the colony; and the difficulties which they encountered in effecting this object seem to have mainly arisen from the disrelish of the people to subject themselves to the necessary taxation for those purposes.

All these provisions and regulations show that while the colonial government intended to allow the free exercise of any particular form of the Christian religion used by Protestants, it was at the same time their wish that the churches to be erected in each parish might be supplied with clergymen of the Established Church of England, and they, therefore, to facilitate that, gave those churches, as near as possible, the officers and form of government of the parish churches of England; and when such a minister should be settled in any church they intimated it to be their intention to compel all the inhabitants of the parish to contribute to his support, however much they might differ from him in judgment upon the matters of religion; and stated it as the conclusion which they had arrived at, that this was no infringement of the liberty of conscience previously granted. They had precedent for this regulation in the uniform practice of the New England colonies, which had then uniformly for years obliged the Episcopalians, or members of the Church of England, to contribute rateably to the support of their Congregational and Presbyterian ministers, and that even where they had a church and ministry of their own to support. The first Episcopalian minister upon this island was the Rev. George Keith, who had formerly been a Quaker. He was sent here by the English Society for Propagating the Gospel in Foreign Parts, soon after its formation in 1701, in order that he might ascertain the best mode of fulfilling the object of the association. He was styled the Rector of Queens County, and was accompanied by the Rev. Peter Gordon, as a missionary for this island, who was afterwards settled at Jamaica in 1702.

The act of 1693, in place of being the first attempt to establish the Episcopal Church on this island, was in some measure a revival of the regulations of 1664, somewhat extended; but this act, in its operation, was confined, on this island, to Queens County. In the year 1700, the people of Jamaica, in that county, who were then generally Presbyterians or Independent, erected a stone edifice for public worship, by a general subscription throughout the town, without restricting it to any particular denomination. After a year or more, they having no minister, the church was not used for Divine service; and Governor Cornbury considering it, from the manner in which the cost of its construction had been raised, as one of the parish churches which had previously been required to be erected at the public expense, delivered possession of it to the Episcopalians, who continued to use it, very much against the will of the Presbyterians, until the year 1735, when they abandoned it, and erected themselves another church in that town, which new church was, in 1761, incorporated by the name of *Grace Church*. When the seats in this new church were sold, in the year 1737, the congregation consisted of twenty-four families.

The above is one way in which the history of this church is narrated. Another is, that the stone church was actually occupied in 1702 by the Rev. John Hubbard, a Presbyterian minister, and his congregation; and that on Sunday afternoon, coming to the church, he found the pulpit occupied by the Rev. Peter Gordon, an Episcopalian minister, and the body of the church in possession of a number of Gov. Cornbury's friends and others, from the City of New York; that this led to a bitter controversy, which, after a protracted and expensive litigation on the trial of the cause before Chief Justice Lewis Morris, resulted in favor of the Presbyterians, and restored the church to them in 1728. Whichever is the true history of this matter, it is certainly to be regretted that any such controversy ever took place.

The Episcopalians were established and a church built in Hempstead in 1704; and the Rev. John Thomas, a missionary of the Society for Propagating the Gospel in Foreign Parts (of England), was their first minister. They erected a new church at that place in 1734, and were then incorporated, and constituted a parish, by the name of "St. George's Church, Hempstead."

On a tombstone now standing in the burying-ground of this church is the following inscription:

"11 June 1764 Died Samuel Seabury Rector of St. George's Church at Hempstead æt. 64."

This Rector Seabury was the father of the Right Rev. Samuel Seabury, the first Bishop of Connecticut, and the first who was consecrated for the United States. He was consecrated by the bishops of the Scottish Episcopal Church, before the English bishops were authorized by act of Parliament to consecrate any bishops for the United Colonies.

The old church of St. George at Hempstead is still (1846) standing, and is one of the most venerable churches in our country; it is beautifully situated, few more so.

Other Episcopal churches were founded on this island at the following named places, and at the periods mentioned:—

At Brookhaven, Caroline church, in 1730.

At Newtown, St. James' church, in 1734.

At Flushing, St. George's church, in 1734.

At Huntington, St. John's church, in 1784.

The first Episcopal church in the town of Brooklyn (which now, 1846, has in it eleven Episcopal churches, and two of them among the most splendid in the country), and, indeed, the first in Kings County, was established in the year 1784, soon after the conclusion of the Revolutionary war. It scarcely took the form of a church; there were but few, very few, Episcopalians in this town or county at that period, so few that they were not able to settle a minister among them, and were supplied with occasional services from the clergymen of the City of New York; for which purpose they assembled in a room of the old one-and-a-half story brick house, known as No. 40 Fulton street, Brooklyn, then called the Old Ferry Road, owned by Abiel Titus, Esq. There is no reason to believe that this little congregation was ever incorporated as a church, or had any regular officers. The first regularly established Episcopal church in this town or county was that formed in the year 1786. The congregation was at first very small, not having in it more than fifteen or sixteen families, and they were not able to go to much expense about erecting a church. They therefore hired the old and long one-story house, owned by Marvin Richardson, on the north-westerly corner of Fulton street and Middagh street, (which old building, or a considerable portion of it, still remains in the interior of the frame buildings now upon that corner,) and taking out the partitions, they seated it with seats with backs to them, and put in a pulpit. The pews they sold, and the tradition is, that a dispute which arose about the sale of one or two particular pews in this little church, was the origin of the Methodist Episcopal church in Brooklyn; and they continued in this edifice about a year or a little over, and their first minister was the Rev. Mr. Wright. This church does not appear to have had any particular name.

A few months before the establishment of the Episcopal church in Brooklyn, a frame building of considerable size for that day had been erected on the present Fulton street, upon what is now the Episcopal burying ground, and was used by a congregation of "Independents." It was incorporated on the 18th of September, 1785, under the name of the "Independent Meeting House," with John Matlock, pastor; George Wall, assistant; John Carpenter, treasurer; George Powers, secretary; and five trustees.

After they had used it for Divine worship something over a year, Mr. John Carpenter, and two or three other gentlemen who had a claim upon the land and building for the money advanced for its purchase and erection, ejected the Independent congregation by fastening up the church, and refusing them admission; and they subsequently transferred the land and church to the Episcopalian congregation, who thereupon left their room on the corner of Fulton and Middagh streets, and occupied it as their church, upon which, on the 23d of April, 1787, they were incorporated under the name of "The Episcopal Church of Brooklyn," and their temporalities placed under the direction of seven *trustees*, the first of whom were Whitehead Cornell, Joshua Sands, Joseph Sealy, Aquila Giles, Matthew Gleaves, John Van Nostrand and Henry Stanton.

The form of government which they had thus inadvertently adopted, not being that suited to the churches and congregations of the Episcopalian church, but intended for the Presbyterian and other congregations, the church was reorganized, and the 22d of June, 1795, newly incorporated, under the name of "St. Ann's Church," and placed under the government of churchwardens and vestrymen.

Many have supposed, and now believe, that the name of "St. Ann's Church" was for the first time applied to the stone church erected on Sands street; but this is an error: it was applied to the old frame church about nine years before the stone church was built.

They remained in this church until the stone Episcopal church on Sands street was erected; also known as St. Ann's church, when the old frame church was taken down about 1805, and from its materials the dwelling house No. 11 Prospect street was erected.

The first organ in any church in Kings County was that in St. Ann's church, Brooklyn, which was first opened April 11th, 1810, and a number of fine pieces of music performed and anthems sung. A sermon was delivered on the occasion by the Rev. R. C. Moore, on the importance of church music. St. Ann's Episcopal church was occupied until the close of the summer of 1825, when it was taken down in the month of September of that year. The first clergyman who officiated in that church was the Rev. John Ireland, a man of a most violent temper, and who was eventually silenced from preaching, or acting as a minister, for some very unseemly exhibitions of it, a restriction after some years removed, and he was appointed chaplain to the United States Navy Yard in this town, which situation he held until his decease.

The new St. Ann's church, constructed of brick, on Washington street, in the rear of the old church, was consecrated in the latter part of the summer of 1825, by the Right Rev. John Croes, Bishop of New Jersey, assisted by the Bishops of Pennsylvania and Rhode Island. At that time it was the only Episcopal church in the town of Brooklyn, or in the County of Kings, except that the chaplain of the Navy Yard then being an Episcopalian, the service in that chapel was of the Episcopal form.

At North Hempstead, in Queens County, an Episcopalian church was founded by the name of "Christ Church" in the year 1803.

FOUNDATION OF METHODIST EPISCOPAL CHURCHES.

The first congregation of this denomination was formed in Brooklyn about the year 1787, but it was some three or four years before they became sufficiently numerous to erect a church or meeting-house, but they had frequent preaching supplied by the itinerant preachers of their connexion, in a small building of one story about thirty-five feet long, and twenty feet broad, which they built on the northerly side of High street, and afterwards used for many years as a school-house.

Their first church on Sands street, near Fulton street, was probably erected in the autumn of the year 1793, as we find it to have been incorporated on the 19th of May, 1794, under the name of the "First Methodist Episcopal Church," and placed under the government of six trustees. This church continued to be used until the year 1810, when being found much too small for the congregation attending there, it was taken down, and a temporary shed of large dimensions erected in the burying-ground immediately in the rear of the church; under which the pulpit and seats were placed, and Divine service performed there until the new church was erected. Which new church was erected upon the site of the old one, and extending much beyond it, both in length and breadth—it was also a frame building, as well as the old church.

This new Methodist church was opened for the first time after its completion, on the 18th of August, 1811, and a dedication sermon preached on the occasion.

This Methodist church erected on Sands street, Brooklyn, in 1793, was not only the first church of that denomination in this town, but also the first erected in Kings County.

FOUNDATION OF ROMAN CATHOLIC CHURCHES.

The first Roman Catholic church founded upon Long Island takes its date from the year 1822.

The corner-stone of this church was laid in the village of Brooklyn, on the 25th of June, 1822, on the corner of Jay street and Chapel street, which was then a large extent of vacant ground, there being then no buildings nearer that spot than High street, and not a single building between the site of the church and the meadows of Wallaboght mill-pond.

This church was incorporated on the 20th of November, 1822, by the name of "St. James Roman Catholic Church," and placed under the government of seven trustees. The church has been very much enlarged every way; the nave of the church, as now used, was all that constituted the original edifice; the front, the tower and spire, the transept and the chancel have all been added. The church, as first erected, was a plain brick edifice, with unfinished walls inside; now it is a very showy building.

OLD HOUSES.

There are several houses still remaining on this island venerable for their antiquity, and for incidents connected with their history. One of them is the house in Southold, known as the "old Young's place," which was built in 1688. It was the mansion house of the descendants of the Rev. John Youngs, the first Christian minister in that part of Long Island. In the same town is also the edifice known as "Cochran's Hotel," which was erected in the year 1700; and there are several others in the eastern part of this island which might be noticed, if time and space permitted. Approaching westwardly through the island, we meet, on Fort Neck, with an old-fashioned brick house, which was many years ago owned and occupied by a Captain Jones, who is reputed to have been a pirate, and in it he died. Tradition says that at the time of his death, a large black crow (which the people supposed to be a demon) hovered over his bed, and when life was extinct, the crow made his exit through the west end of the house. This story is still told by the oldest inhabitants as a fact, and they also state that the hole through which the crow made his departure cannot be stopped, and that as often as it is closed it is opened by some unknown means.

I saw the house in July, 1827; it was a venerable-looking building, but fast hastening to ruin. It was then pointed out to me as the "haunted house," by persons in the vicinity. Capt. Jones was buried not far from the house, and his grave is designated to this day as the "Pirate's Grave."

This grave is about half a mile south of the house, on the banks of a creek, in a small piece of ground surrounded by an earth wall. The tombstone is of red freestone. The ground also contains the graves of his wife, his son, and his son's wife. There are no other persons interred there but these four. It is quite a solitary spot.

The mansion of the Hon. George Duncan Ludlow, at Hempstead Plains, now called Hyde Park, was one of the largest and best houses of its day on this island. It was destroyed by fire accidentally, in the month of December, 1773, and the loss sustained was estimated at not less than £3000. With it was also consumed a library estimated to be worth twelve hundred pounds, which must have been a very large and valuable library for the colonies. This house was immediately rebuilt upon the same spot, and again destroyed by fire in 1817, while in the occupation of the celebrated William Cobbett.

In the town of Flatbush are several of these relics of former days; among them is an old one-story brick dwelling-house erected in the year 1696, situate at the corner of the Flatbush turnpike road and the road leading to New Lotts. This house has the following figures and devices, containing the date of its erection, and the initials of its original proprietor, on its front, formed with blue bricks inserted between the red bricks.

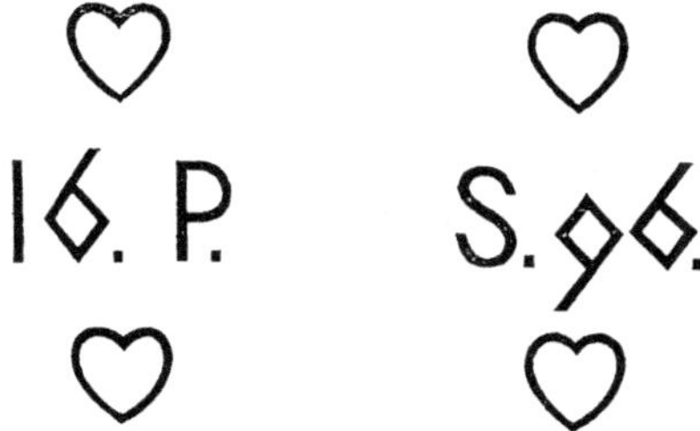

In the same town is a very old frame house, covered with cedar shingles, the date of which is unknown, but we should not be surprised, judging from its appearance, if the date of this building was prior to that of the one above mentioned.

The oldest house in the town of Brooklyn is supposed to be the house which was known as No. 64 Fulton street, in the village of Brooklyn, and owned and occupied by Mr. Jacob Patchen. Mr. Charles Doughty, who has been dead about twenty-five years, and was about eighty-five years of age when he died, said that this was an old house when he was a boy. Mrs. Rapalje, the mother of John Rapalje, whose property in Brooklyn was confiscated during the Revolutionary war, said that this house was built by a family of the Remsens who came from Holland. This house was removed by order of the corporation of the village of Brooklyn, for the purpose of opening Market street in that village, and now stands on Jackson street in said village, now city.

There was also recently an old brick house standing on Fulton street, in Brooklyn, near the corner of Nassau street, which was occupied by the Colonial Legislature as a sessions house during the prevalence of the small-pox in New York in 1752; and at this house, on the 4th of June, 1752, 2,541 bills of credit issued by this Colony, amounting to £3,602. 18s. 3d., were cancelled by the Colonial Commissioners. This house was subsequently occupied by General Israel Putnam as his headquarters during the stay of the American army on Long Island, in the summer of 1776.

The house was taken down in May, 1832, and its timbers, which were all of oak (as were those of all the old buildings of that early period), were so perfectly sound and hard that they could not be cut without much difficulty; and most of them were worked into the new brick buildings which now occupy the same site.

What an idea does this simple fact afford us of the strength and permanency with which every thing was done by our ancestors. They did not build in haste, or run up houses during the frosts of winter, but all was done with much care and forethought; they were building for their posterity as well as for themselves. In building, as in every other matter, much time was spent in examining the project in all its probable bearings before it was adventured upon; and when once undertaken, it was persisted in with a force and spirit almost unknown to the present age. To this peculiar characteristic of our forefathers we owe all the blessings arising from our institutions of government. A slight and even partial examination of the history of the United States for the half century preceding the Revolution of 1776, will show us how many years of patient thought and unwearied toil were deemed necessary by the patriots of that day to precede the great event of the Declaration of Independence, and to give to it the desired stability. They did not dream of getting up a revolution in a few hours, days or months, now so common in this world, and whose effects, of course, are as evanescent as were the deliberations which gave them birth. The house on Brooklyn Heights recently owned by Henry Waring, Esq., was at the same time occupied by General Washington as his headquarters.

There is a very old stone dwelling house near the water at Gowanus Bay, and next to the house of Simon Bergen. It was formerly the old Bergen mansion house, and near the well of this house, Mr. Bergen, the proprietor, was shot during the Revolutionary war by an English soldier. Another memorial of antiquity which still remains to us in Brooklyn is an old stone house owned by the family of Cortelyou, at Gowanus, which bears on its gable end, in iron figures, the date of 1699. It is a venerable looking edifice; and when viewing it, our minds are imperceptibly led to think how much of human joy and sorrow, what scenes of happiness and misery, must have occurred under the roof-tree of that old mansion since the date of its erection; and if it were in our power to learn its entire history without the slightest embellishment, what a strange romance would even the plainest narrative of the facts which have transpired within its walls now appear to us! So true it is that fact is often much stranger than any romance which the mind of man ever conceived. This house was the residence of the American general, Lord Stirling, prior to his capture by the British forces in the battles of Long Island.

The house No. 27 Fulton street, opposite Front street, in Brooklyn, and for many years occupied as a tavern, was built in 1780, entirely of Long Island timber, and the frame of oak, as was formerly the case with many houses; it was taken down about the year 1830. In digging the cellar of this house a large rock was found, which in endeavoring to sink slipped, and one of the men fell under it and was crushed to death, and his bones remain under it to the present day: so says tradition.

The houses mentioned were among the largest and most important dwellings in the colony at the time of their erection, and serve to show us what the more wealthy and noble of the land then thought sufficient for all their wants, and for the accommodation of their families and friends. In the century following there was an evident change in sentiment in this respect; the houses were larger, and from being long and narrow, with two front doors, not unfrequently side by side, and one or one and a half stories high, they became square and two stories in height, affording double the amount of room, and often more, than in the old style of building in the century immediately preceding. Of this more modern style, many of the houses would even now be regarded highly respectable in appearance; it was an adaptation, to some extent, of the English style, as its predecessor was of the Dutch mode of building; there are however but few, very few, of this second order of our old mansions now in existence: a few of them are mentioned in the following pages.

The first Lighthouse erected on Long Island

was the Lighthouse on Montauk Point, which was built in 1796. It is a very massive and durable tower of stone, and it is said to be one of the best lights in the United States.

GOVERNOR MARTIN'S HOUSE.

Prior to the Revolution of 1776, Governor Martin, of the province of South Carolina, came on from that province to New York, and built the large old house at Rockaway Beach, now (1833) occupied as a boarding-house, where he resided with his family. In the large room on the lower floor, now used as a dining-room, there is a painting on a panel over the fire-place, representing a child playing with a dog. It is a splendid piece of painting, the dog especially is admirable: it is a spotted dog. This painting was done by Sir John Copley, then without his title, and an inhabitant of Boston, in Massachusetts, and the child represented a member of Governor Martin's family. The house is a very fine specimen of the old style of mansion-house building. Mrs. Martin, the widow of Governor Martin, lived and died in the city of New York, in Broadway, on part of what is now the site of Astor's great hotel; she was a daughter of Sir John Copley, and sister of Lord Lyndhurst, the

English Lord Chancellor; she says the painting before mentioned was from the pencil of her father. She died about the year 1825, and quite wealthy; she gave eight thousand dollars by her will to Bishop Hobart of New York. In the comptroller's office of Trinity Church, on the corner of Fulton and Church streets, New York, is another painting by Sir John Copley. It is a likeness of the Rev. Mr. Ogilvie of Trinity Church, assistant minister with the Rev. Mr. Auchmuty, the rector of that church. Mr. Ogilvie died before the Revolutionary war, on Fulton street, in Brooklyn, near its junction with Jackson street, and about fifty feet southerly of that junction, on the east side of the street, is (1830) a relic of the olden time which has been there some considerable time before the Revolutionary war It is a wood medallion, but profile likeness of King George III., of England, crowned with a laurel wreath. It is well done and a creditable specimen of wood carving not only for that day, but for any day, and judging from the engraved likeness of that monarch, it is a very good representation of him. It is now, and I believe always has been, on the front of the hay scales, near the top, which are now kept by Charles Poling. It should be preserved as a memento of our ante-Revolutionary history. In

1820 there was another of these old-fashioned hay-scales in Brooklyn; it stood on the westerly side of Fulton street, a little southerly of the corner of that street and Buckbee's alley, and between the front of those hay-scales and the opposite side of the street was only about thirty-five feet. On the top of these hay-scales was a small cupola in which hung the fire-bell of Brooklyn, then the only bell in the village for an alarm in such cases, except the bell of St. Ann's church, which was but a poor one, and the small bell of the old Dutch Church, which then hung in the belfry of the Dutch Reformed Lecture-room in Middagh street. At this period all the houses on Fulton street, between the corner of Front street, and the junction of Fulton street and Main street, were old frame buildings of one and two stories high, with the exception of the stone dwelling-house of two stories, occupied by Jacob M. Hicks and John M. Hicks, on the corner of Hicks street and Fulton street; and the two-story brick dwelling of Burdett Stryker, opposite Front street; and the long old one-story brick dwelling of Abiel Titus, on the east side of Fulton street. Hicks street then was only about fifteen feet wide at its junction with Fulton street, and was a steep, ugly hill to get up with a loaded cart, and gullying very much with every rain. About this time the trustees of the village attempted its first regulation, by building a high stone wall along from the rear of the Messrs. Hicks' house for 600 or 700 feet (outside of it being then all vacant ground, used for garden purposes), and then cutting off the top of the hill some four or five feet, they filled in the bottom and along even with that stone wall; and then, to prevent its gullying, paved it with a gutter in the centre of the street.

On the westerly corner of Front and Fulton streets stood the old Rapalje mansion-house, a large stone building of two stories, about forty feet front on the street. This house was second to none upon Long Island, when it was built, for size and elegance. It was taken down about 1807.

The next house west of that upon the Old Ferry street, now Fulton street, was the large, old, stone two-story building, occupied as a tavern, known as the "Corporation House;" it belonged to the Corporation of the City of New York, and was originally erected by them as an inn or tavern some twenty or thirty years before the Revolution, and was occupied as such all through that war, and was a noted resort of the British officers stationed in New York, and many of them mention it in their published travels in this country.

That house was destroyed by fire in the year 1815, and its desolate walls remained standing for some two or three years after, when the Corporation of New York had a new survey made of their property there, and new division of lots, upon which they leased the same, and brick stores and dwellings were erected.

Another noted house in Brooklyn was the mansion-house of Philip I. Livingston, afterwards a member of the Continental Congress. This was a large frame building, actually forming two dwellings. The larger part, which was about forty feet square, Mr. Livingston erected for his son, who was a young man then travelling in Europe; who, upon his return, was to be married to a lady to whom he was engaged before he left home, and occupy that new house; but he was taken sick, and died abroad only a few months before his return was expected.

This mansion, both the old and the new part, was finished throughout in the best and most costly style of that period, having much beautiful carved wood-work and ornamented ceilings, and also Italian marble chimney-pieces sculptured in Italy. Most beautiful specimens they were; we have often admired them. This house, upon the death of its last owner and occupier, Judge Joralemon, in 1842, was about to be taken down, and these marble chimney-pieces were packed up for removal, when it took fire, and they, with the house, were destroyed. The gardens attached to this mansion, when the British took possession of it and converted it into a naval hospital in 1776, are said to have been among the most beautiful in America.

OLD MONUMENTAL STONES AND FUNERAL CUSTOMS.

The oldest monumental tombstones bearing inscriptions are to be found on the east end of the island, although there were settlements made on the west end at an earlier date than on the east. The reasons for this we conceive to be these: Among the Dutch settlers the art of stone-cutting does not appear to have been used until within comparatively a few years, with but few exceptions, and their old burying-grounds are strewn with rough headstones which bear no inscriptions; whereas the English people immediately on their settlement introduced the practice of perpetuating the memories of their friends by inscribed stones. Another reason for not finding any very old tombstones in the Dutch settlements is, that they early adopted the practice of having family burial-places on their farms, without monuments, and not unfrequently private burials, both of which the Governor and Colonial Legislature, in 1664 and 1684, deemed of sufficient importance to merit legislative interference, and declared that all persons should be publicly buried in some parish burial-place; but as there was no specific penalty attached to the breach of these laws, the custom of burying in private burial-places still continued, and is practised to a considerable extent at the present day.

In the old grave-yard at East Hampton are said to be several ancient tombstones, and that in that grave-yard are buried many of the first settlers.

The first English settlement in the town of East Hampton (excepting Gardiner's Island) was made in the spring of 1648, and the first interments were made in the south burial-ground of that town, where yet may be seen monuments of red cedar wood, which are probably as ancient as any other now existing.

The public cemeteries on the east end of the island were uninclosed, indicating that the settlers regarded with no religious veneration the resting-places of the dead; not that they had no respect for *the memories* of their deceased relatives and friends, but that they esteemed all measures for setting apart the final resting-place of *the body*, by enclosures and other acts, as relics of superstitious observances, which should, as an act of duty, be avoided, and they, therefore, in their great care to abstain from anything which might have the appearance of acceding to the ceremonies and requirements of Prelacy and Papacy, ran into the opposite extreme.

On the west end of the island, on the contrary, care was taken to secure the burial-places from all intrusion, by fencing them, and allowing but one place for their entrance; and although no particular ceremony was used in setting them apart, or upon interring the dead in them, except by the few members of the Church of England, or Episcopalians, yet all here regarded the grave-yard as a species of hallowed ground, not to be trod upon lightly or without cause.

In the church burying-ground at Southold is a tombstone bearing the following inscription:

"Here lies ye body of William Wells of Southold, gent, justice of ye peace, and first Sheriffe of New Yorkshire upon Long Island, who departed this life November 13th, 1671, aged 63."

"Yea here hee lies, who speaketh yet, tho' dead,
On wings of faith his soule to Heaven is fled,
His pious deedes and charity was such,
That of his praise no pen can write too much.
As was his life so was his blest decease,
He lived in love and sweetly dy'd in peace."

The oldest tombstone in the Dutch church-yard at Brooklyn, having any mark, is one which bears the date of 1730.

The oldest tombstone at present in the Bushwick burying-ground is one erected to the memory of Cornelius Bogart, and bears the date of 1769. There are inscriptions in Dutch on tombstones in this burial-place bearing date as late as 1780.

In the burying-ground in Flatbush village, among the earliest grave-stones, is one now standing about eighteen inches in height from the ground, made of the white sandstone which is usually found in the woods. It is inscribed to the memory of Helen Vanderbilt, wife of one of the Martenses, and has cut on it, near the top, a rough representation of a cherub's head. There is a tradition in the Martense family, that this monumental stone cost ten pounds of the currency of the colony at that period. A most enormous sum, being equal to the whole salary of the Clerk of Kings County for a year, that being also ten pounds currency at that time, and explaining to a certain extent the reason why so few gravestones of an ancient date are to be found in the burying-grounds on the west end of the island; and taken in connection with the fact of the private burial-places, affords, perhaps, a complete solution to the whole question. There were unquestionably but few persons who here followed the business of stone-cutting, and consequently the price was too high for any but those who were comparatively wealthy, and the most of those having been interred in their private cemeteries, but few of those stones are to be found in the public grave-yards.

The Legislature of the State of New York, on the 6th of April, 1796, passed an Act authorizing the inhabitants of Flatbush to establish a night watch in that town. The object designed by this watch was to prevent the taking up of recently buried dead bodies from their graves in the church-yard, to be used for anatomical examinations in the city of New York and elsewhere; which it was said had been previously done in some instances, and caused much excitement in the community, as well as grief to the surviving relatives; for there is nothing that the old-fashioned Dutch people so much dread and abhor as the idea of having their own bodies, or those of their friends and relatives, subjected to the dissecting knife of the surgeon for any such purpose.

This watch was usually kept every night in the burying-ground, for eight or ten days after the interment, depending on the season of the year. The friends of the deceased supplied the watch each night with provisions and refreshments to be consumed during their vigils.

Formerly the funerals upon this island were of a very expensive character, and it was a custom in the old families to lay up a stock of superior wine to be used on such occasions; and frequently at those funerals you would meet with wine so choice and excellent that it could scarcely be equalled by any in the land, although our country has always been celebrated throughout the world for its excellent Madeira wine. Christopher Smith, Esq., of Jamaica, on this island, who died about half a century since, had stored away a large quantity of the most superior wines in the country, which were used at his funeral; and an old friend of ours who attended the funeral of General Curtenius, in the city of New York, several years ago informed us that from the great profusion of excellent wines, liquors, segars, etc., it resembled more a wedding feast than it did a funeral; this, however, was not peculiar to this instance; it was the general custom at that period and for a very long time previous upon Long Island and in the city of New York. Also, and not very many years since, among us a custom universally existed of handing around wine to all persons attending a funeral; and it was also usual, when the estate of the deceased would afford it, and even in many cases where it could not, to give to each of the pall-bearers, clergymen and physicians attending, a scarf of white linen (sufficient in quantity to make a shirt), which was worn by them across the shoulder; and also a pair of gloves, either of silk or kid. If the deceased was old or married, the scarf was tied with a black ribbon, and the gloves were black; but if the deceased was young and unmarried, the scarf was fastened with a white ribbon and the gloves were white. The custom of giving gloves and scarfs at funerals is not yet entirely gone out of existence. At a still earlier period it was the custom, at the more superior order of funerals, to give gold mourning rings to each person who attended, and we have seen still preserved on Long Island, in the family of the gentleman to whom it was presented, a ring which was thus given at the funeral of the Earl of Bellamont, who died the Governor of the Colony of New York; it was a very heavy, massive gold ring, and has upon it the inscription, "Comes De Bello-mon."

And even within the present century it was likewise the custom at funerals in the country parts of Long Island, for the relatives of the deceased, at the house from which the funeral was to proceed, to prepare a large quantity of cold provisions, such as roast turkeys, boiled hams, roast beef, etc., which were set upon a table in a room opened for the purpose, and every one went there and helped himself as he pleased. Also rum, brandy and gin, with pipes, tobacco and segars, were handed around among the people during their stay at the house, it being considered inhospitable not to do so; and it was not an unusual thing to see the farmers congregate together, in warm weather, under the shade of trees, about the vicinity of the house, smoking their long pipes and drinking, hearing and telling the news, and laughing and talking together for two or three hours before the funeral would move. This long stay at the house previous to proceeding to the place of interment, together with the great plenty of spirituous liquors distributed about, sometimes occasioned scenes of much noise, and very inappropriate to the purpose for which they had assembled. The change which has since been produced in this practice is mainly to be credited to the exertions of one gentleman, the Rev. Evan M. Johnson, then the Rector of the Episcopal church at Newtown, who some years since proposed to the vestry of that church, that thereafter, at all funerals in that congregation, the friends should be bidden or invited at one hour, and the interment should take place the next succeeding hour, so as to allow them sufficient time to assemble and no more, and to induce its acceptance the rector agreed to relinquish his claim to a scarf on such occasions; he also proposed that the use of spirituous liquors at funerals should be discontinued; to all these propositions the vestry assented, recommending that in place of spirituous liquors, wine should be handed around among the people; this was a great reform, when we consider that it was long before the temperance movement commenced. This plan being seen to work well in that congregation, was also adopted by other congregations in other parts of the island, and after a while the use of wine itself at funerals was dispensed with.

But expensive as was the character of the funeral on this island, and in New York, they could not compare in that respect with those among the Dutch inhabitants of the city of Albany. Judge Benson, in his memoir read before the New York Historical Society, describes the funeral of Lucas Wyngaard who died in that city in the year 1756, a bachelor, leaving some estate. The invitation to that funeral was very general, and those who attended returned after the interment, as the custom then was, to the house of the deceased, towards the close of the day; and a large number of them never left it until the dawn of the ensuing day. In the course of the night a pipe of wine, which had been stored in the cellar for some years before the occasion, was drank; dozens of papers of tobacco were consumed; grosses of pipes broken; scarce a whole decanter or glass was left; and, to crown the whole, the pall-bearers made a bonfire of their scarfs upon the hearth of the room where they were carousing. This may have been a little more uproarious than most of the funerals of that period, as the deceased was a bachelor, and had no widow and children in the same house to control, and, in some degree, to modify their proceedings; but yet all the funerals of that time were more than enough so under any circumstances. Even down to within the last fifty years Albany was noted for the expensive character of its funerals; a funeral, in a respectable old Dutch family at that place and especially of the head or any principal member of it, often cost from three to four thousand dollars. That of the first wife of the late Patroon, Hon. Stephen Van Rensselaer, it is said, cost him not less than twenty thousand dollars! All his tenants were invited, and most of them were in Albany two or three days at his expense, and two thousand linen scarfs were given on that occasion. It was formerly the custom there for a young man immediately previous to his marriage, to send to the Island of Madeira for a pipe or two of the best wine; a portion of which being used in the rejoicings consequent upon his marriage, and the remainder stored away for his funeral and that of his wife.

It was also the practice in that city to send out special funeral invitations for all the friends and acquaintances of the deceased, being about the same age, and likewise for all the clergy and professional men of the city and neighboring country, and general invitations from the pulpits of the churches for the citizens at large. To the house of each person thus specially invited was sent a linen scarf, a pair of black silk gloves, a bottle of old Madeira wine, and two "*funeral cakes*," which were round, and about the size of a dinner plate; this was done previous to the funeral, and was in addition to the great quantity of spiced wine and other liquors, which, with tobacco and pipes, were distributed and used at the house of the deceased immediately preceding and after the interment. When General Schuyler died in that city, all the clergy, lawyers, physicians, and even students, in Albany and its neighborhood for many miles, were invited specially, and a scarf, gloves, a bottle of wine, with funeral cakes, given to each one of them. So particular were they about the linen of which to make these scarfs, that in several instances they sent down by land to New York, in the depth of winter, to purchase it, and paid two dollars a yard. Common linen would not answer; the finer it was the better it was liked for that purpose. These customs have now all died away in that city; the only relic of them remaining we noticed at a funeral there during the winter of 1840, when the persons attending in large numbers, after the interment, accompanied the relatives of the deceased in procession on their return to the house, and when they had arrived at the door they all dispersed without going in.

Among the Dutch inhabitants on Long Island, it was recently, and had been from time immemorial, if it is not even yet, customary to convert the first money that a young man obtained by his labor or services, after he became of age, into gold coin, and then lay it by for the purpose of burying him, until a sufficient sum was thus procured to bear the expense of a "respectable funeral"—they esteeming it a great reproach to have it said that either of them died after attaining about the age of twenty-three years, without leaving money sufficient to pay the expenses of their burial, unless under very peculiar circumstances. We have seen a large number of guineas of the reign of George II., and Spanish gold pieces of a later date, which had in one family been collected from one generation to another, and laid by for that purpose, being esteemed as something sacred, and not to be disposed of in any other way, but to be preserved for the emergency, if required. It was also formerly the custom with them, the Dutch farmers, when the head of a family died, to kill an ox or steer, and to buy a barrel of wine, upon which they had a great feast among the relatives and friends. We have been informed by a gentleman now living, that some years ago, he had charge of the funeral of one of the old Dutch inhabitants of this island, a very respectable farmer, and that the expense attending that funeral was between seven and eight hundred dollars, and that it was the particular request of the surviving relatives that it should be so, their attachment for the deceased impelling them to desire that his funeral should be a generous one, and have nothing mean or inhospitable about it.

It was also the practice on this island, and still is so, to appropriate a new linen shirt, handkerchief, etc., for each member of the family, for the purpose of burying them in, and which articles are never worn, but are left clean for that use. And in the country parts of Long Island it is usual, or was until very recently, when a woman died in childbed, to carry the corpse to the grave, with a white sheet spread over the coffin, in place of a pall.

This last-mentioned custom gave rise to the only instance of second-sight we have ever heard of upon this island. A gentleman, who is now deceased, a man of veracity and high standing in the community, and who for many years of his life was in public office, informed us that some years previous, coming up a road leading into the village of Flatbush (we think that from New Utrecht), he met or rather overtook, within about a mile of the village, a funeral of a female who had died in childbed, for the white sheet was spread over the coffin; the road being quite wide he passed them, and some time after, in the same day, he inquired what female had been buried in the church-yard that day. He was told there had been no interment on that day, and that no funeral had passed through the village; he also inquired along the road on which he had seen the funeral procession moving, and all the people, to his great surprise, declared that no funeral had passed on that day, or they would have seen it, nor was any one dead in the neighborhood, or they would have heard of it. He now began to think his eyes might have deceived him, but could not imagine how that could be, when the following day he heard of the death of the w'fe of one of his friends not far from Flatbush, who had died that morning in childbed; and the next day at the same hour in which he had seen it, the funeral procession did come along the same road on which he had thus before seen it, with the white sheet spread over the coffin; and then he began to conclude that he had experienced an instance of that nature called by the Scotch second-sight. He said he was in good health at the time, and was in no way excited, for he had no idea it was a vision he was looking upon, but believed it to be a real funeral.

SCHOOLS AND EDUCATION.

The reputation of the schools in New York under the Dutch government was so high that it was not an unfrequent occurrence for the English settlers in Virginia, and other southern colonies, to send their children to New Amsterdam, now New York, for the purposes of education.

One of the very first regulations made by the Dutch government upon the settlement of the colony of the New Netherlands was to provide for the education of the youth, as well as for the religious instruction of the colonists. In the "Conditions offered by the Burgomasters of the City of Amsterdam, etc., to all who are willing to settle in New Netherland," that city having, under the Dutch West India Company, the arrangement of the terms and conditions upon which the colonists should be transported to, and seated in the new colony, was the following on the subject of schools:—

"The City of Amsterdam shall send there a proper person for a schoolmaster, who shall also read the Holy Scriptures in public, and set the Psalms."

"The City of Amsterdam shall also, as soon as they conveniently can, provide a salary for the said schoolmaster."

The colonists were probably very soon after their settlement in a situation to relieve the Fatherland from this engagement on their behalf, and to provide a salary for their schoolmaster themselves. For we find that by 1650, and probably some time earlier, there was a school established in each town under the Dutch government, and the schoolmaster's salary formed part of the regular town expenses.

In each of these towns the schoolmaster was also the chorister and sexton of the church, and in the absence of the minister was required, by the terms upon which he was engaged, to read prayers and a sermon in the church to the congregation. Thus, when the Rev. Henricus Selwyn, on the 23d of July, 1664, took leave of his church at Brooklyn, on this island, to return to Holland, after his departure Charles Debevoise, the schoolmaster of this town, was required to read prayers and a sermon from an approved author every Sabbath, in the church, for the improvement of the congregation, until another minister was called.

This connection between the schoolmaster and the church in the Dutch towns existed not only under the Dutch administration in this colony, but was also continued under the English government for a long period after its establishment in the colony, as will be seen by a reference to the agreement made between the Consistory of the Dutch Reformed church at Flatbush, and Johannis Van Eckellen, the schoolmaster of that town, on the 8th of October, 1682.

Who is it that does not see that the peculiar aptitude always manifested by our people for self-government, from a period long anterior to our Revolutionary contest, resulted mainly, under Providence, from the great care manifested by our forefathers for the establishment of schools, and their support in each town, both under the Dutch and English governments?

Long Island, at a very early period of its settlement, was peculiarly blessed in this respect. By the articles of agreement for establishing the boundary line between the United English Colonies of New England and the New Netherlands, made at Hartford by the Commissioners of the New England Colonies and Governor Stuyvesant, on the 19th of September, 1650, and which was ratified and confirmed by the States General of Holland, on the 22d of February, 1656, it was agreed that the boundary line on Long Island, between the Dutch and English, should be "a line drawn from the westermost part of Oyster Bay, and thence in a direct course of the sea-shore, shall be the line of division between the Dutch and English on Long Island, the eastern part for the English, and the western part for the Dutch."

By this arrangement, the eastern part of this island came under the government of the colony of Connecticut, and received the benefit of the New England common-school system, which was established at that early period; and the western part, remaining under the Dutch government, had the advantage of their system of establishing a school in each town.

Few, and indeed none but those who have made our early history their study, can duly appreciate the causes which led to the American Revolution, and gave us existence as an independent nation. None tended more to that event than the universal diffusion of education among our people, which enabled them to judge accurately of public measures and foresee their consequences.

With any other people upon earth at that period the British Ministry might have successfully tried their experiments of arbitrary government without meeting with resistance, and have effectually enslaved a whole country before its inhabitants would have been aware of their ultimate design.

That the Dutch colonists were very particular in all their arrangements about their schools, and in making their agreements with their schoolmasters, is clearly shown by the following:

"Articles of agreement made with Johannis Van Eckellen, schoolmaster and clerk of the church at Flatbush," translated from the Dutch language.

"Art. 1st. The school shall begin at 8 o'clock in the morning, and go out at 11 o'clock. It shall begin again at 1 o'clock, and end at 4 o'clock. The bell shall be rung before the school begins.

"2d. When the school opens, one of the children shall read the morning prayer, as it stands in the catechism, and close with the prayer before dinner. In the afternoon it shall begin with the prayer after dinner, and close with the evening prayer. The evening school shall begin with the Lord's Prayer, and close by singing a Psalm.

"3d. He shall instruct the children in the common prayers and the questions and answers of the catechism, on Wednesdays and Saturdays, to enable them to say their catechism on Sunday afternoons in the church before the afternoon service, otherwise on the Monday following, at which the schoolmaster shall be present. He shall demean himself patiently and friendly towards the children in their instruction, and be active and attentive to their improvement.

"4th. He shall be bound to keep his school nine months in succession, from September to June, one year with another, or the like period of time for a year, according to the agreement with his predecessor; he shall, however, keep the school nine months, and always be present himself."

His predecessor, John Tebout, was not bound to keep the school the three summer months, unless twenty scholars attended; he was, however, at liberty to keep the school for ten or a less number at the stated price.

CHURCH SERVICE.

Art. 1st. He shall be chorister of the church, ring the bell three times before service, and read a chapter of the Bible in the church, between the second and third ringing of the bell; after the third ringing he shall read the ten commandments and the twelve articles of Faith, and then set the Psalm. In the afternoon, after the third ringing of the bell, he shall read a short chapter, or one of the Psalms of David, as the congregation are assembling. Afterwards he shall again set the Psalm.

2d. When the minister shall preach at Brooklyn or New Utrecht, he shall be bound to read twice before the congregation a sermon from the book used for the purpose. The afternoon sermon will be on the catechism of Dr. Vander Hagen, and thus he shall follow the turns of the minister. He shall hear the children recite the questions and answers of the catechism, on that Sunday, and he shall instruct them. When the minister preaches at Flatlands, he shall perform the like service.

3d. He shall provide a basin of water for the baptisms, for which he shall receive twelve stuyvers, in wampum, for every baptism, from the parents or sponsors. He shall furnish bread and wine for the communion, at the charge of the church. He shall furnish the minister, in writing, the names and ages of the children to be baptized, together with the names of the parents and sponsors; he shall also serve as a messenger for the consistories.

4th. He shall give the funeral invitations, and toll the bells, for which service he shall receive, for persons of fifteen years of age and upwards, twelve guilders; and for persons under fifteen, eight guilders. If he shall invite out of the town he shall receive three additional guilders for every town; and if he shall cross the river to New York, he shall have four guilders more.

SCHOOL MONEY.

He shall receive for a speller, or reader, in the day school, three guilders for a quarter, and for a writer, four.

In the evening school, he shall receive for a speller or reader four guilders, and five guilders for a writer, per quarter.

SALARY.

The residue of his salary shall be four hundred guilders in wheat, of wampum value, deliverable at Brooklyn Ferry; and for his service from October to May, two hundred and thirty-four guilders, in wheat, at the same place, with the dwelling, pasturages, and meadow appertaining to the school, to begin from the first day of October. Signed by the Constable and Trustees. Done and agreed on in Consistory, in the presence of the Constable and Trustees, this 8th day of October, 1682. Signed by Casper Van Zuren M. and the Consistory.

I agree to the above articles, and promise to observe the same to the best of my ability.

JOHANNIS VAN ECKELLEN.

Under the Dutch government of this colony, great care was used in the selection of the schoolmaster for each town; and no man was appointed to that office unless upon the recommendation of the Governor. Thus we find, in the month of May, 1661, Governor Stuyvesant recommended Charles Debevoise as a suitable person for the schoolmaster of the town of Brooklyn, and clerk and sexton of the church in this town; and upon that recommendation he was employed in those offices. It may seem a matter of surprise to us, that the Governor of the colony should employ his time in selecting suitable persons for such an office as a schoolmaster; but our Dutch ancestors entertained a different view of the matter; they, from the first period of their settlement, were fully convinced that an intelligent and educated community could alone make the colony of any value to themselves or to the Fatherland; and that crime and unhappiness among a people resulted in a great measure from ignorance. With them, therefore, it was a cardinal principle to diffuse the means of education as widely as possible; but to establish schools was not of itself sufficient, unless they also secured the services of the proper men to conduct them. To effect this latter purpose, which they regarded as all important to the successful advancement of the colony, the policy was adopted of employing no one as a schoolmaster who did not previously satisfy the Governor as to his competency, and procure his recommendation for his appointment to that office. When once appointed the records show that the schoolmasters retained their situations, almost without exception, for a number of years in succession.

ANCIENT NAMES OF PLACES.

The following is a list of ancient names upon Long Island, with the dates affixed opposite to them, of the time when they were used, viz.:

IN THE TOWN OF BROOKLYN.

1667. *Gowanus*, which still retains the same name.

1667. *Cripplebush*, which still retains the same name.

1686. *Wallaboght*, which still retains the same name.

1686. *Marchwick*, and in 1722 called *Martyr's Hook*, which was the point of land forming the present United States Navy Yard.

1689. *Lubbertse's Neck*, which was sold by Peter Corsen to Cornelius Sebringh, March 28, 1698, for £250, and Sebringh to find Corsen in meat, drink, washing, lodging, and apparel during his life. In 1690 the same place was called *Graver's Kill*. This place was recently known as *Cornell's Red Mills*, and is about five hundred feet north of the Atlantic dock.

1700. *Gowanus Mill Neck*, sometimes called *Mill Neck*, and known by this latter name in 1785. In 1680, a lot of land in this town was called an *Erffe*.

About the period of the Revolution the people were in the habit of distinguishing the large lots into which their farms or plantations were divided, by particular names, and these names they retained for many years. Thus in this town, near the road leading from Brooklyn Ferry to Flatbush, were the "Geele Water's Caump," the "Erste Caump of Derrick's land," the "Kline Caump," the "Twede Caump of Derrick's land," the "Middleste Caump," the "Benen Caump," and the "Agterse Caump."

IN THE TOWN OF MIDWOUT, OR FLATBUSH.

1660. Canarsee Landing, Canarsee Woods, which places still retain the same names.
1679. Third Kill.
1687. Minsehoele Hole.
1698. Rush Swamp.

IN THE TOWN OF BUSHWICK.

1690. The Norman Kill.

IN THE TOWN OF AMERSFORT, OR FLATLANDS.

1636. *Kaskutensukin*, the westernmost flat of land of the three flats.
1646. Mutelar's Island.
1687. Stroom Kill.
1687. Jurianses Hook.
1687. Fries Hook.
1690. Hogg's Neck.
1694. Albertse's Island.
1695. Mayise land.
1704. Fresh Kill.
1711. Bestevaar's Kill.
1712. Craven Valley.

IN THE TOWN OF NEW UTRECHT.

1660. Nayack, which name it still retains.
1685. The Fountain at Yellow Hook.
1690. Turk's Plantation, afterwards called Bruynenbergh.

IN THE TOWN OF GRAVESEND.

1692. Hoogh Penne Neck.
1693. Gysbert's Island.
1695. Ambrose Strand.
1697. Garretsen's Neck.
1698. Cellars Neck.
1704. Great Woods.
1718. Harbie's Gat.
1718. Brown's Creek.
1718. Robin Poyneer's Patent.

IN THE TOWN OF NEWTON.

1656. The west branch of *Mespatt Kills*, called *Quandus Quaricus.*

Dosaris, the name of a place on this island, has its origin from the circumstance of the original owner of it, as a farm, or plantation, having obtained it through his wife, and he being a scholar, called it *Dos uxoris*, the *Wife's Gift*, which the people subsequently corrupted to its present name of *Dosoris.*

Quogue, in Suffolk County, is probably a corruption of the Indian name of a favorite shell-fish known to us as the *clam*, *Quohaug*—these shell-fish having been very abundant, and probably of a choice kind, as is indicated by the immense ancient shell banks in all the surrounding region. At this place is the only point from which the Great South Beach can be reached on foot from the mainland of the island, for the immense stretch of coast reaching from Fire Island to the inlet of Shinecoc Bay. In all other places you have to pass in a boat over many miles of water; and it is this circumstance which renders a shipwreck upon that beach in winter so frequently dreadful in its consequences from the loss of life; for even if the crew and passengers should succeed in reaching the beach alive, they will find no shelter there, and having from ten to twenty miles of water to cross before they can experience any relief, and their boats being almost invariably destroyed or lost in the shipwreck, if the storm is very heavy and the cold severe, as is frequently the case, they perish from the exposure. It may be asked by those not acquainted with this beach, Why is this not provided against? The answer is, It is almost, if not quite impossible to do so, the character of the beach being such, and the distance from the mainland, and the difficulties and dangers of communication often so great that men could not live there at the times when their services would be most required. The formation and position of this beach is, however, such that the great loss of life is usually sustained before the shipwrecked persons have the chance of reaching the land, from the immense seas thrown over them by the whole swell of the Atlantic Ocean, which, by the rapid evaporation it causes, comparatively soon chills them to death.

NAMES OF FAMILIES IN BROOKLYN.

Ancient.	*Modern.*
Courten.	
Defforest,	Deforest.
Ffilkin.	
Gulick.	
Hansen,	Johnson.
Harsen.	
Houghawout,	Lefferts.
Abranse.	
Aerson.	
Amertman,	Amerman.
Blaw.	
Beeckman,	Beekman.
Casperse.	

Ancient.	***Modern.***
Dehart.	
Depotter.	
Ewetse.	
Hooghland.	
Janse,	Johnson.
Jarisse.	
Jurianse.	
Lambertse,	Lambertson and Lamberson.
LeFoy.	
Lubbertse.	
Middagh.	
Schaers.	
Seberingh.	
Symonse,	Simonson.
Staats.	
Van Cortlandt.	
Van Eckellen.	

Of all these families there are now but seven remaining in Brooklyn, viz.: Beekman, Deforest, Johnson, Lambertson, Lefferts, Middagh and Simonson. Within the last five or six years the emigration from Continental Europe has brought back some of the old names as in New York, merchants of the name of Courten. The name of Middagh is Dutch, and means, in English, midday or noon.

NEW UTRECHT.

Ancient.	*Modern.*
Van Westervelt.	
Mattyse,	Martense.
Coorten.	
Salom.	
Smack,	original of Martense.
Van Thinhoven.	

GRAVESEND.

Garretse,	Garretson and Gerritson.
Remmerson,	Remson.

FLATLANDS.

Tiehuynon,	Terhune.
Lucasse.	
Kenne.	
Elbertse.	
Harmanse.	

BUSHWICK.

Vanderschaez.
Schamp.
Loysen.

FLATBUSH.

Ditmarse,	Ditmas.

The practice of giving people what would now be called *nicknames*, by which they became known, not only to the public generally, but also in the official records, was very common under the Dutch Colonial Government, and it also continued for a considerable period under the English administration in this colony. In 1644, in the Dutch records we have John Pietersen, alias Friend John. In the Newton purchase from the Indians, dated April 12, 1656, one of the boundaries is, "by a Dutchman's land called *Hans the Boore;*" and in the Bushwick patent, dated October 12, 1667, one of the boundaries is "John the Swedes Meadow." In 1695, in the Kings County records a man is named living at Gowanus, as "Tunis the Fisher."

And we also find that by the records of the Common Council of the City of New York, on the 25th of March, 1691, they ordered that "fish be brought into the dock, over against the City Hall [then standing in Pearl street, at the head of Coenties slip], or the house that *Long Mary* formerly lived in."

And also on the 9th of April, in the same year, they directed "that *Old Bush* deliver into the hands of the treasurer, the scales and weights that he hath in his hands belonging to the city, being first satisfied for the making of them."

Again, on the same day, the order "that *Top Knot Betty* and her children be provided for as objects of charity, and four shillings a week allowed." And further, that "the treasurer let *Scarebouch* have a new suit, and assist him in what's wanting."

All the preceding orders, from the date of April 9th, inclusive, were made in one day, so that our city functionaries of that period seem to have had a most charitable disposition, as well as a strange propensity for giving nicknames to people. But we are not yet done; this Common Council were not so mean as to apply such nicknames to those only to whom they afforded charitable relief, as some might otherwise suppose—they also used them when discharging their debts. Thus, on the 8th of December, 1691, the city records contain an order that "the treasurer pay *English Smith*, £1, 13s. for three cords of wood, which he bought for the use of the city this day."

Strange as it may now seem to us for the Common Council of a city to place such names upon the public records, yet we have seen that this practice extended to the highest functionaries of the Colonial Government, and that the Governors, both Dutch and English, used it in their patents for towns, and other official documents.

The explanation of it, in many cases, undoubtedly was, that in many instances the parties either had no surname, or family names (for family names were not so common then as now), or if they had, they did not themselves know it, and that which now appears like a nickname was from necessity adopted as a means of distinguishing them, and was usually taken from some personal characteristic, and which subsequently became, some part or other of it, the surname of the children as *Long* and *Betty.*

The manner in which names of families sometimes become changed in this country is truly curious. There was previous to the middle of the last century, among the Dutch settlers in the southern part of this colony, and particularly upon Long Island, a regular systematic change of the family name with every generation, so that the son never bore the family name of his father; thus, if the father's name was Leffert Jansen, and he had a son named Jacobus, this son's name would not be Jansen, but it would be written Jacobus Leffertsen—suppose the old gentleman would have a grandson by his son, who was christened Gerrit, his whole name would be Gerrit Jacobsen. Thus we would have in the three generations of that one single family, the following different names, viz.:

1. The father, named Leffert Jansen.
2. The son, named Jacobus Leffertsen.
3. The grandson, named Gerrit Jacobsen.

This strange custom does not seem to have prevailed among the Dutch in Albany; there they preserved their family names from the first settlement, and many of them may therefore be traced back without difficulty.

In other parts of our country, as well as among the Dutch, great changes have occurred in family names. Edward Livingston, Esq., in his answer to Mr. Jefferson, in the case of the New Orleans Batture, furnishes us with the following singular instance of this nature:

An unfortunate Scotchman, whose name was Feyerston, was obliged, in pursuit of fortune, to settle amongst some Germans in the western part of the State of New York. They translated his name literally into German and called him Fourstein. On his returning to an English neighborhood his new acquaintances discovered that Fourstein, in German, meant Flint in English; they translated, instead of restoring his name, and the descendants of *Feyerston* go by the name of *Flint* to this day. I ought, however, says Mr. Livingston, to except one of his grandsons who settled at the Acadian coast, on the Mississippi, whose name underwent the fate of the rest of the family; he was called, by a literal translation into French, *Pierre-a-fusil*, and his eldest son returning to the family clan, his name underwent another transformation, and he was called *Peter Gun!* This is about equal to the Dutch transmutation of names, although wanting its system. Here we have the following result:

1. The father's	1st Name,	Feyerston.
	2d Name,	Fourstein.
	3d Name,	Flint.
2. The son's	Name,	Flint.
3. The grandson's	1st Name,	Flint.
	2d Name,	Pierre-a-fusil.
	3d Name,	Peter Gun.

The old practice formerly so common among the Dutch settlers on Long Island, seems also to have been at one time in use in Iceland. Mr. Hooker, who was there in the summer of 1809, speaking of the family of Olaf Stephenson, the former governor of that island, observes: "In naming his children, the Stiftsamptman (governor), as well as his sons, have abolished the custom, which is otherwise, I believe, very general in Iceland, of calling the child after the Christian name of the father, with the addition *sen* or *son* to it; thus the son of the Etatsrœd (chief justice) Magnus Stephenson ought by this rule to have been *Magnusen*, to which any Christian name might be subjoined. If it had been *Olaf Magnusen*, his son would bear the name of *Olavsen*, or rather *Olafsen*, as I believe it is generally written. The females had the addition of *datter* to the Christian name of the father."

This was precisely the old Dutch custom in this colony; and it has led to great difficulty in tracing the descent of our early Dutch families, and also in examining our old records, as there are but few who are conversant with this peculiarity in their change of names. Thus, amongst the Dutch the original name of the present family of the Lefferts was *Houghawout*. Leffert Houghawout's son James was called Jacobus Leffertsen, or Leffertse, as it was often written, dropping the letter *n*; and when this custom was abolished about the middle of the last century, this latter name Leffertse was retained as the family name. So also the original family name of the Martenses was *Smack*. Mattyse Smack's son received Mattyse as his surname, which eventually became the present name of Martense, although as now written only within the last half century. This is also the origin of the present family names of Johnson, or Jansen (which are both the same name), Remsen, Gerritsen, etc. It is strange that such a custom should have been identically the same with those two different nations; but it shows their common origin.

Upon this island, and especially in the central portions of it, are very many families of the name of Smith, and so numerous did they become at an early period of the settlement, that it was thought necessary to distinguish the various original families by some peculiar name. Thus we have the Rock Smiths; the Blue Smiths; the Bull Smiths; the Weight Smiths, and the Tangier Smiths. Of the Rock Smiths there are two distinct families: one originally settled between Rockaway and Hempstead, some ten or fifteen years before the settlement of the first white inhabitant in Setauket, who derived their name from their contiguity to Rockaway; and the other located themselves in Brookhaven, and obtained their appellation from their ancestor erecting his dwelling against a large rock which still remains in the highway of that town. The Blue Smiths were settled in Queens County, and obtained their peculiar designation from a blue cloth coat worn by their ancestor; whether because a cloth coat was then an uncommon thing in the neighborhood, or that he always dressed in a coat of that color, does not appear. The Bull Smiths of Suffolk County are the most numerous of all the families of the name of Smith upon this island; it is said there are now at least one thousand males of that branch on this island. The ancestor of this branch of the Smith family was Major Richard Smith, who came from England to New England, with his father Richard, in the early part of the seventeenth century; and afterwards came to this island, and became the patentee of Smithtown. The sobriquet of this class of Smiths is said to have arisen from the circumstance of the ancestor having trained and used a Bull in place of a horse for riding. The Weight Smiths derived their name from being possessed of the only set of scales and weights in the neighborhood of their residence, to which all the farmers of the country around resorted for the purpose of weighing anything they wished to sell or buy; at least so says the tradition. The Tangier Smiths owe their origin to Colonel William Smith, who had been the English Governor of Tangier, in the reign of Charles the Second,* and emigrated to this colony in the summer of the year 1686, where he settled in the town of Brookhaven, on the Neck known

* Tangier, in Africa, was about that period an English colony, having come to the British Crown as part of the dowry of Queen Catharine of Portugal; and was, in 1683, abandoned by the English to the Moors, in consequence of the great expense and small value of the colony.

as Little Neck, and afterwards as Strong's Neck, which, together with his other purchases, were erected into a manor by the name of St. George's Manor, by a patent granted to him in 1693, by Governor Fletcher. Most of the Tangier Smiths are now in that town, scattered through it from the north to the south side of the island.

These different appellations of the families of the Smiths became as firmly settled as if they were regular family names; so that when any inquiry was made of any person on the road, man, woman, or child, for any particular Smith, they would at once ask whether he was of the Rock breed, or the Bull breed, etc.; and if the person desiring the information could say which *breed*, he at once was told of his residence. In truth there are so many of the same name in that most numerous family of the Smiths upon this island, that without adopting some such plan it would be almost impossible to distinguish one from the other. Among these Smiths, and at Smithtown, upon this island, have occurred two of the most marked instances of longevity known in this country.

Richard Smith, the patentee of Smithtown, of the Bull breed, purchased at New York a negro man named Harry, who lived with him, with his son, and then with his grandson, and died at

Smithtown in the month of December, 1758, aged at least one hundred and twenty years. This remarkable individual said he could remember when there were but very few houses in the city of New York; his memory must have extended back to the administration of the Dutch Governor Kieft. His health and strength of body continued almost unimpaired until very near his death, and he could do a good day's work when he had passed one hundred years.

There appears to have been another negro man in the same town, who even exceeded him in the point of age. In a note to Moulton's *History of New York*, it is stated, that an obituary article appeared in a newspaper, printed in 1739, of the death of a negro man at Smithtown, on Long Island, reputed to have been *one hundred and forty years* old; who declared that he well remembered when there were but *three houses* in New York. The memory of this man must therefore have extended back to the founding of New Amsterdam, in the year 1626, as New York was then called, and he must have come into this country with some of the first Dutch settlers.

MANNERS AND CUSTOMS.

There are a number of interesting facts connected with the antiquities of this island, which are not easily reducible under any of the previous heads, which we have thought should be preserved, as matters of considerable moment connected with the first settlement and condition of Long Island, and we have therefore made for them this distinct head. Among them is the following extract from the official records of Rhode Island, which show how early a jealous and unfriendly feeling sprang up between the English and Dutch colonies in this country. We have always viewed it as an unfortunate circumstance for the preservation of this colony to the Dutch, that Peter Stuyvesant was not the governor here when that ill-feeling began first to manifest itself, some considerable time anterior to the period referred to in the following record. His mode of conducting the difficult negotiation with the English commissioners at Hartford; the manner in which he settled the disputes between the Dutch and English colonists, and also between their respective governments in this country, in reference to the settlement at Hartford and in its vicinity, which had been for years a serious and acrimonious controversy between his predecessor in the Colonial government and the United Colonies of New England; and his settlement and defining of an established boundary, in which all acquiesced, between the New Netherlands and the English colonies, all serve to show, in our judgment, that if he had had the control and management of those controversies in the first instance, they would have been all adjusted in an amicable and satisfactory manner long before they attained that violent and hostile character which had induced in the minds of the leading men of New England the settled conviction that it was necessary to their peace to get rid of the Dutch government in the colony next adjoining them; and by such a course the colony would have been preserved to Holland, at least for very many years to come. But Governor Stuyvesant unfortunately arrived here after the commissioners of the United Colonies of New England had not only come to that conclusion, but had also made representations to that effect to their home government, and the whole effect of Governor Stuyvesant's peaceful and wise administration of affairs was to procrastinate for some few years the English attempt at the subjugation of this colony; a design which the latter, however, never abandoned, as is clearly shown from the communication which Gov. Stuyvesant made to the church of Brooklyn, on this island, on the last of June, 1663, directing the *fourth day of July* following, to be observed as a day of thanksgiving, because, among other things, the

English had been defeated in their attempt to take possession of the whole of Long Island by the timely arrival of a Dutch fleet of armed ships in the bay of New Amsterdam (New York)—this occurrence, it will be observed, is more than a year anterior to the actual capture of New Netherland and the taking of New Amsterdam (New York) by the English fleet and forces under Gov. Richard Nicolls. Here follows the Rhode Island record, above mentioned:

"Acts and orders of the General Assembly, held at Newport, May 17, 18, 19, 1653—Mr. Nich. Eaton, moderator."

II. A committee of two men of each town, or eight men, be chosen, for ripening matters that concern Long Island, and in the case concerning the Dutch. Mr. Rich. Eaton, Mr. John Eaton, Mr. Rich. Burden, Mr. Randall Holden, Mr. John Smith, Mr. Robert Field, Richard Few, John Roome, act upon these.

"12. *First*, That we judge it to be our duty to afford our countrymen on Long Island what help we can safely do, by virtue of our commission from the Right Honorable the Council of State, either for defending themselves against the Dutch, the enemies of the commonwealth, or for offending them, as by us shall be thought necessary.

"*Second*, That they shall have two great guns,

and what murtherers are with us, on promise of returning them, or the due valuation, and to be improved as by instructions given by this Assembly's authority, this or what else, provided they engage to the Commonwealth, and confirm by subscription to do their utmost to set themselves in a suitable posture of defence against all enemies of the Commonwealth of England, and to offend them, as shall be ordered.

"*Third*, That there be allowed twenty voluntaries out of the colony, provided they be such as be under no fixed relations or engagements.

"13. That for trial of prizes brought in according to law, the general officer, with three jurors of each town, shall be authorized to try it; the President and two assistants shall have authority to appoint the time, but if any fail at the time appointed, either officers or jurors shall be made up in the town of Newport (where they shall be tried); in case any of the officers fail, then they that appear shall proceed according to the law of allaroon.

"13. Commissions granted to Capt. John Underhill and Mr. William Dyre.

"14. That Edward Hall shall have a commission granted him to go against the Dutch, or any enemies of the Commonwealth of England."

The following notes are necessary to a full understanding of this interesting record:—

The two great guns here spoken of were cannon, and the murtherers, or *murderers*, were pieces of small cannon, fitted into a wooden stock for the convenience of being carried about, and were used for firing stones instead of balls. They are also sometimes called in the old record "stone-pieces."

The muskets of that day were of a very much heavier and more clumsy make than those of the present day, and of a larger bore; they were at this period fired by laying upon a rest, with a slow match, as they had no locks; the rest was an upright rod of iron, about five feet long, with a pike end to stick into the ground, and a crotch at the other end for the musket to lie in. The soldier, when marching, carried this rest in his right hand, and the musket upon his left shoulder. The present cartridge-box was supplied by a bandalier, as it was called, being a belt over the shoulder and across in front; attached to it hung a dozen small leather or copper cases, each containing one charge of powder and ball for the musket: he also carried a sword. A man thus armed was considered a part of the stationary or heavy force of an army of that day, as much so as the artillery, and they were both certainly sufficiently unwieldy. It is only in comparatively modern times that soldiers armed with muskets have been considered as infantry, or light troops.

The "engagement to the Commonwealth" means the Commonwealth of England, under Oliver Cromwell; and they also required that the Long Islanders should enter into a similar written subscription as that required from all the functionaries in England, to support the Cromwellian administration.

The meaning of the provision concerning "twenty voluntaries" is that twenty volunteers were authorized to be raised in Rhode Island for this service upon Long Island; but that they must be particular, and enlist no men who were married, or engaged to be married, or who were bound to service.

The "trial of prizes" is believed to be the first admiralty court established in the New England colonies; the establishment of which courts by the English government about a century later, was a source of great dissatisfaction in those colonies. But there was this difference between the two cases; in the first, the people themselves, by their own immediate representatives, organized and made choice of its judges and officers from their own people, and directed that it should proceed with a jury; and in the last case the

9*

courts were organized by the British Parliament, in which the colonies had no representation whatever; the judges and officers were most of them strangers, selected and chosen by the King in Council from abroad, or from other colonies, and they were required to proceed without the intervention of a jury; differences enough assuredly to give reason for dissatisfaction to the full as strong as any shown on the subject. The laws of *Allaroon* referred to as the code for the government of this admiralty court in its proceedings, is undoubtedly meant for the laws of Oleron.

It was undoubtedly under the Edward Hall Commission from Rhode Island, and with the volunteer force from that colony, joined by some of the Long Islanders, that Capt. John Underhill, in this same year, 1653, stormed and captured the Indian fort upon Fort Neck, in Queens County, and broke up and dispersed the Indian force, which had seriously threatened the desolation of this part of Long Island.

William Dyre seems to have remained upon Long Island until near the period of the arrival of the English expedition under Gov. Richard Nicolls, when he joined that force and accompanied it to the capture of New Amsterdam (New York). After which he settled in this colony, and became one of its distinguished men.

He was for a long period one of the Governor's council, and frequently acted as the President of the Court of Sessions for the West Riding of Yorkshire upon Long Island.

The Convention of Deputies assembled at Hempstead, on this island, during the year 1664, for the adoption of the code of laws afterwards known as the *Duke's Laws*, after concluding their labors, adopted the following address, which they sent to James the Duke of York and Albany, subsequently King James II. of England: "We, the deputies duly elected from the several towns upon Long Island, being assembled at Hempstead in general meeting, by authority derived from your Royal Highness unto the Honorable Colonel Nicolls, as Deputy-Governor, do most humbly and thankfully acknowledge to your Royal Highness the great honor and satisfaction we receive in our dependence upon your Royal Highness, according to the tenor of his sacred Majesty's patent, granted the 12th day of March, 1664, wherein we acknowledge ourselves, our heirs and successors forever, to be comprised to all intents and purposes as therein is more at large expressed. And we do publicly and unanimously declare our cheerful submission to all such laws, statutes, and ordinances which are or shall be made, by virtue of authority from your Royal Highness, your heirs and successors forever; as also that we will maintain, uphold, and defend to the utmost of our power and peril of us, our heirs and successors forever, all the rights, title, and interest granted by his sacred Majesty to your Royal Highness, against all pretensions or invasions, foreign or domestic, we being already well assured that in so doing we perform our duty of allegiance to his Majesty, as free-born subjects of the kingdom of England, inhabiting in these his Majesty's dominions. We do further beseech your Royal Highness to accept of this address as the first-fruits in this general meeting, for a memorial and record against us, our heirs and successors, when we or any of them shall fail in our duties. Lastly, we beseech your Royal Highness to take our poverties and necessities, in this wilderness country, into speedy consideration; that by constant supplies of trade, and your Royal Highness' more particular countenance of grace to us, and protection of us, we may daily more and more be encouraged to bestow our labors to the improvement of these his Majesty's western dominions under your Royal Highness, for whose health, long life, and eternal happiness we shall ever pray, as in duty bound."

The people of Long Island were so much exasperated against the deputies of the convention at Hempstead, for making that address to the Duke of York, which they regarded as too base and servile to come from representatives of freemen, and expressed their disgust in such a plain, open manner, that the court of assizes (composed of the governor and his council, and a justice of the peace of each town), at a term held at New York, in 1666, in order to save those deputies from abuse, if not in some instances from personal violence, deemed it expedient to declare, that, "Whosoever hereafter shall any ways detract or speak against any of the deputies signing the address to His Royal Highness, at the general meeting at Hempstead, they shall be presented to the next court of sessions, and, if the justices shall see cause, they shall from thence be bound over to the assizes, there to answer for their slander, upon plaint or information."

The deputies, also, subsequent to their address to the Duke of York, made one to the people, in which they set forth their reasons for agreeing to the code called the Duke's Laws, and endeavor to show that they had done nothing in that, or in their address, incompatible with the duty they owed to their country as freemen; they were not, however, very successful in this attempt to ward off the public indignation, which they certainly richly merited for their address to the Duke.

In consequence of a serious dispute which existed between Governor Nicolls and the colony of Connecticut relative to the boundary-line between New York and Connecticut (Connecticut seems to have thought if she and the other colonies of New England could dispossess the Dutch, she could then extend her boundary towards the south, which she much desired to do), in the month of December, 1664, Connecticut sent commissioners to New York to settle this difference, which appeared materially to affect the peace of both colonies. By the arrangement entered into on this occasion, the eastern part of Long Island, which became a part of Connecticut by the treaty made with the Dutch, on the 19th of September, 1650, was surrendered by Connecticut to New York, and the Mamaroneck river, and a line drawn from it north-northwest to the boundary line of Massachusetts, was declared to be the eastern boundary of New York. So that Connecticut, instead of being the gainer, was the loser, by dispossessing the Dutch from the government of the colony of New Netherlands.

Governor Richard Nicolls, in the month of November, 1665, wrote a letter to the Duke of York, in which he informed him: "My endeavors have not been wanting to put the whole government into one frame and policy, and now the most factious republicans cannot but acknowledge themselves fully satisfied with the way and method they are in. My resolutions are, to send over to your Royal Highness this winter, a copy of the laws as they now stand, with the alterations made at the last general assizes, which, if you shall confirm and cause to be printed at London, the country will be infinitely obliged to you." The laws were accordingly sent and confirmed by the Duke of York, being the code adopted by the convention at Hempstead, and the alterations and amendments made to that code by the court of assizes, in September, 1665, but whether they were printed or not, we do not know, never having seen or heard of a copy; if they were printed, it must be a very rare book, indeed.

Governor Nicolls, in a letter which he addressed to the Duke of York two or three months after the capture of New York in August, 1664, says: "Such is the mean condition of this town (New York) that not one soldier to this day has lain in sheets, or upon any other bed than canvas or straw." Soldiers must have had much more dainty lodgings in those days, and must have been much nicer in their taste than at present, if a bed of canvas and straw in the warm season of the year is complained of, as from this letter seems to have been the fact. It is not, however, in this view of the case that we have adduced this extract from Gov. Nicolls' letter, but to show something of the situation of the city when it passed from the hands of the Dutch, and came under the English government. The changes which have taken place since that period in the city of New York, and on the west end of Long Island, are without example in history; and these become the more marked and striking when we extend our comparison some twenty-five years further back, when Kieft became the Dutch governor of this colony, and a full and minute examination into its condition was made and recorded, showing us changes truly wonderful, and all occurring in about two centuries, a period during which many of the important cities and towns in Europe and Asia have remained, in comparison, almost stationary. Here, on this little spot, then known as New Amsterdam, where in the year 1639 there was but one magazine, or store-house, for wares and merchandise, but one small church, one blacksmith shop, two saw-mills and a grist mill, and where one hundred and twelve years later there were but ten thousand souls, is now congregated a population of about four hundred thousand, engaged in a commerce which sends its messengers to the ends of the earth, and is now a place which might well be characterized, as was ancient Egypt by the inspired prophet and poet Isaiah, as "the land shadowing with wings," "that sendeth ambassadors by the sea;" for the sails of its shipping overshadow the ocean, and there is no part of the habitable globe, and scarcely of that portion locked up in the eternal frosts of the arctic and antarctic zones that is not visited by those sent on missions of trade or peace from this city. The immense increase of the trade or commerce of this city has occurred in such a short space of time, that we now have its whole history in our existing public records. We find that at the period first referred to, 1639, the revenue of the entire colony amounted to $31,220 per annum, while the annual expenses of the colonial government, civil and military, were $40,500, leaving a yearly deficit of about nine thousand dollars to be made up by the Dutch West India Company, and which they could well afford to bear, as they had all the commerce of the colony in their own hands, and from the single article of beaver alone (then exported in large quantities) were realizing a profit of one hundred and twenty per cent. Now this city carries on more than half of the foreign commerce of the whole United States, and now collects more than half of all the duties paid upon imports into the same, being the main revenue of the general government. This will become apparent from the following statement derived from official sources:

In 1836 the whole amount of imports into the United States was........................	$189,980,035
Of which amount there was imported at New York.........	118,253,416
Leaving to be imported in all the other portions of the United States......................	71,726,619

In 1837 the whole amount of imports into the United States was	$140,989,217
Of which amount there was imported at New York..........	79,301,772
Leaving to be imported in all the other portions of the United States......................	61,687,445

This great commercial preponderance of New York has grown up within the last thirty-five years. At the middle of the last century, Newport, in Rhode Island, was a much more important place in a commercial point of view than New York; and Boston was very much its superior in every respect. As regards Philadelphia, in point of size, appearance or trade, there was then no comparison, and no one thought of making any; Philadelphia was then a city, and New York, in comparison, but a village. And thus continued the relative positions of the two places until some time after the close of the Revolutionary war; evidence of any jealousy on the part of the former did not begin to manifest itself until about 1806, and even then no Philadelphian would ever believe that New York could ever equal Philadelphia in population. But when every succeeding census of the General and State Governments showed a rapid and steady increase of New York in population, in a ratio far beyond that of Philadelphia, and the reports of the Secretary of the Treasury showed an annual and great increase of her trade, so that at last she equalled and then far outstripped Philadelphia in both cases, the Philadelphians at first vented their mortification in bitter sarcasms against New York and its inhabitants, and in illiberal comparisons between the two cities. But finding these unheeded and disregarded both by the New Yorkers and the inhabitants of the great West who went to New York to trade, that city from its immense foreign commerce offering them a better market to make their choice in, Philadelphia induced the State of Pennsylvania to embark in the immense system of railroads and canals traversing that State in various directions, and which almost entirely, from their great cost, prostrated the credit of that powerful State, and has crippled their resources for a long period of time yet to come, in order to divert that Western trade from New York, and to bring it to Philadelphia, where the most of it formerly was transacted; and yet, strange as that may seem, although those works have undoubtedly benefited both that State and city, scarcely a railroad or canal has been made by them that has not materially increased the trade of New York; has brought their coal to New York at a cheap rate, where it was much wanted, and by connecting with the Ohio river, has, by means of the Alleghany river and the Ohio canal, opened the western part of their own State to the trade of New York.

But these are all changes in our own days: when we look back for about a century and a half, a period scarcely recognized by change in many portions of the old world, and we find our Dutch progenitors assembled in this goodly city of New Amsterdam, goodly then in prospect, if not in fruition, declaring, in 1656, that, "*The widow of Hans Hansen, the first-born Christian daughter in New Netherland*, burdened with seven children, petitions for a grant of a piece of meadow, in addition to the twenty morgen granted to her at the Waale-Boght," in the town (now city) of Brooklyn, opposite New York, we can scarcely realize that in this, and the examinations made into the state and condition of New Amsterdam in 1639, before referred to, we are looking upon the beginning of the great City and State of New York; and when we cast our eye over the assessment roll of that city for raising the sum of five thousand and fifty guilders from her wealthier citizens in 1653, and compare it with the assessed value of her real and personal estates in 1838, amounting to two hundred and sixty-four millions of dollars, it seems more like the story of some minstrel of Arabia or Hindostan, than sober matter of fact.

All this immense increase of New York City, and the western extremity of this island, dates from the year 1817—its main commencement. From the close of the Revolutionary war to 1812, Boston was the first importing city of the United States, and there it was that the New York merchants purchased the most of their goods of British and India manufacture. From 1812 to 1815, that city maintained its commercial preponderance, from the policy which the British Government imagined it their interest to adopt, in leaving Boston comparatively a free port. Whatever may have been their reasons for this policy, or the causes operating to produce, which it is no part of our object or design to inquire into, it is certain that Boston during the war was the market from whence the Union principally derived their supplies of European and East India goods. After the peace of 1815, the foreign trade of our entire country manifested a tendency to centre in that city, and the greater part of the capital of the United States engaged in commerce collected in Boston and its vicinity. The general decrease of business in the City of New York, caused by the accumulation of this trading capital in Boston, induced the merchants of our city to inquire into the reasons of this state of affairs; and upon making this inquiry they arrived at the conclusion, that the auction business was highly injurious to the trade of New York, and that if this branch of business was destroyed, the trade and commerce of this city would become prosperous, and with that view they petitioned the Legislature to impose a duty of ten per cent. on all auction sales, which would, in fact, amount to a prohibition of them. There were some few persons, however, who entertained a different opinion as to the causes of this depression of trade in New York; and among them one of the prominent was Abraham G. Thompson, Esq., who had been for many years an enterprising and successful merchant in that city. He saw that one reason operating in favor of Boston was that India goods could be sold in that city and pay a duty of only one per cent., while at the same time, if those goods were sold at New York, they would be obliged to pay a duty of two and a half per cent., and that to increase the duty upon auction sales was only to increase more widely the difference in favor of Boston and against New York, and the existing duties should be, on the contrary, diminished in this State. With that view he went to Albany and submitted the result of his experience and judgment to the Legislature, assuring them that by establishing the duties at one per cent. upon East India, and one and a half per cent. on European goods, the interests of the City of New York, and also of the State, would be greatly promoted, and the revenue increased by this reduction. It was difficult at first to satisfy those with whom the matter rested that this effect would result from the proposed change; so many hundreds of the merchants and citizens of New York had petitioned for this great increase of duties upon auction sales, that it was almost impossible to think that they could be mistaken in their view of the subject. Eventually, however, Governor Tompkins did become satisfied that the project of Mr. Thompson was the correct one, and gave his influence to secure the enactment of the law reducing the rates of duties as proposed, in place of increasing them. Previous to the passage of the law reducing the rates of duties, for the *two* best years between 1783 and 1812, this State had received from duties upon auction sales of India goods between five and six thousand dollars, averaging between twenty-five hundred and three thousand dollars per annum; and to show his confidence in the opinions he had expressed, Mr. Thompson offered the Governor, that upon the passage of the law reducing the rate of duties, if the State would convey to him the duties alone upon India goods, he would pay into the State treasury, in advance, for the first year the sum of six thousand dollars, being more than the State had received for duties for any two years subsequent to 1783. The results following that reduction of duties more than justified all his anticipations, and more than fulfilled all his predictions; for soon after the passage of that law, in place of selling all East India cargoes in Boston, as had been previously the case, a Boston ship from the East Indies was sent to New York, and the auction duties upon her cargo alone amounted to upwards of six thousand dollars; and the revenue received by this State upon India goods, for the first year after that reduction of duties, amounted to between thirty-two and thirty-three thousand dollars. All the India ships after the enactment of that law were sent to New York; and from that time to within the last four years, but one attempt has been made to sell a cargo of India goods east of New York, and that was a failure, nothing being sold but the sample packages, and the bulk of the cargo was afterwards sent to this city and sold here. The reduced rate of duties being still continued, the revenue arising from that source to the State treasury has gradually increased until it has reached to between two hundred and three hundred thousand dollars. The effect of this reduction of the duties upon auction sales has not only multiplied the business of this city to the shipper, the importer, the jobber, and the mechanic; it has not only by this increase of business made New York the commercial emporium of the nation, and thus has drawn to us merchants and purchasers from all parts of our widely extended country; and tended directly to enhance the value of houses, stores, and lots, and filled our city with palaces, and made our merchants princes; it has not only materially aided the

State in the payment of her debt incurred from the system of internal improvements; but it also afforded an impetus to the prosecution of the project for the great Erie canal, without which it would probably have been delayed for very many years. When the friends of the Erie canal urged the connecting of the waters of Lake Erie with those of the Hudson river, they were met not only with the sarcasms and ridicule of those who would not bestow the time requisite to a proper examination and understanding of the subject, but also by the unanswerable objection, that the State had no settled revenue upon which it could rely for the payment of the interest of the debt that must be incurred in the making of this canal; and that it would be an unwise step to rely alone upon the prospective revenues of an untried project, and that, too, through a region of country entirely unsettled and in its native forest state, as was a large portion of the country at that period now traversed by the Erie canal. When this act was passed reducing the auction duties, and the successful result that immediately followed, placed into the State treasury such an immensely increased amount of duties, compared with the previous receipts from the same source, that objection was obviated, and the State at once embarked upon the prosecution of this canal, which has poured and continues to pour untold wealth into the city and State of New York.

The following is a copy of Governor Sir Edmond Andros' proclamation, issued upon taking the surrender of the colony of New York from the Dutch authorities in November, 1674, taken from an official copy sent to Long Island.

"By the Governor. Whereas it hath pleased his Majesty and his Royal Highness to send me with authority to receive this place and government from the Dutch, and to continue in the command thereof, under his Royal Highness, who hath not only taken care for our future safety and defence, but also given me his commands for securing the rights and properties of the inhabitants; and that I should endeavor by all fitting means the good and welfare of this province and dependencies under his government. That I may not be wanting in any thing that may conduce thereunto, and for the saving of the trouble and charge of any coming hither (to New York City) for the satisfying themselves in such doubts as might arise concerning their rights and properties upon this change of government, and wholly to settle the minds of all in general, I have thought fit to publish and declare that all former grants, privileges or concessions heretofore granted, and all estate legally possessed by any under his Royal Highness, before the late Dutch government, as also all legal judicial proceedings during that government, to my arrival in these parts, are hereby confirmed; and the possessors by virtue thereof to remain in quiet possession of their rights. It is hereby further declared, that the known book of Laws, formerly established and in force under his Royal Highness's government, is now again confirmed by his Royal Highness, the which are to be observed and practised, together with the manner and time of holding courts therein mentioned, as heretofore; and all magistrates and civil officers belonging thereunto to be chosen and established accordingly. Given under my hand, in New York, this ninth day of November, in the twenty-sixth year of his Majesty's reign, Annoque Domini 1674.

"E. Andros."

The first general market for the sale of commodities, upon the principle of the English fairs and *Markets overt*, was established at Brooklyn on this island in 1675, by an order of the court of assizes (then the legislative authority of the colony) at their session held in the City of New York on the 13th of October, in that year, as follows:

"Upon a proposal of having a fair and market in or near this city, it is ordered that after this season there shall yearly be kept a fair and market at Brooklyn, near the ferry, for all grain, cattle, or other produce of the country, to be held the first Monday, Tuesday and Wednesday in November; and in the City of New York the Thursday, Friday and Saturday following."

SLAVERY: The following exhibits one of the regulations which the existence of slavery amongst us rendered necessary upon the west end of this island, as early as the summer of 1706:

"By his excellency, Edward Lord Viscount Cornbury, Captain-General and Governor in Chief of the Provinces of New York, New Jersey, and the territories depending thereon, in America, and Vice-Admiral of the same, etc. Whereas, I am informed that several negroes in Kings County have assembled themselves in a riotous manner, which, if not prevented, may prove of ill consequence; you and every of you are therefore hereby required and commanded to take all proper methods for the seizing and apprehending all such negroes in the said county as shall be found to be assembled in such manner as aforesaid, or have run away or absconded from their masters or owners, whereby there may be reason to suspect them of ill practices or designs, and to secure them in safe custody, that their crimes and actions may be inquired into; and if any of them refuse to submit themselves, then to fire on them, kill or destroy them, if they cannot otherwise be taken; and for so doing this shall be your sufficient warrant. Given under my hand at Fort Anne in New York, the 22d day of July, 1706.

"CORNBURY.

"To the Justices of the Peace
in Kings County, and to any
or every of them."

Although there were some instances of unruly slaves upon this island, as is indicated by the preceding proclamation of the Governor, yet as a general thing they were a peaceable, orderly race, much attached to the families in which they were owned, and where they would remain from generation to generation; the only separation that was known was when some of the younger members of the family would marry and leave the homestead to keep house for themselves, one or two of the younger slaves would voluntarily accompany them to form the new household, and in some instances where an old negro wench had acted as the dry nurse of her young master or mistress, she would insist upon accompanying them, which was almost invariably consented to, although her services would be of little value, unless it might be as a kind of oracle for the family in all matters of old family history, or of the weather, which she would deliver with great show of importance and no little pride, from the kitchen chimney-corner, a seat appropriated to her use, knowing that all the other members of the household were too young to know much, if anything, about it. And she, together with the other old negroes of the family, would become high authority in all the numberless superstitions which are accustomed to congregate about a farmer's kitchen fireside; where the younger members of the household, white and colored, would delight to assemble on the long winter evenings to hear their stories.

An intimate association with nature, with an exclusion from the more busy haunts of men, insensibly tends to make people superstitious, as the world calls it, and we have observed that the more pure and virtuous the mind under such an association of circumstances, the more likely it is to be superstitious. So that we have learned to look with great respect on this trait of human character, as an indication that the heart is right, and most probably worthy of our high esteem.

This is no imaginary picture, as any one can assure us who has been brought up on the western part of Long Island, even within the last forty years. The general docility of these slaves, and their long connection with the families, caused them to be highly valued when an occasion did offer for a sale or a valuation, as upon the event of the death of the proprietor. In an inventory taken on the 16th of December, 1719, in Kings County, on this island, of the estate of a deceased person, a negro wench and child are valued at £60, while five milch cows, five calves, three young bulls and two heifers were collectively valued at £20.

Previous to our Revolutionary war there were, besides negro slaves, a species of white servants from Europe, who, upon emigrating to this country, sold their services for a certain number of years. By some they were called apprentices, but that term, as now used, will not convey a proper idea of the situation of those persons. They were as much the subject of sales during the period of their service as the negro slaves. So we find in the *New York Gazette* of December 24, 1767, the following advertisement: "To be disposed of, the remaining time, being about three years, of three German servants, one a baker by trade, one a butcher, and the other a laborer.

They are very industrious, good men, whose honesty has been tried, and may be had on reasonable terms. Inquire of the printer hereof." On examining the old journals of the General Assembly of the Province of New York, from 1691 to 1763, I found, particularly between 1691 and 1725, many regulations in relation to "negro and Indian slaves." Before meeting with these provisions we had no idea that the Indians were ever made slaves, and indeed had all along supposed the Indian character would not brook slavery. We are satisfied that they were never treated as slaves under the Dutch government in this colony, and that they were not subjected to that state until many years after the conquest of this colony by the English, in August, 1664; and we still believe that none of the Indians in the immediate vicinity of New York, or under the English government, were ever made slaves, as that would have been contrary to the policy which they pursued towards the aborigines in conciliating them, and forming alliances with them for the protection of their frontiers from the French in the Canadas, and through the valleys of the Ohio and Mississippi rivers; and that these slaves were probably French Indians captured by the Iroquois in their excursions, and sold by them to the English inhabitants. If so, it was a humane arrangement, by which the lives of the captives were preserved, and they were saved from a death of the most excruciating torture, which, as is well known, it was then the custom of the Iroquois and many other Indian nations, to inflict upon their captives unless redeemed.

SAMP PORRIDGE.—It is now, and has been for very many years past, customary on Long Island, in the latter part of the week in autumn, to pound their Indian corn in samp mortars. The corn thus pounded is called *samp;* they put the corn the night before in a weak ley of wood ashes, to take off the husk of the grain. This preparation they use in making their celebrated "samp porridge," a high favorite among culinary articles on this island. It is formed by boiling the samp with salted beef and pork, with potatoes, and such other vegetables as may be desired, according to the taste. It requires much boiling to make it perfect, and is said to be better on the second day, after another cooking, than it is on the first, and that it even improves in taste and goodness to the third or fourth day, being heated up and partially re-cooked on each day. In order to provide for this, they make it in a very large pot or kettle; and we have heard of people having enough cooked for a week. By these various processes of cooking, the porridge acquires a very stout crust on the outside next the pot; so much so that we have been told of the porridge, towards the end of the week, being lifted out of the pot bodily by the crust, which was then used as a dish or bowl to eat the interior from.

The samp mortar is constructed by selecting the sound stump of a large white oak tree—if rooted in the ground, so much the better; then burning it out until the cavity is formed of the desired size and shape, which is carefully scraped to remove all the charcoal. This being done, a block of white oak, weighing some fifty pounds, is selected, which is rounded at the lower end to fit the mortar, through which block a hole is bored near the top, and through it is a pin, projecting about a foot on each side, by which to take hold of. A sapling is then selected contiguous to the mortar, which is bent over without breaking, and its top attached by a strong wythe or cord to the upper end of that block, and this completes the pestle. The spring of the sapling assists in raising the pestle, but is not so strong as to prevent a man or a stout boy from bringing down the block or pestle with sufficient force upon the Indian corn in the mortar, to break it and pound it fine enough for the purpose designed.

Some captains of vessels, well acquainted with

the harbor of New York and the surrounding country, and with the manners and customs of the people, jocularly say they can tell when they are coming upon the Long Island coast during a fog in autumn, by hearing the sound of the *samp mortars* when the breeze is wafted off the shore. Their faculty of hearing is equally acute with that of the strollers on the Battery in the City of New York, mentioned by the worthy Diedrich Knickerbocker in his veritable *History of the New Netherlands*, who, on a calm summer evening, just after the sunset had dyed our western horizon with all the gorgeous colors of the famed Italian skies, could hear the joyous laugh of the negroes at thè little primitive Dutch settlement of Communipaw wafted across the bay when its waters were scarcely disturbed by a ripple.

When the western and south-western portions of this State were first settled, there being but very few mills, and in many places none for grinding the grain of the inhabitants, they adopted as a substitute these samp mortars, which were found to answer a valuable purpose. This process, however, was slow, it being a day's work to convert half a bushel of corn into coarse meal. The settlers who owned a few slaves employed them in this work; and hence, this process was vulgarly called in that part of the State " nigger ing corn." On Long Island, however, this duty was performed by the young men and stout boys in the family, although in some cases there it was also done by the negroes. Slavery existed upon Long Island, and also in most other parts of this State, only in name, for no distinction as to the kind of work to be performed was made between the slaves and the white young men and boys of the household. They were almost universally treated with great kindness, and were a careless, happy race of mortals, and when they became too old for work, they were not cast off, but cherished and taken care of by the family, in whose service they had spent their best days.

Home Habits.—For a long period anterior to the Revolution, and down to within the last forty years, the style of furnishing their houses among the most wealthy and the most respectable on this island, was the acme of simplicity compared with the present style. Then a white floor sprinkled with clean sand drawn into various figures by the broom, large tables, and heavy high-backed chairs of walnut or mahogany, decorated with brass nails along the edge of the leathern back and cushioned seat, furnished the parlor genteelly enough for anybody; and most comfortable chairs they were truly, as all know who have ever seen or tried them. Sometimes a carpet was seen upon the dining-room, not, however, covering the whole floor. This room, although called the *dining-room*, was, in reality, a show parlor, and only used on great occasions, and then not to dine in. The houses, then, were abundantly provided with necessary and substantial furniture; but with nothing that was merely for show, and not for use. Pewter-plates and dishes were in general use, and it was a long time after china and earthenware had been introduced into this country before they superseded the pewter; very many of the inhabitants, and especially among the elderly and old-fashioned, preferring their pewter dining-sets, and urging as a reason for that preference that they could not keep their knives sharp and in good order if they used the new-fangled plates and dishes, but it was otherwise if they continued the pewter. It does one's heart good to see the sets of bright pewter-plates, dishes, porringers, tankards, etc., still kept among some of the old Dutch families.

There was no trade from the colonies to China or the East Indies, and the porcelain of the former country came from Europe, and much of it had been preserved in the families for several generations. It was not unfrequently in the shape of beautiful plates, highly ornamented; of which a strange use was sometimes made by drilling two holes in the edge of the plate, through which a ribbon was passed, and it was hung up against the wall as a picture; we have seen over half a dozen beautiful china plates thus hanging in a single room. Occasionally a very beautiful article, known in that early period as *burnt China*, was to be seen in some families, but always in the form of plates; all the porcelain, if seen at all on the dinner table, was only displayed on very extraordinary occasions. Silver-plate, more or less, was to be seen in every family in anything like easy circumstances; it was a matter of pride to possess it, and once in, it scarcely ever went out of the family, but descended as an heirloom. This plate was not in all the various shapes you will now see it, but in massive waiters, bowls, tankards, cans, etc. Glass was then but little used. Punch was the most common beverage, and was drank by the company from one large bowl of china or silver; and beer or cider from a silver tankard. Many of the wealthy old Dutch families on this island had casks expressly made to contain their wines and liquors, with brass hoops and much ornamented, which were placed upon permanent racks in their cellars; and when they bought a cask of Holland gin, Jamaica rum, sherry and Bordeaux wines, and English beer or porter, or the latter from Philadelphia, where it was made very good long before the Revolutionary war, it was turned into the cask appropriately marked; for all liquors were then used from the wood, and they did not know the distinction of wines in wood, and wines in glass. The preceding were the liquors in common use; Madeira wine was only used on extraordinary occasions, as on the birth of a child, a marriage, and at a funeral. When a young man of any wealth among the Dutch settlers was about to be married, the first thing to be done was to send to Madeira for a pipe of the best Madeira wine, a portion of which was drank on the occasion of his marriage, another portion on the birth of his first son, and the remainder was stored away in the cellar, to be consumed at his funeral. At the close of the last century, on the west end of this island, at an invitation to dinner at the house of the wealthy and respectable inhabitants, the entertainment would be as follows: Punch, warm and cold, before dinner, excellent beef and pork, with the table abundantly and solidly served in other respects; and at the dinner, spruce beer, cider and Philadelphia porter were the drink. After the meats a dessert of puddings and pies, with sherry and Bordeaux wines.

About the period alluded to a matron would drink tea with her friends, return home by candle-lighting, tie on her *check apron*, and put her children to bed, and then pass her evening by her fireside in company with her husband, together with some friend or neighbor who might casually drop in to chat away an hour with them.

Tea-drinking in our cities was a great favorite among the ladies about the middle of the last century. Its introduction and progress in this country are easy to be traced; in 1720, Bohea tea was selling at Philadelphia for fifty shillings a pound, and for some time after it was varying in price, from twenty to thirty shillings a pound, so that it is evident but little of it could have been used in this country at that time. It was not until some twenty-five or thirty years later that its use became anyway general in the community. It may with some be difficult to imagine what substitute they used in its place; they indeed used no substitute; our ancestors had no such meal as we know by the name of tea. An old gentleman, who was living on Long Island in 1820, aged eighty-seven, recollected perfectly well that when he was a young man, just grown up, tea-drinking was first introduced in the town of Gravesend and its vicinity on this island. The original china tea-cups, then first brought there, were some of them still preserved in that year. They were for some considerable time after their introduction passed around from neighbor to neighbor when their friends visited them, for the convenience of tea-drinking; for tea was then considered the greatest treat which could be offered by one friend to another. These cups, as were all other tea-cups of that period, were very small, being not much, if any, larger than an egg-shell.

From a very early period until within the last twenty-five years, a custom existed on Long Island of visiting each other in parties on Sunday afternoon; which, coming to be regarded as an evil demanding a speedy change, and the clergy and some of the strictest of the sect insisting upon it, a change was effected, and the custom is now to a great extent broken up, if not entirely so. In extenuation of this practice it may be observed that the people, necessarily engaged in their agricultural pursuits during the week for a large portion of the year, had little time to visit their relatives and friends, who not unfrequently lived at a considerable distance from them; and that, after attending to the religious services of the day, being dressed in their best apparel, and having been obliged to use their vehicles and horses in transporting the family to church, it seemed almost natural, in meeting their friends, that they should go with them, or take them to their own residences, to enjoy the pleasant and important meal in the country of *taking tea*, and also to pass the early evening in social intercourse; and it might also be urged that considering the manner in which the Sabbath had been kept under the whole Jewish economy, and also its observance by the entire Christian Church from the earliest period of the Church down to the sixteenth century, it seems more like modern Puritanic rigor, than as an exhibition of Christian feeling, to break up such kindly and social meetings as these, after the religious services of the day have been performed. It may probably be said that it was not so much this part of the custom which induced this visiting to be regarded as an evil, as it was the later evening visits of the young men to see the girls, which had been engrafted on it. If this be so, why was not the distinction made; there was certainly ample room for it?

The following table exhibits the prices at which the articles enumerated were sold on this island at the various periods mentioned, and will enable the reader to form some idea of the expense of living in former times.

	In 1770.	In 1790.	In 1815.
Mason's work, per day	$0 44	$0 60	$1 75
Carpenter's work, do.	40	56	1 50
Common laborers, do.	25	37	1 00
Beef, per pound	03	04	12½
Pork, do.	03	04	10
Butter, do.	06	09	30
Eggs, per dozen	04	06	18
Labor, per day, for mowing and getting in hay	30	37	1 00
Labor, per day, in harvest	37	50	1 25
Wheat, per bushel	50	75	2 00
Indian corn, per bushel	30	37	1 12
Rye, per bushel	37	50	1 25

At the beginning of the present century a very large tulip, or white wood tree, existed in Brooklyn, on the bank of the East river, a short distance northeasterly from the Main street ferry. It was a very old tree and hollow, large enough inside to hold eight men comfortably; and was a splendid sight in the spring when in blossom, with its large flowers evaporating their perfume over most of the then little settlement of Brooklyn. Under this tree was a beautiful green sward, and the tree being full of large leaves it cast a most extensive and grateful shade in the warm season. It was so well known in the city of New York, that it was usual among the old-fashioned inhabitants of that city, to make up parties of three or four families, to cross the East river in their own boats, carrying their provisions with them, directly after their early dinner hour of twelve or one o'clock, and to pass the long summer afternoon in laughing, talking, smoking, and drinking under the shade of this tree. The women would boil their tea kettle in the hollow of the tree; and then between four and five o'clock they would sit down to drink tea, with the smooth grass for their tea-table, after which the men would again smoke their long pipes, and after some social chat, and planning another excursion into the country (as it was then called, but how different now!), they would return to the city about sunset, without the fear of being run over by steamboats in their long and slow row across the river, amusing themselves with looking at the gentlemen playing at bowling upon the smooth lawn in the front of the Belvidere club-house, on the height of land south of Corlears Hook; and wondering whether the fishermen in the small boats, anchored a little way from the beach, between the foot of George street (now Market street) and Corlears Hook, had caught any fish; also admiring the gorgeous beauties of the sunset; but at times they would hasten their speed as they looked upon this splendid scene, because the lower cloud that the sun has just disappeared behind, and tinged its edges with living gold, exhibited a very black and ominous appearance, as if it had a thunder shower in its bosom, which idea became strengthened by seeing, almost directly after, the crinkling lightning playing along its surface; and they were also startled by the rushing past them of several porpoises, every few minutes showing their curved backs far above the surface of the water, which, smooth and still as if it were glass, reflected upon its surface all the heights of land, the wharves, buildings, and even lamps of the neighboring city, all which they say to each other is a sign that the storm is near at hand; but they reach home in safety just as the first drops of rain begin to fall. Such parties as these were of very frequent occurrence during the summer. Some may feel an interest in knowing what became of this interesting tree, so identified as it was with many of the purest and most pleasurable enjoyments of our ancestors. One Sunday morning, in the early part of summer, about forty years ago, when the few people who lived at "Brooklyn ferry" (as a large part of the present city was then called) were at church, an alarm of fire was given by the only bell in the place (the Dutch church was then at Brooklyn parish, or Brooklyn proper), which was the fire bell hanging on the Old Ferry road. All ran out to see where the fire was, and observing a smoke in that direction, they passed on until they discovered it was the great tree in flames. For a long time no one dared go near it, under the apprehension that a powder magazine, which then stood in the vicinity, would blow up. The tree was so large and the smoke so great, that for near an hour the inhabitants were much alarmed lest the fire might be communicated to the magazine, and all their houses, if not their lives, destroyed by the explosion, they believing a large quantity of gunpowder to be stored there. After some time, four or five of the most courageous taking pails, and dipping water from the river, threw it into the hollow of the tree and extinguished the fire. It was supposed to have originated from the carelessness of some fishermen, who, having cooked their breakfast there, as was then not an unfrequent occurrence, had neglected afterwards to put out the fire with as much care as was usual. This, however, did not destroy the old tree; it still continued in leaf, and was resorted to during the warm season by the Knickerbockers for their accustomed tea and smoking parties. But when the gales and storms came in the autumn, the tree was so much weakened by the loss of the wood which had been burnt from the inside, that it was blown down, to the great regret of all the inhabitants of Brooklyn and also of New York, to whom, and especially the latter, it had long been a very pleasant resort.

The habits and manners of the people on this island were quite primitive until a very recent period. This arose in a great measure from their seclusion from the travelling world, by reason of the imperfect modes of conveyance throughout a large portion of the island. Old Mr. John Moore, of Newtown, in Queens County, who was aged ninety-seven years in 1826, says, that his mother was the first white woman who came by land from Newtown to Brooklyn. She came with her husband on horseback, riding on a pillion behind him (as was then the custom), through an Indian path, then the only road, and at that time this journey was considered a very arduous undertaking, and her friends wondered much that she should have the courage to think of it. As late as 1793, there was no post-office on any part of Long Island and no mail carried on it; the people on the west end received all their letters and sent them (and few they were) through the post-office in New York, except those on the east end of the island who used the tri-weekly mail from New London to New York, they having frequent communication with New London and other parts of Connecticut, by means of their small sailing vessels, a communication kept up to the present day.

The first post-route upon Long Island, with the first post-offices, was established on the memorial of Abraham G. Thompson and Jonathan Thompson, Esqs., with a few others of the other inhabitants of this island, about the commencement of the present century; and Abraham G. Thompson, Esq., was the first postmaster at Babylon, and held that office for about six years, until he removed to the city of New York and commenced his successful mercantile career in that city. About ten or twelve years previous to the establishment of the post-route on this island, a respectable old Scotchman, named Dunbar, was in the habit of riding a voluntary post between the city of New York along the south road to Babylon, and from thence a few miles to the east, and then across the island to Brookhaven. He thus brought the inhabitants of the central portion of this island their letters and newspapers about once a week or once a fortnight, depending upon the state of the weather.

Mr. Dunbar appears to have ridden his voluntary post even as early as near the commencement of the Revolution. *Rivington's Royal Gazette*, printed in New York, for February 16th, 1778.

establishes this fact by the following article of news: "At two o'clock last Thursday morning a party of twelve rebels seized, at Coram, in Suffolk County, two wagons loaded with dry goods, the property of Obediah Wright of Southampton, These maurauders had been several days on the island, visited most parts, and committed many robberies, especially at the house of Colonel Floyd, Setauket, which they robbed of goods and cash to a considerable amount, and took some property of *Mr. Dunbar, who rides down the island occasionally*, and happened to lodge in the house that night."

It would not answer to be more explicit about Mr. Dunbar, for although there was no mail-route upon the island, yet the king had his deputy postmasters for North America, who were alone authorized to transmit letters to any part of the country, and the people of Long Island, from one end to the other, were presumed to receive their letters at the post-office in the city of New York; Mr. Dunbar's business being an illegal one subjected him to severe penalties, and was only winked at by reason of its absolute necessity.

A mighty change has been produced in Long Island within the last few years, by the introduction of the railroad; now by its means travellers leave New York city, after breakfasting, and arrive in Boston between five and six o'clock the same evening. Only as late as 1835, the regular mail-stage left Brooklyn once a week, on Thursday, having arrived from Easthampton and Sag Harbor the afternoon of the previous day; and this was the only conveyance travellers could then have through this island, unless they took a private carriage. The practice then was to leave Brooklyn about nine o'clock in the morning—they were not, however, particular as to a half hour—travel on to Hempstead, where they dined; and after that, jog on to Babylon, where they put up for the night. A most delightful way this was to take a jaunt—there was no hurry, no fuss and bustle about it; no one was in haste to get to his journey's end, and if he was, and intended going the whole route, he soon became effectually cured of it. Every thing went on soberly and judiciously, and you could see all there was to be seen, and hear all that was to be heard, and have time enough to do it all in; no mode of travelling ever suited our taste better; it was the very acme of enjoyment. The next morning you left Babylon just after daylight—which in the summer was of itself worth living for—journeyed on to Patchogue, where you got your breakfast between nine and ten o'clock, with a good appetite for it, we warrant you. You would get no dinner this day, nor would you feel the want of it after your late and hearty breakfast; but travel along slowly and pleasantly until you reached the rural post-office at *Fire Place*, standing on the edge of a wood; here, if you have a taste for the beautiful in Nature, you would walk down the garden to look at the trout stream filled with the speckled beauties. Here you need give yourself no uneasiness about being left by the stage, as is the case in some of the go-ahead parts of our country —in this particular region the middle of the road is sandy, and the driver, like a considerate man, gives his horses an opportunity to rest, so that they may the better travel through this piece of heavy road. You might, therefore, after enjoying yourself at this spot, walk on leisurely ahead of the stage, with a friend, and some one who is conversant with the country and its legends, and this walk would prove by no means the least pleasant part of your excursion, for many are the tales that you would hear of awful shipwrecks, of pirates and their buried wealth, of treasures cast up by the sea, and of all those horrors and wonders of which the ocean is the prolific parent. After walking for some two or three miles upon the green sward at the edge of the road, gathering and eating the berries as you strolled along, until you were tired, you would find the stage a short distance behind you, the driver very complaisant, for you have much eased his horses in their journey through the heavy sand, and the passengers pleased to see you back in your seat again, that is, if you have done as every traveller ought to do, studied the comfort and convenience of your fellow-passengers as well as your own. Shortly after sunset you would stop for the night, the second one of your journey, at a place called Quagg or Quogue. Here you might, after supper, on a moonlight night in the beginning of August, if you were so fortunate as to be there at such a time, as we were, cross the meadows with a guide, and walk down to the sea-beach, where, with no sound but the beating of the waves upon the shore, swelling in from a waste of waters of three thousand miles, and making the earth tremble under your feet, with scarcely a breath of air to move the hair upon your forehead, and nothing in sight for miles upon miles but the white sand hills glistening in the moonbeams on one side, and this world of waters on the other, you would more than at any other time realize the immensity of creation, and your own comparative insignificance. The following morning you would breakfast at Southampton, after passing through a pine forest, in a portion of which, from the early hour and blindness of the road, you would probably require a guide to go ahead of the horses with a lighted lantern. You would also, this morning, before arriving at Southampton, cross the remains of the first canal constructed in what is now the United States, by Mongotucksee, the chief of the Montauk Indians, long before the white settlement of the country, and also traverse a region of hills known as the Shinecoc Hills, on which not a tree has grown since they were known to man, certainly not since the European settlement of this island; and if you are wise, you would leave the stage near this canal, and with your friend cross these hills on foot, for the stage has to make a long circuit around their base, and you may leisurely walk over them in nearly a straight line, enjoying some most delightful views, which are not to be seen from any part of the road, and reach the road on the opposite side before the stage has completed the circuit. Sag Harbor would be reached in time for dinner, after which the mail stage would travel on to its final destination at Easthampton, arriving there just before sunset on Saturday afternoon; thus occupying nearly three days to traverse a distance of one hundred and ten miles; but most pleasant days they were, and no one has ever tried this mode of journeying through Long Island who had pleasure in view, who did not wish to try it again. It would afford recollections for a life to make such a tour of this island to Montauk Point, going by the south road and returning by the north side; to stroll along the great south beach near Ammagansett, on the hard level sand near the water's edge, with nothing in view but the white sand hillocks crowned with scrubby bushes, and occasionally, at long intervals, small thatched huts or wigwams on the highest elevations, with a staff projecting from the top. These huts were occupied at certain seasons by men on the watch for whales, and when they saw them blowing, a signal was hoisted on this staff. Immediately the people would be seen coming from all directions with their whaling boats upon wagon-wheels, drawn by horses or oxen, launch them from the beach and be off in pursuit of the great fish. You would see all through this region these whaling-boats turned upside down, lying upon a frame under the shade of some trees by the road-side, this being the only way in which they could keep them, having no harbors; four or five families would club together in owning one of these boats and in manning them.

This journey was then a most interesting one, from the variety of scenery and curious out-of-the-way occurrences. The whole south side of the island, and also portions of the northern side, are full of legends and stories of pirates, shipwrecks, and strange superstitions, of murders and buried treasures, which are revived from time to time by the actual discovery of Spanish dollars along the beach, after unusually heavy storms; a large amount was found in this way, as late as March, 1842. It was worth the trouble of such a journey then, to witness the primitive manner of the post-office arrangements in various parts of the island, manifesting a degree of honesty in the whole community, and confidence in each other, to be met with in few other places in this world. The villages were in some instances a mile or two off the post road; in such cases the driver would stop and lay his package for the place intended on a particular rock inside of the fence by the road-side, and would take up anything left there for him; at other times, as he was jogging along, he would throw out two or three newspapers, under a certain tree or shrub, all of which were sure to find their true destination. One morning on our journey down the island, we came to an old tree standing at the intersection of two roads, with a box fastened to it without a lock; this was the post-office of that district; our driver deposited in it the letters and papers for that place, and took out those intended for carriage further east. These were the mail arrangements on Long Island even at that late period, and yet no instance was known of any letter or paper having miscarried. But those things are all now passed, and such a jaunt can never again be taken; the old mail route is broken up, and now, in place of travelling soberly along, we, by means of railroads and turnpikes, fly rapidly through the island. Now we will meet with hundreds of tourists for pleasure, where we met one at that period. It was then something of an undertaking to go to Montauk Point—now almost everybody goes there. Then there were few taverns, and in many places none; the inhabitants were delighted to see strangers, and learn from them the news of the world; they were plain and hospitable in their manners, so that it was a peculiar pleasure to visit them. Now there are taverns or hotels everywhere, and in the summer they are filled. The people have ceased to offer their hospitalities, except to those with whom they are somewhat acquainted, otherwise from the great influx of strangers they might be much imposed upon. In place of that kind, openhearted reception which you then met with from all the girls and young men in the eastern part of the island, you will find they have now the manners of the young people of our towns; and in order to have any intercourse with either sex, a previous formal introduction is necessary, and even after that, the frolicking, kind, good-humored attention you then received are now supplied by manners tinctured with distance and reserve. This change may have been inevitable, and, in fact, absolutely necessary, from their change of circumstances and situation, with reference to the travelling world, but yet it is much to be regretted.

From 1664, down to the close of the British government in this colony, a period of more than a century, almost all the marriages upon this island (which were not of unfrequent occurrence, judging from the statement of Major Rogers, that more than a hundred ladies from this island were annually married, about the middle of the last century, into the neighboring plantations), and also in New York, took place under the Governor's license, thus adding very much to his income; it was, in fact, esteemed rather disreputable to be married by the publication of the banns for three Sabbaths, in church, or by putting up the notices required by law. The following extract from a New York newspaper, under the date of December 13, 1765, will show how strongly that prejudice existed in the community, and that the occurrence of a marriage by the publication of the banns, even at that late period, was so uncommon as to call forth a special notice in the public journals of the day:

"We are credibly informed (says the editor) that there were married last Sunday evening, by the Rev. Mr. Auchmuty, *a very respectable couple*, that had been published three different times, in Trinity Church. A laudable example and worthy to be followed. If this decent, and, for many reasons, proper method of publication, was once generally to take place, we should hear no more of clandestine marriages, and save the expense of licenses, no inconsiderable sum these hard and depressing times."

At the same time that our ancestors provided all the necessary facilities for entering the marriage state, a state of peculiarly high moment to a newly settled colony, they also made provision for arranging and disposing of the disputes which sometimes arise from that condition of life, and we find, in 1673, at New York City, an officer styled, "The first commissary of marriage affairs,"—whose duty it was to hear and determine all matrimonial controversies, and whose jurisdiction extended to Long Island. Notwithstanding there was undoubtedly some business for this officer and his successors to perform, yet our history from the first settlement of this colony to the year 1786, presents no instance of divorce *a mensa et thoro*, and but one single instance of a divorce *a vinculo matrimonii*, and that was obtained by Rebecca Leveridge from her husband Eleazer, in the Court of Assizes, held in the City of New York on the 22d of October, 1670. This certainly speaks well for the morals of our ancestors. And they were indeed a moral, honest race, notwithstanding they were fond of good living, and indulged in many sports and amusements, which we have, from the requirements of fashion, suffered to become obsolete. Our records show the extraordinary fact, that from the year 1786 there has not been a single instance of any person executed for a capital offence in Kings County; which, considering its numerous population, and its immediate proximity to one of the greatest commercial cities in the world, is a phenomenon in the history of morals. We cannot form a correct opinion as to the inhabitants of this island, or indeed of any country, without looking into their festival amusements, their sports, and the manner in which their fireside enjoyments were conducted. In this we have the advantage of almost any other people, for we were so fortunate as to have a "*Fatherland*," *Vaderlandt* as well as a "*Mother Country*," and our ancestors coming, in the good "olden time," from those countries, introduced with them the customs and festivities of their different nations, which have since become domesticated among us, and with some others, originating in our own land, now of right form a portion of our history as a people. It is true that at first there was not so good a state of feeling existing between the Dutch and English settlers as might have been desired, but this feeling has all died away long since, and the Dutch and English, by living as neighbors and coming better to understand each other's characters, and by frequent intermarriages, have become one people; and the Dutch talked English, and the English talked Dutch; and they eat sour-krout, smoked goose and kolichees, and roast beef and plum pudding together, and everything has since gone as comfortably as could be wished.

Christmas was a season of great festivity on Long Island from its first settlement. Formerly among the English families on this island it was customary on Christmas eve to place on the fire a large log of hickory wood, which had been previously selected and prepared for the occasion, called the "Christmas log;" this was the "*Yule cleugh*" of the Saxons. Etymologists have long puzzled themselves to find the meaning of this expression as applied to this log of wood burnt upon the hearth on Christmas eve, and during Christmas day. It was formerly the general belief from a very early period, that on Christmas eve the evil spirits, by reason of their spite and malice being increased by the birth of the Saviour, who was destined ultimately to destroy their power, were unusually busy in their efforts to injure mankind; and that it was necessary to use some extraordinary precautions to thwart their designs. These logs being cut some time before, and destined for the hearth on that particular occasion, were supposed to acquire a degree of sanctity from that fact, and also being sufficiently large to burn through the night and the succeeding day, the light from their burning was believed to drive away all evil influences of a supernatural character, such spirits fearing light and loving darkness; the expression as thus used, therefore, means a log burnt to drive away the evil spirits. In Rolle's translation of some of the Psalms of David, made in the fourteenth century, we have the word *Yule* used in that sense, viz.: "I shal not dreede Yueles," which we now translate, "I will fear no evil" (see Psalm 23). This word, *Yuele*, is evidently the same as that written *Yule*, the orthography of the language not being, by any means, in a settled state at that early period.

So universal is this belief that the evil spirit fears light, that even the aborigines of New Holland will never venture from their fires at night because of the horror they entertain of an evil spirit, whom they represent as a gigantic black man, always prowling about at night, ready to seize and devour any unfortunate wanderer, except from the most urgent necessity, when they always carry *a firebrand* to intimidate the monster. (Wilkes' *United States Exploring Expedition*, vol. II., page 198.)

All nations appear to have the idea of repelling their spiritual enemies by means of light; and it is certainly a very curious circumstance that the declaration of Scripture that evil loves darkness and hates light, should find such a full confirmation in the belief of all nations, as well the lowest and most ignorant, as the most civilized and intelligent.

This Christmas log has been several times placed upon the hearth, in our family, within our memory, but the custom is now nearly discontinued. The children, also, formerly had their candles, made in different shapes, at that season, often three branches from one body, called "Christmas candles," and which they burnt on Christmas eve, and were allowed to sit up until they were burnt out.

Among the Dutch settlers, Christmas was always a great festival; and a day on which Saint Nicholas was in high repute, who, according to the belief of the children, on Christmas eve, came down the chimney in his little wagon, and deposited his gifts in their nice, clean, woollen stockings, hung in a row near the fire-place, for the good saint's convenience; for he was mighty busy on that night, and had no time to waste in hunting about the room for their stockings. A firm belief in these annual domiciliary visits of St. Nicholas was formerly universal among the children on this island and vicinity; and even now exists to a very considerable extent. Formerly, if any child should happen, in the presence of other children, to express a disbelief in this annual visit of the saint, he was sure to be looked upon by the others as little better than a heretic, or anything that was bad, and he would be referred at once to the indisputable evidence of Santa Klaas' veritable existence afforded by the tracks of his wagon-wheels upon the ashes of the hearth. No persons but those who, in their youthful days, have experienced it, can realize the anxiety with which the youngsters look forward to the eves of Christmas and New Year, when they could hang up their stockings. After which they went to bed, and dreamed, if they could get asleep, which, at such times, was a very difficult matter to accomplish, about St. Nicholas, in the form of a pleasant little old gentleman in a cocked hat and breeches, with a large bag full of sugar-plums and toys. When they got up in the morning, for they were all early risers on that morning, the first thing was to go to the stockings, which, if they had been good, they would find full of cakes, sugar-plums, toys, and some small pieces of money; but if they had been bad, they tremblingly expected to find a small birch twig, symbolical of what they deserved. We have no doubt but that this belief, where it was prevalent among children, had a considerable tendency to check any vicious dispositions or inclinations which they might have.

The Dutch children upon this island used to have a hymn, written in the Dutch language, in praise of St. Nicholas or "Santa Klaas," as they call him; which hymn commences with:

> "Sanctus Klaas, goedt heyligh man;"
> Saint Nicholas, good holy man;

and which hymn they sang on Christmas eve and Christmas day.

The New Year's eve and New Year's day were also seasons of great festivity upon this island, and still continue to be; in few parts of the world are they observed with more hospitality and kind feeling than among us. Paulding, in his *New Mirror for Travellers*, speaking of the celebration of New Year's eve in the good old Dutch way, and observing that it also is under the especial patronage of St. Nicholas, exclaims: "To whom (St. Nicholas) whoever fails in due honor and allegiance, be his fate never to sip the dew from the lips of the lass he loveth best on New Year's eve or New Year's morn; never to taste of hot-spiced Santa Cruz; never to know the delights of mince pies and sausages, swimming in the sauce of honest mirth and homefelt jollity."

The New Year's day with us, almost from time immemorial, was ushered in with great noise and rejoicing, which was formerly continued throughout the day and even the day following. The inhabitants used to go from house to house with their guns and fire salutes; and at every house thus saluted, it was customary to invite them in to partake of the good things of the season. After enjoying themselves for a time, in eating and drinking, they would depart accompanied by the men of the house, and thus they would pass through the whole neighborhood, until every house was saluted, and all the men of the vicinity were collected together—then they would go to some convenient spot and pass the remainder of the day in firing at the mark and in athletic sports.

This custom of firing guns on this occasion, was attempted to be stopped by an act passed by the Colonial Legislature, on the 8th of March, 1773, in which they state that "great damages are frequently done on the eve of the last day of December, and on the first and second days of January, by persons going from house to house with guns and other firearms." And after the close of the Revolution, and on the 22d of April, 1785, the Legislature of the State of New York found it necessary to revive that enactment of the Colonial Legislature, and they further extended it to prevent the firing of guns, pistols, rockets, squibs, and other fireworks on *Christmas eve;* for about this period the people began also to celebrate the eve of Christmas in this noisy manner—this last, however, continued but a short time, and never became very prevalent.

It has been with us, for very many years past, and is yet customary with the clergy, to visit their congregations during the holidays, and to partake with them of the good cheer of the festal season. This is a good custom; it brings the pastor and his flock more intimately connected, and endears them to each other.

About the middle of the last century, and for

some time previous, it was the custom among the Dutch inhabitants, when a negro woman's child attained the age of three years, solemnly to present it to a son or daughter, or other young relative of the master's family, who was of the same sex as the child thus presented. The child to whom the young negro was given, immediately presented it with some piece of money and a pair of shoes; and from that day the strongest attachment existed between the domestic and the destined owner. It is scarcely possible to meet with instances of friendship more tender and generous than that which often existed in this colony between the slaves and their masters and mistresses; extraordinary proofs of which were not unfrequently given in the course of hunting and Indian trading, then matters of common occurrence.

About the same period, when the change of the Style took place in 1752, and in 1753, many people, and it may be said, the larger portion of them, refused to observe the Christmas and New Year according to the new Style, and insisted upon keeping those festivals eleven days later, according to the *good old style*, as they called it; for, said they, Parliament may, if they please, alter the names of the months and of the days, but it is out of their power to change the seasons. It has been frequently asserted, and with much truth, that in no part of the Union is the New Year celebrated with greater cordiality and more hospitality than with us, which continues to be the case even to the present period. Private families are prepared to receive visits of congratulation on this day from all who have even the slightest acquaintance, and indeed also from those who have none, and who are obliged to be introduced for the first time, and sometimes to introduce themselves. These visits are understood to be tokens of respect to the ladies; unless in the case of some gentlemen of high official rank, or of some poor fellow of a bachelor who has no lady to do the honors of his house. This is a blessing which we derive from our honest, good-natured Dutch ancestors, who in their time were satisfied with the *Oly Cookes*, *Pretzies*, *Kiskatomas-nuts* and *Spitzenburgs*, with hot spiced *Santa Cruz*, *good strong Christmas beer* and *cider*, with which their ample oaken tables were filled on New Year's day. In place of these, it is true, we have substituted the splendid iced and ornamented plum cake, with almost numberless other cakes, confectionaries and fruits, not forgetting the true *New Year's cake*, and a variety of other choice edibles, together with Madeira and other wines, cordials and liquors, yet we have retained much of the kind feeling and heartfelt welcome which so much distinguished them on this jubilee of the year. The temperance reformation has worked some change in our holiday customs recently, in causing wines and cordials, and indeed all kinds of liquor, to be banished from the social board in the great majority of cases, on this occasion, and hot coffee and lemonade have been substituted in their places. That it may be long, a very long time, ere we shall forget to keep up our holiday customs, should be the sincere wish of all who desire the happiness of our people. It is a good thing for us all to have a day of mutual friendship and forgiveness when those who have been estranged from each other for months by wide separation or some foolish misunderstanding, are expected to meet each other with the kind feelings adapted to the season, and when friends and relatives, whose business and vocations have parted them asunder for a long period, meet and revive the best affections of the human heart.

In enumerating our holidays and festivals, the 14th day of February, St. Valentine's day, cannot be omitted. No! St. Valentine, thou love-making prelate, though most writers do unworthily unsaint thee, thou must not be forgotten. For thou, with our fair countrywomen, art an especial favorite, and thy festival is duly observed by making of true-love knots, which are often more difficult than the Gordian knot to untie, in the writing of valentines; by the seeking for favorable dreams; by throwing whole apple parings (which are taken off from a fair apple, standing before a looking-glass) over the right shoulder, thereby to show by its formation on the floor the first letter of the future husband's name, and by many other rites and mysteries which are known alone to and practised by the gentle lover.

Among our early Dutch settlers this day was called "*Vrouwen dagh*," *Women's day*, and was celebrated in the following singular manner: Every girl provided herself with a cord, without a knot in the end, and on the morning of this day they would sally forth, and every lad whom they met was sure to have three or four smart strokes from the cord bestowed on his shoulders. These, we presume, were in those days considered as "love-taps," and in that light answered all the purposes of the "valentine" of more modern times, as the lasses were not very likely to favor those with their lashes whom they did not otherwise prefer.

Easter among our Dutch ancestors was a festival of high note, and as such observed by them with religious services, as well as by merry-making. In a volume of sermons by Hadrianus Visscherus (Adrian Fisher), printed in Dutch, 4to, Amsterdam, 1667, is one entitled "Het Paesschen-Feest der Christelijcke Kercke, ofte de Evangelische historie van Jesu Christi Triumphante opstandinge," etc., being a discourse preached on the feast of Easter. Easter day was called among our Dutch inhabitants, and also by many of the English, until the last twenty-five years, *Paessch*, pronounced *Paas;* and from thence the same appellation became transmitted to Easter Monday, to which it was applied even after the word *Easter* became generally adopted.

Anciently, the Dutch people, and also some of the English, were in the habit of making presents of eggs to each other on Easter day and Easter Monday—the egg being considered an emblem of the Resurrection, from the fact of its yielding animal life, after remaining for a considerable space of time in an inert and apparently dead condition. The only relic of this custom now is that observed by the boys on Easter Monday, and which a few years ago was general among them, of cracking the points and butts of eggs together, and whoever cracked the other's egg won it. This sport was followed up with great zeal, and sometimes with a little knavery; as in getting the Guinea hen's eggs, which have a harder shell than the common hen's egg, and taking off the spots with vinegar, and thus by those winning the eggs of their opponents, and also by emptying through a small hole and then filling it up with rosin; and at other times by getting a piece of white marble, fashioned like a hen's egg; this last trick, however, was easily detected. The boys' eggs at this season were frequently stained various colors; and these colored eggs were invariably exhibited for sale at the small shops during Easter week, and for some days previous. This is a sport which excites much more interest in the boys than can be well imagined by those who are unacquainted with it; this we say from experience, having been an adept in this species of amusement when a school-boy.

The first Monday in June, or as the Dutch call it, *Pinckster*, was formerly considerable of a festival among the Dutch inhabitants of Long Island; and they celebrated it by treating their friends to an abundance of good cheer, among which, and peculiar to this festival, was the "*Soft Wafels*," and by riding in parties about the country making visits. But now poor *Pinckster* has lost its rank among the festivals, and is only kept by the negroes; with them, however, especially on the west end of this island, it is still much of a holiday. For many days before it arrives, the negroes come into the City of New York with their sassafras and swingled tow for sale, in order to raise money with which to keep this day. The day has sunk lamentably low, and without any apparent reason; to ridicule *whistling*, it is called *Negro Pinckster Music.*

> "With hurried step and nodding knee,
> The negroes keep their jubilee;
> While Cuffee, with protruding lip,
> Bravuras to the darky's skip."
> [*Whistles.*]

Considering its origin, this festival, from its singular mode of observance, was one of the strangest of the American customs. From a very early period, probably from the first settlement of the country, until about the commencement of the present century, *Pinckster* was a holiday among our Dutch inhabitants. It was celebrated as the day of *Pentecost*, the day upon which occurred the miraculous descent of the Holy Spirit upon the apostles. In the volume of sermons by Adrian Fisher, before referred to, when treating of Easter, printed in 4to, at Amsterdam, in 1667, is one entitled, "Het Eerste Tractact: Van de Uystortinge des Heyligen Geests over de Apostelen op den

Pinckster dagh." (A Discourse on the Descent of the Holy Spirit upon the Apostles on Pinckster day.)

Although this day was a species of negro jubilee upon Long Island at the same time that it was observed as a festival by the white population, and eventually became entirely left to the former, yet it never was with us the perfect saturnalia that was for a long period exhibited in its observance at Albany. In that city, about forty years ago, and for ages previous, it was a day of much note, and the negroes used to assemble from the city and the surrounding country for a long distance, to celebrate it in booths upon the hill at the head of State street, where the Capitol now stands. These booths were filled with edibles, cakes, and fruits of every description which could then be procured at the season of the year, and also liquors; and the carousal continued for the space of three days and nights. It was indeed a real saturnalia; about these booths on the green, the negroes were in the habit of dancing what was then known as the "Toto dance," which is described by those who have witnessed its performance as having been the most indecent dance that can well be imagined; and yet such was the state of public sentiment, and the liberty allowed to their slaves at that time, for they were so then that respectable females would stand by and witness this dance as a mere matter of course. Some may say, on reading this, that the state of public morals has greatly improved since that period; that however is questionable, for we must bear in mind that there is a possibility of being so virtuous as not to see evil in that which would bring the blush at once to the cheek of a female of immoral heart, although of outwardly moral conduct.

The music which usually accompanied this dance was the "banjo drum," formed of a hollow log, with a skin of parchment stretched over one end, the other being left open, on which they beat with a stick, making a rough, discordant sound. Both the dance and the drum were most probably introduced from Africa by the Guinea negroes. They had also a great procession through the public streets of the City of Albany during those three days. The head man in all these dances and processions was an old Guinea negro, aged eighty-five years, whom they called *King Charlie.* His official costume on such occasions was a scarlet coat and an old-fashioned cocked hat, and he rode a horse at the head of his array. His will was law among all the negroes, and if there was any dispute, as would frequently be the case in so large an assemblage of such people kept together for so long a period, he had only to decide, and the matter was settled, and his fiat, whatever it might be, was quietly submitted to.

The frolickings on that occasion were not confined to the negroes, but the younger portion of the white population also shared in them, and had frequent balls and dances, not with the blacks, however, although at the same time.

The Evacuation day, November 25th, the day on which the British army left Brooklyn, on this island, and also the City of New York, in the year 1783, has been observed as a species of holiday on the west end of Long Island; and good cause they had to rejoice at it, for Brooklyn at that time was little more than a garrison, being covered with fortifications, there being no less than five distinct forts, and also a line of fortifications more than six miles in length, within the present City of Brooklyn, which were occupied by British and Hessian troops.

The 4th day of July, the national festival, is observed among us with great spirit; in describing it we are obliged to extend our view beyond the region of this island, the customs attending its celebration with us being so mixed up with those other sections as to render this unavoidable. This birthday of our nation is celebrated with all "the pomp and circumstance of" martial display and civic honors from Maine to Texas; but the manner and mode of its observance in some parts of our country sometimes has that about it which, although it manifests honorable feelings and stern independence in the people, is yet calculated to excite mirth. The following ode, though a little distorted, is, withal, a pretty fair description of some country celebrations; it is said to be "composed for the 4th of July, calculated for the meridian of some country towns in Massachusetts, and Rye, in New Hampshire;" it was written about the year 1800, and made its appearance in the *Farmer's Museum*, printed in Massachusetts:

"Squeak the fife and beat the drum,
Independence day is come!!
Let the roasting pig be bled,
Quick twist off the rooster's head,
Quickly rub the pewter platter,
Heap the nut cakes fried in butter,
Set the cups and beaker glass,
The pumpkin and the apple sauce.
Send the keg to shop for brandy;
Maple sugar we have handy.
Independent, staggering Dick,
A noggin mix of *swinging thick;*
Sal, put on your *russel skirt*,
Jotham, get your *boughten* shirt,

To-day we dance to tiddle-diddle—
Here comes Sambo with his fiddle;
Sambo, take a draw of whiskey,
And play up Yankee Doodle frisky—
Moll, come leave your witched tricks,
And let us have a reel of six—
Father and mother shall make two;
Sall, Moll, and I stand all a row,
Sambo, play and dance with polity;
This is the day of blest equality,—
Father and mother are but men,
And Sambo is a *citizen.*
Come, foot it, Sal; Moll, figure in,
And, mother, you dance up to him;
Now saw as fast as e'er you can do,
And, father, you cross over to Sambo.
—Thus we dance and thus we play,
On glorious Independence Day.
Rub more rosin on your bow,
And let us have another go—
Zounds! as sure as eggs and bacon,
Here's Ensign Sneak and uncle Deacon,
Aunt Thiah, and their Bet's behind her
On blundering mare, than beetle blinder—
And there's the Squire, too, with his lady—
Sal, hold the beast! I'll take the baby!
Moll, bring the Squire our great arm-chair,
Good folks, we're glad to see you here—
Jotham, get the great case bottle,
Your teeth can draw the corn-cob stopple—
Ensign, Deacon, never mind;
Squire, drink until you're blind."

NOTES

GEOGRAPHICAL AND HISTORICAL,

RELATING TO THE

TOWN OF BROOKLYN

IN KINGS COUNTY, ON LONG ISLAND.

By Gabriel Furman.

"They are worthy of reprehension who contemn the study of antiquity, (which is ever accompanied with dignity,) as an arid curiosity."—LORD COKE.

BROOKLYN:
PRINTED BY A. SPOONER.
1824.

ADVERTISEMENT.

The Compiler offers these notes to the inhabitants of his native town, in the hope that they may be in some small degree useful and entertaining in discussions relating to the history and rights of this thriving place. He claims no merit for this performance, and neither does he write from the vanity of being considered an author, but is only actuated by a desire to rescue from oblivion such facts as may be interesting to his fellow-citizens. The Compiler would consider himself guilty of ingratitude, if he did not in this public manner, acknowledge the obligations he rests under from the kind assistance afforded him whilst collecting these notices, by Jeremiah Johnson, Abraham Vanderveer. Silas Wood. and John Doughty, Esqrs.

NOTES, ETC.,

OF THE

TOWN OF BROOKLYN.

SITUATION.

THIS town is situated in Kings County, on the west end of Long Island, in the State of New York. It is bounded north by the City and County of New York; east by the township of Bushwick; south by the township of Flatbush and New Utrecht; and west by New York Bay; and contains the village of Brooklyn, which is about a mile square. This town formerly composed part of a powerful Indian Sachemdom; and with the other parts of the Island bore the Indian name of Matowcas.

This part of the island, as far as Jamaica, was inhabited by the Canarsee tribe of Indians. The old Dutch inhabitants in this county have a tradition, that the Canarsee Indians were subject to the Mohawks, as all the Iroquois were called, and paid them an annual tribute of dried clams and wampum. When the Dutch settled here, they persuaded the Canarsees to keep back the tribute; in consequence of which a party of the Mohawks came down and killed their tributaries wherever they met them. So great was the dread that these Indians afterwards entertained of the Iroquois, that when a party of the Iroquois, during the French war, were taken prisoners and imprisoned in the Jail of this county, the Canarsees avoided them with the greatest care, and seemed to be afraid even to come where they should see them. The Canarsee Indians are at this time totally extinct; not a single member of that ill-fated race is now in existence.

There was also a small tribe of the Nyack Indians near the Narrows.

In this town is also the United States Navy Yard, containing about 40 acres, which was purchased of John Jackson, Esq., by Francis Childs, Esq., for $40,000, and on the 23d day of February, 1801, was conveyed by said Childs to the United States.

ANCIENT NAMES AND REMAINS.

In 1667, this town was known by the name of Breucklen. In the act to divide the province of New York into shires and counties, passed Nov.

1, 1683, it is mentioned by the name of Breucklyn. It is also called Broucklyn in the act to divide the province into shires and counties, passed Oct. 1, 1691. The present name Brooklyn does not appear to have been generally adopted until after the Revolutionary war.

Heads of Indian arrows, beds of oyster and clam shells, denoting the former residence of the aborigines, are frequently found in different parts of this town.

Among the most ancient remains are two houses, one owned by the family of Cortelyou, built in 1699; the other standing on Fulton-street, in the village of Brooklyn. The last mentioned house was occupied by the Colonial Legislature as a Sessions-house, during the prevalence of the small-pox in New York, in 1752; and at this house on the 4th of June, 1752, 2,541 bills of credit, issued by this Colony, amounting to £3,602, 18, 3, were cancelled by the Colonial Commissioners. This house was also occupied by Gen. Putnam as his head-quarters during the stay of the American Army on Long Island, in 1776. But the oldest house in the town of Brooklyn is supposed to be the house known as No. 64 Fulton-street, in the village of Brooklyn, and now owned and occupied by Mr. Jacob Patchen. Mr. Charles Doughty, who has been dead about twenty-five years, and was about eighty-five years of age when he died, said that this was an old house when he was a boy. Mrs. Rapalye, the mother of John Rapalye, whose property in Brooklyn was confiscated during the Revolutionary war, says that this house was built by a family of the Remsens, who came from Holland.

SOIL AND CLIMATE.

The soil of this town appears to be mostly alluvial, though some few primitive rocks are to be met with. Several years since, in digging a well on some of the highest ground in Brooklyn, a hemlock board was found at the depth of thirty feet, and again at the depth of seventy-three feet oyster and clam shells were met with, which crumbled on being exposed to the air.

The shores of Brooklyn, where they are not defended by wharves, are undergoing continual and rapid changes, in consequence of the velocity of the current in the East River. The tide rises here about five feet.

There is very little doubt but that Governor's Island was formerly connected with Red Hook point in this town. It is an established fact, that previous to the Revolutionary contest, cattle were driven from Red Hook to Governor's Island, which places at that time were only separated by a very narrow channel, which is called Buttermilk channel, and is now wide and deep enough to admit of the largest size of merchant vessels passing through.

The climate is very changeable, but cannot be called unhealthy. People in this town live to as great age as in almost any other part of the United States; as instances of which, April, 1823, Mr. Tiebout died in this town, aged one hundred years and ten months. The same year, Mr. Schoonmaker died, aged eighty-four years; and in 1824, Mary Peterson, a colored woman, died, aged one hundred and three years. It is not an uncommon thing for the inhabitants to live beyond the "three score years and ten."

This town has at different periods been visited by the yellow fever. Between July 10th and September 10th, 1809, twenty-eight persons died of that disease. During the prevalence of the yellow fever in the city of New York, in the summer of 1822, seven persons died of that disease in Brooklyn. In the summer of 1823, the yellow fever made its appearance in the village of Brooklyn, and nine persons fell victims to that dreadful pestilence in the space of one month, during which time its ravages continued. Every year that this disease made its appearance amongst us, it could be distinctly traced to some foreign cause; as, in 1809, it was brought in the ship Concordia, Captain Coffin, on board of which vessel the first case and death happened. In 1822, it was introduced from the City of New York—and in 1823, it was traced to two or three vessels which had arrived a short time previous from southern latitudes. Indeed, the high and airy situation of Brooklyn almost precludes the idea of its being engendered among us.

ANCIENT GRANTS AND PATENTS.

In the year 1638, William Kieft, Director General and Counsellor for their high mightinesses the States General, and his highness the Prince of Orange, granted to Abraham Rycken, a tract of land in the present town of Brooklyn.

September 11, 1642, William Kieft, Director General, &c., patented to Jan Manje, a piece or parcel of land containing twenty morgan, or forty acres, in the town of Brooklyn. A copy of which patent is hereto annexed as a specimen of those ancient instruments:

By William Kieft, Director General and Counsellor, about the high and mighty Lords, the States General of the United Low Country, and his highness of Orange, and the Lords Commanders of the privileged West India Company, residing in the New-Netherland, do ratify and declare by these presents, that we upon the date hereinafter written, did give and grant to Jan Manje, a piece of land, greatly twenty morgan stretching about south-east one hundred and ninety rods inward the woods towards to Sassians maise land—long is the limits of the said maise land fifty rod, and then again to the water side, two hundred and twenty rod, about north north-west, well so northerly and along the strand or water side, seventy rod. Which abovesaid land is lying upon Long-Island, between Andries Hudde and Claes Janse Ruyter.—With express conditions, &c. Dated at Fort Amsterdam, in the New-Netherland, the 11th day of September, 1642.

WILLIAM KIEFT.

By order of the Lord the Director General, and Counsellor of New-Netherland.

CORNELIUS VANTIENHOVEN, Sec'ry.

January 29, 1652, Pieter Linde, having married the widow of Jan Manje, transported or sold the above tract of land to Barent Janse. August 23, 1674, before Nicasius de Sille, admitted Secretary of the Dutch towns appeared Jan Barentse,* and

* The custom of changing the names of sons, or rather substituting the surnames for the Christian name, prevailed at

Auke Janse, with Simon Hausen as Guardian of the other children of Barent Janse, deceased, "procured by his wife Styntie Pieterse deceased, all living within the town of Midwout Fflackbush," and declared that they transported the above tract of land to Dirck Janse Woertman.

September 12, 1645, William Kieft, Director General, &c., patented to Andries Hudden, "a piece of land lying upon Long-Island against over the fort, lying to the south-west to Jan Manje," containing 37 morgan. December 10, 1651, "Pieter Cornelissen, by virtue of a procuratie of Andries Hudden," for the consideration of 400 guilders, transported to Lodewyck Jongh the above tract. July 19, 1676, Lodewyck Jongh transported to Jeronimus de Rapalje, eight morgan of the above tract. February 12, 1679, Harmatie Jansen, relict of Lodewyck Jongh, transported to Dirck Janse Woertman, 12 morgan of the above tract. May 3, 1685, "Dirck Janse Woertman, transported to the heirs of Jooris Dirckse, a small stroke off land lying at the east side off the highway being all the claime they can pretende by virtue off the abovesaid Pattent."

---

this period; as in the above instance, the father's name was Barent Janse, and the son was called Jan Barentse.

September 30, 1645, William Kieft, Director General, &c. patented to Claes Janse, from Naerder, a piece of land, containing 20 morgan, lying south-east, a little easterly, just over against the Fort, upon Long Island. March 11, 1660, the above tract of land was transported by Claes Janse Ruyter, to Machiell Tadens, who transported the same to Machiell Hainielle.

The three patents to Manje, Hudde, and Janse, from Naerder, were located near the Ferry in this town, and all subsequently were purchased by Derick Woortman, alias Dirck Janse Woertman, and were by him sold to Joras Remsen, on the 10th day of October, 1706, for the sum of £612 10s. current money of New-York.

There is great reason to believe that there was a General Patent of this town under the Dutch Government, which patent is now lost. What strengthens this idea is, that the first by Governor Nicolls under the English is confirmatory of some former grant.

August 10th, 1695. The Patentees and freeholders of this town sold unto Stephanus Van Cortlandt, the neck of land called Red Hook, containing by estimation 50 acres; which they state in their deed "was formerly given and granted to the town of Broocklyn, in the year

1657, by Governor Stuyvesant, the Dutch Governor then at that time, and since confirmed by the English Governors, Governor Nicolls, and Governor Dongan." Which is very strong proof of there having been a general Dutch Patent for this town.

October 18, 1667, Richard Nicolls, the first English Governor of New York, granted to the inhabitants of Brooklyn, the following full and ample patent, confirming them in their rights and privileges.

L. S. "Richard Nicolls, Esq. Governor General under his Royal Highness James Duke of Yorke and Albany, &c. of all his Terretorys in America, To all to whom these presents shall come, sendeth Greeting.—Whereas there is a certain town within this government, situate lying and being in the West Riding of Yorkshire upon Long-Island, commonly called and known by the name of Breuckelen, which said town, is in the tenure or occupation of several freeholders and inhabitants who having heretofore been seated there by authority, have been at very considerable charge, in manuring and planting a considerable part of the lands belonging thereunto and settled a competent number of families thereupon. Now for a confirmation unto the said freeholders and inhabitants in their possessions and enjoyment of the premises, Know ye, That by virtue of the commission and authority unto me given by his Royal Highness, I have given, ratified, confirmed, and granted, and by these presents, do give, ratify, and confirm and grant, unto Jan Everts, Jan Daman, Albert Cornelissen, Paulus Veerbeeck, Michael Eneyl, Thomas Lamberts, Tuenis Guysbert Bogart and Joris Jacobson, as patentees, for and on the behalf of themselves and their associates, the freeholders and inhabitants of the said town their heirs successors and assigns, all that tract together with the several parcels of land which already have or hereafter shall be purchased or procured for and on behalf of the said town, whether from the native Indian proprietors, or others, within the bounds and limits hereafter set forth and exprest, viz. that is to say, the town is bounded westward on the farther side of the land of Mr. Paulus Veerbeeck, from whence stretching south-east, they go over the hills, and so eastward along the said hills to a southeast point which takes in all the lotts behind the swamp, from which said lotts they run north-west to the River* and extend to the farm, on the

* According to the New-York doctrine, this boundary of the town can only be correct when the tide is flood, for when

t'other side of the hill heretofore belonging to Hans Hansen over against the Kicke or Looke-out, including within the said bounds and limitts all the lotts and plantations, lying and being at the Gowanis, Bedford, Wallabouclit and the ferry.—All which said parcels and tracts of land and premises within the bounds and limitts aforementioned, described, and all or any plantation or plantations thereupon, from henceforth are to bee appertaine and belong to the said town of Breucklen, Together with all havens, harbours, creeks, quarryes, woodland, meadow-ground, reedland or valley of all sorts, pastures, marshes, runs, rivers, lakes, hunting, fishing, hawking, and fowling, and all other profitts, commodities, emoluments, and hereditaments to the said land, and premises within the bounds and limits all forth belonging, or in any wise appertaining,—and withall to have freedome of commonage for range and feed of cattle and horse into the woods as well without as within these bounds and limitts with the rest of their neighbours *—as

the water is low, the town is bounded by property belonging to the Corporation of the City of New-York, and not by the River.

* This town enjoyed this privilege in common with the other towns on Long-Island, and their cattle which ran at large were marked with the letter N.

also one-third part of a certain neck of meadow ground or valley called Sellers neck, lying and being within the limits of the town of Jamaica, purchased by the said town of Jamaica from the Indians, and sold by them unto the inhabitants of Breucklen aforesaid, as it has been lately laid out and divided by their mutual consent and my order, whereunto and from which they are likewise to have free egress and regress, as their occasions may require.* To have and to hold all and singular the said tract and parcell of land, meadow ground or valley, commonage, hereditaments and premises, with their, and every of their appurtenances, and of every part and parcell thereof to the said patentees and their associates, their heirs, successors and assigns, to the proper use and behoof of the said patentees and their associates, their heirs, successors and as-

---

* At the annual town meeting, April, 1823, a committee was appointed to inquire if this town at present had any, and if any, what right to the above-mentioned tract of meadow ground called Sellers neck; what progress this committee made in their investigation, the Compiler is uninformed. This meadow called Sellers neck, the Compiler thinks was apportioned among the patentees and freeholders, and what leads him to this conclusion is, that on the 10th of May, 1695, John Damen, who was one of the patentees of this town, sold to William Huddlestone all his interest in the said meadow.

signs forever. Moreover, I do hereby give, ratify, confirm and grant unto the said Patentees and their associates, their heirs, successors, and assigns, all the rights and privileges belonging to a town within this government, and that the place of their present habitation shall continue and retain the name of Breuckelen, by which name and stile it shall be distinguished and known in all bargains and sales made by them the said Patentees and their associates, their heirs, successors and assigns, rendering and paying such duties and acknowledgments as now are, or hereafter shall be constituted and established by the laws of this government under the obedience of his Royal highness, his heirs and successors. Given under my hand and seal at Fort James, in New York, on the Island of Manhattat, this 18th day of October, in the nineteenth year of the reign of our Sovereign Lord, Charles the second, by the grace of God, of England, Scotland, France and Ireland, King, Defender of the faith, &c. Annoque Domini, 1667.

RICHARD NICOLLS.

Recorded by order of the Governor, the day and year above written.

MATTHIAS NICOLLS, Sec'ry.

1670. The inhabitants of this town desirous of enlarging the bounds of their common lands, and extinguishing the Indian claim to the same, applied to Governor Lovelace, and obtained from him the following permission to purchase of the Indians.

"*L. S.* Whereas the inhabitants of Breucklyn, in the west Riding of Yorkshire upon Long-Island, who were seated there in a township by the authority then in being, and having bin at considerable charges in clearing ffencing and manuring their land, as well as building ffor their conveniency, have requested my lycense for their further security to make purchase of the said land of some Indians who lay claim and interest therein; These are to certify all whom it may concerne, that I have and doe hereby give the said inhabitants lycense to purchase their land according to their request, the said Indians concerned appearing before me as in the law is required, and making their acknowledgments to be fully satisfyed and payed for the same. Given under my hand and seal at ffort James, in New-Yorke, this ffirst day of May, in the 22nd yeare of his Majestyies reigne, Annoque Dom. 1670.

FFRANCIS LOVELACE."

The purchase was accordingly made and the following is a copy of the deed from the Indians for the same.

"To all people to whom this present writing shall come, Peter, Elmohar, Job, Makaquiquos, and Shamese, late of Staten Island send Greeting: Whereas, they the said Peter, Elmohar, Job, Makaquiquos, and Shamese, afore-mentioned, doe lay claime to the land now in the tenure and occupation of some of the inhabitants of Breucklyn, as well as other lands there adjascent as the true Indian owners and proprietors thereof, Know Yee, that for and in consideration of a certaine sum of wampum and diverse other goods, the which in the Schedule annext are exprest unto the said Sachems in hand payd by Monsieur Machiell Hainelle, Thomas Lambertse, John Lewis, and Peter Darmantier, on the behalf of themselves and the inhabitants of Breucklyn, the receipt whereof they doe hereby acknowledge, and themselves to be fully satisfyed and payed therefore; have given, granted, bargained and sold, and by these presents doe fully, freely and absolutely give, grant, bargain and sell, unto the said Monsieur Machiell Hainelle, Thomas Lambertse, John Lewis and Peter Darmantier, ffor and on behalf of themselves, and the inhabitants aforesaid, their heyrs and successors; all that parcell of land and tract of land, in and about Bedford, within the jurisdiction of Brucklyn, beginning ffrom Hendrick Van Aarnhems land by a swamp of water and stretching to the hills, then going along the hills to the port or entrance thereof,* and soe to Rockaway ffoot path as their purchase is more particularly sett fforth; To have and to hold all the said parcell and tract of land and premises within the limits before described unto the said Monsieur Machiell Hainella, Thomas Lambertse, John Lewis, and Peter Darmantier, ffor and on the behalf of the inhabitants aforesaid, their heyres, and successors, to the proper use and behooff of the said inhabitants, their heyers and successors forever; In witness whereof the partyes to these presents have hereunto sett their hands and seales, this 14th day of May, in the 22nd yeare of his Majestyes reigne, Annoque Dom. 1670.

Sealed and Delivered in the presence of Ma-

---

* This "port or entrance," as it is called, is situate in the valley on the Flatbush Turnpike, near the "Brush" or "Valley Tavern," and a short distance beyond the 3 mile post from Brooklyn ferry.—A freestone monument has been placed here, to designate the patent line between Brooklyn and Flatbush.

thias Nicolls, R. Lough, Samuel § Davies, John Garland.

his marke

The mark of þ Peter. (L. S.)
The mark of o Elmohar. (L. S.)
The mark of ✕ Job. (L. S.)
The mark of ❜ Makaquiquos. (L. S.)
The mark of 7 Shamese. (L. S.)

"This Deed was acknowledged by the within written Sachems, before the Governor in the presence of us, the day and year within written.

MATHIAS NICOLLS, Secretary.
The mark of § SAMUEL DAVIES.

"Recorded by order of the Governor.

MATHIAS NICOLLS, Secretary.

The Inventory, or Schedule referred to in the Deed.

"The payment agreed upon ffor the purchase of the land in and about Bedford, within the jurisdiction of Breucklyn, conveyed this day by the Indian Sachems, proprietors, is, viz.:—

100 Guilders Seawant,
Half a tun of strong Beer,
2 half tuns of good Beer,
3 Guns, long barrells, with each a pound of powder, and lead proportionable—2 bars to a gun,
4 match coates."

May 13, 1686. Governor Dongan granted to the inhabitants of Brooklyn the following confirmatory patent:

L. S. "Thomas Dongan, Lieutenant Governor, and Vice Admiral of New York, and its dependencies under his Majesty James the Second, by the grace of God, of England, Scotland, France and Ireland, King, Defender of the Faith, &c.—Supreme lord and proprietor of the Colony and province of New York and its dependencies in America, &c. To all to whom this shall come sendeth greeting, whereas the Honorable Richard Nicolls, Esq. formerly Governor of this province, did by his certain writing or patent under his hand and seal, bearing date the eighteenth day of October, Annoque Domini, one thousand six hundred and sixty-seven, ratifie, confirm and grant unto Jan Evarts, Jan Damen, Albert Cornelissen, Paulus Verbeeck, Michael Enyle, Thomas Lamberts, Tunis Gisberts Bogart, and Joris Jacobsen, as patentees for and on behalf of themselves and their associates, the freeholders and inhabitants of the town of Breucklen, their heirs, successors, and assigns forever, a certain tract of land, together with the several parcels of land which then were or thereafter should be purchased or procured for and on behalf of the said town, whether from the native Indian proprietors, or others within the bounds and limitts therein sett forth and expressed, that is to say, the said town is bounded westward on the further side of the land of Mr. Paulus Verbeeck, from whence stretching south-east they go over the hills, and so eastward along by the said hills to a south-east point, which takes in all the lotts behind the swamp, from which said lotts they run north-west to the River, and extend to the farm on the other side of the hills heretofore belonging to Hans Hansen, over against Keak or Look-out, including within the said bounds and limitts all the lots and plantations, lying and being at the Gauwanes, Bedford, Wallabocht and the ferry, all which said parcells and tract of land and premises within the bounds and limitts aforementioned described, and all or any plantation or plantations thereupon, from henceforth are to be, appertain and belong to the said town of Breucklyn, Together with all harbor, havens, creeks, quarries, woodland, meadow ground, reed land or valley of all sorts, pastures, marshes, waters, rivers, lakes, fishing, hawking, hunting, fowling, and all other profits, commodities, emoluments and hereditaments to the said lands and premises within the bounds and limitts set forth, belonging, or in any wise appertaining, and with all to have freedom of commonage for range and feed of cattle and horses, into the woods with the rest of their neighbours, as also one third part of a certain neck of meadow ground or valley, called Seller's neck, lying and being within the town of Jamaica, purchased by the said town of Jamaica from the Indians, and sold by them unto the inhabitants of Breucklen aforesaid, as it was laid out aforesaid, and divided by their mutual consent and order of the Governor. To have and to hold unto them the said patentees and their associates, their heirs, successors and assigns forever, as by the said patent reference being thereunto had, doth, fully and at large appear. And further, in and by the said patent, the said Governor, Richard Nicolls, Esq., did erect the said tract of land into a township by the name of Breucklen aforesaid, by that name and style to be distinguished and known in all bargains, sales, deeds, records and writings whatsoever; and whereas the present inhabitants and freeholders of the town of Breucklen aforesaid, have made their application to me for a confirmation of the aforesaid tract of land and premises in their quiet and peaceable possession and enjoyment of the aforesaid land and premises. Now Know Ye, That I, the said Thomas Dongan, by virtue of the commission and authority derived unto me, and power in me residing, have granted, ratified and confirmed, and by these presents do grant, ratifie and confirm, unto Teunis Gysberts, Thomas Lamberts, Peter Jansen, Jacobus Vander Water, Jan Dame, Joris Jacobs, Jeronimus Rapelle, Daniel Rapelle, Jan Jansen, Adrian Bennet, and Michael Hanse, for and on the behalf of themselves and the rest of the present freeholders and inhabitants of the said town of Breucklen, their heirs and assigns forever, all and singular the afore-recited tract and parcels of land set forth, limited and bounded as aforesaid; together with all and singular, the houses, messuages, tenements, fencings, buildings, gardens, orchards, trees, woods, underwoods, pastures, feedings, common of pasture, meadows, marshes, lakes, ponds, creeks, harbors, rivers, rivulets, brooks, streams, highways and easements whatsoever, belonging or in any wise appertaining to any of the afore-recited tract or parcells of land and divisions, allotments, settlements made and appropriated before the day and date hereof. To Have and To Hold, all and singular, the said tract or parcels of land and premises, with their, and every of their appurtenances unto the said Tunis Gysberts, Thomas Lamberts, Peter Jansen, Jacobus Vander Water, Joris Jacobs, Jeronimus Rappelle, Daniel Rappelle, Jan Jansen, Adrian Bennet and Michael Hanse, for and on behalf of themselves and the present freeholders and inhabitants of the town of Breucklen, their and every of their heirs and assigns forever, as tenants in common without any let, hindrance, molestation, right of survivorship or otherwise, to be holden in free and common socage according to the tenure of East Greenwich, in the county of Kent, in his Majesty's kingdom of England. Yielding, rendering and paying therefor yearly, and every year, on the five and twentyeth day of March, forever, in lieu of all services and demands whatsoever, as a quit rent to his most sacred Majesty aforesaid, his heirs and successors, at the city of New York, twenty bushels of good merchantable wheat. In testimony whereof, I have caused these presents to be entered and recorded in the Secretary's office, and the seal of the Province to be hereunto affxed this thirteenth day of May, Anno. Domini, one thousand six hundred and eighty-six, and in the second year of his Majesty's reign.

THOMAS DONGAN."

Quit rents to the following amounts and at the following periods have been paid on the Brooklyn patents.

June 8, 1713. Paid to Benjamin Van de

Water, Treasurer, the sum of £96 7s 1d. for upwards of 16 years quit rent.

April 6, 1775. Charles Debevoise, Collector of the town of Brooklyn, paid to the Receiver General of the Colony of New York, 20 bushels of wheat, for one year's quit rent, due from said town.

November 9, 1786. Fernandus Suydam, and Charles C. Doughty, two of the Trustees of the town of Brooklyn, paid to the Treasurer of the State of New York, the sum of £105 10s. in full for arrears of quit rent due from the said town.

TOWN RIGHTS AND FERRIES.

The difference between this town and the city of New York relative to the water rights of the former, has deservedly excited the attention and interest of our inhabitants, as involving property to a great amount, and unjustly withholding from our town a revenue which would enable it to improve with almost unparalleled rapidity. In order that each person so interested may form a correct opinion of the subject matter in dispute, the Compiler has thought proper, under this head, to lay before them the foundations of the claims on both sides of the question.

October 18, 1667. In the reign of Charles 2d Richard Nicolls, Esq., Governor General of the

Province of New York, under his Royal Highness James, the Duke of York, &c., afterwards James 2d of England, granted to the inhabitants of this town a confirmatory patent, acknowledging that they were rightfully, legally and by authority in possession of the property and privileges they then enjoyed. The patent after naming the patentees, and describing the bounds of the town, and binding by the *River* and not by high water mark, proceeds to say, "Together with all *havens*, *harbors*, creeks, marshes, *waters*, *rivers*, lakes, fisheries." "Moreover, I do hereby give, ratify and confirm unto the said patentees and their associates, their heirs, successors and assigns, all the *rights* and *privileges* belonging to a town within this government." Under this patent the town of Brooklyn justly claims the land between high and low water mark on their shore, in opposition to the claims of the Corporation of the City of New York; and an equal right with them to erect ferries between the town of Brooklyn and the City of New York.

It does not appear that there was any adverse claim on the part of New York, until the 27th of April, 1686, *nineteen years* after the date of the Brooklyn patent, when the Corporation of New York obtained a charter from Governor Dongan, by which the ferries were granted to them, but not a word mentioned about the land between high and low water mark on the Brooklyn side. From the reading of this charter it appears as if the Governor was doubtful as to his right even to grant the ferry, for it contains an express saving of all the rights of all other persons, bodies politic and corporate, their heirs, successors and assigns, in as ample a manner, as if that charter had not been made.

May 13, 1686. The freeholders and inhabitants of Brooklyn somewhat apprehensive of encroachments by New York, obtained from Governor Dongan, a patent under the seal of the Colony, fully confirming that granted them by Governor Nicolls.

May 6, 1691. An act was passed by the Governor, Council and General Assembly of the Colony of New York, "for settling, quieting and confirming unto the cities, towns, manors, and freeholders within this Province, their several grants, patents and rights respectively." By this act the freeholders and inhabitants of the town of Brooklyn were confirmed in the rights they possessed and enjoyed under their two several patents.

October 12, 1694. The Corporation of New York, not thinking their foothold on the Brooklyn side sufficiently secure, purchased of one

William Morris, for no specific consideration, a piece of land in Brooklyn near the ferry. This deed is the foundation of the Corporation claim to their land in the village of Brooklyn. A copy of which will be found in the appendix marked with the letter A.

Bent on unjustly wresting from the town of Brooklyn their water right, the Corporation, on the 19th of April, 1708, obtained from Governor Cornbury, a man infamous for his vices and disregard of justice, another charter, in which they came out more openly than before, and claimed the *vacant* land to high water mark, on Nassau Island, reserving to the inhabitants of Brooklyn the right of transporting themselves in their own boats ferriage free, to and from New York.* By this charter, no matter how ample soever they might have considered it at the time, they obtained nothing but *vacant* land to high water mark; that is the land which was not already granted, and in the possession of some other person or persons, which was not the fact as to the land on the Brooklyn side, it being vested in the patentees, their heirs, successors, and assigns forever; so that the only power or authority remaining in

---

* Although the bounds of this grant commences about 250 yards in the town of Bushwick, the Corporation of New York have made no claim to land beyond the Wallabought.

the Governor was to grant the Corporation of New York, the privilege of buying the water rights of the inhabitants of Brooklyn. But that would not answer their purpose, for those rights could be bought cheaper of Governor Cornbury than they could of this town.

This proceeding on the part of New York stimulated the inhabitants of Brooklyn to obtain from the Colonial Legislature, in 1721, an act confirming their patent rights.

To obviate the effects of this law, and strengthen the charter of Cornbury, which from the circumstances under which it was obtained, the Corporation feared was invalid, on the 15th of January, 1730, they procured from Governor John Montgomerie, a new charter confirming their pretended right to the land to *high water mark on our shore.**

* There was some peculiar circumstances attending the consummation of this charter, which the Compiler thinks ought to be known. A short time previous to obtaining the charter, the Common Council of the City of New-York resolved that the sum of £1400 was necessary for the procuring of that instrument; £1000 of which sum they determined to raise immediately by a loan on interest for one year; which they accordingly did, and gave a mortgage for that amount to James De Lancey, Esq., dated January 14, 1730. Directly after the execution of this mortgage they resolved to address the Governor, "for the great favour and goodness

The grants from the Corporation of New-York, under their two charters for the water lots on the Brooklyn side, are very artfully and ingeniously drawn. By those grants are only conveyed "all the estate, right, title, interest, property, claim, and demand whatsoever, in law and equity" of them the said Corporation; and their covenant for quiet possession only extends to them and their successors, and not against any other persons lawfully claiming premises. These grants in order to save the Corporation harmless against the claims of Brooklyn, also contained a covenant to the following effect: "It is hereby covenanted, granted and agreed upon by and between the parties to these presents (that is the Corporation of New York and the person to whom they give the grant), and the true intent and meaning hereof also is, and it is hereby declared, that this present grant,

---

shown to this Corporation in granting their petition, in ordering and directing his Majesty's letters patent for a new charter and confirmation to this Corporation," and probably informing him that they had obtained the money. The consequence was, that on the next day, January 15, 1730, the charter was completed; and on paying the £1000 was delivered to them on the 11th day of February, 1730, almost a month after its date. By which it appears that the Corporation of New York still continued purchasing the right of the town of Brooklyn from the Colonial Governors. See list of Corporation Charters and grants, 1747.

or any words, or any thing in the same expressed, or contained, shall not be adjudged, deemed, construed or taken to be a covenant or covenants on the part and behalf of the said parties of the first part (that is, the Corporation of New York), or their successors for any purpose or purposes whatsoever, but only to pass the estate, right, title, and interest they have or may lawfully claim by virtue of their several charters, of, in, and to the said premises. Which covenant evidently shows a want of confidence in the validity of their title on the part of the Corporation.

October 14, 1732. An act was passed by the General Assembly of this Colony, "confirming unto the City of New York its rights and privileges." By this act no addition was made to their former pretended rights.

November 14, 1753. The freeholders and inhabitants of this town appointed Jacobus Lefferts, Peter Vandervoort, Jacob Remsen, Rem Remsen, and Nicholas Vechte, Trustees, "to defend our patent where in any manner our liberties, privileges, and rights in our patent specified is encroached, lessened, or taken away by the commonality of the City of New York." A copy of the proceeding of the town meeting at which the above trustees were elected, will be found in the ppendix marked B.

Not satisfied with the encroachments they had made, the Corporation began to question the right of the inhabitants of Brooklyn to cross to and from New York ferriage free in their own boats, and to carry over the inhabitants in those boats;—the result was, that in July, 1745, a suit was commenced by one of the inhabitants of Brooklyn, named Hendrick Remsen, against the Corporation of New York, which was tried before a jury in Westchester County. A special verdict was found setting forth all its patents and charters, and among other things, that the road from which the said Hendrick Remsen ferried the inhabitants of Brooklyn to and from New York, "then and long before was laid out for a public highway leading down to *low water mark* on the East River, between the places aforesaid called the Wallabouclit and the Red Hook on Nassau Island, and the jurors aforesaid, upon their oath aforesaid, do further say, that the river called the East River, over which the said Hendrick did carry the persons and goods aforesaid, from the said lands, between the Wallabocht and the Red Hook, is a large and public and navigable river used by his Majesty's ships, and other ships, and smaller vessels employed in trade and commerce, and hath always been so used from the first settlement of this Colony." On argument, judgment was rendered by the Supreme Court of this Colony in the month of October, 1775, in favor of Hendrick Remsen, that he recover his damages against the Mayor, Aldermen, and Commonality of the City of New York, and the sum of one hundred and eighteen pounds, fourteen shillings and tenpence half-penny for his costs and charges. An appeal to the King and Council, from this decision, was brought by the Corporation, which was not determined in consequence of the Revolutionary war. There is a tradition in this town that the Corporation of New York were so apprehensive of this claim on the part of the town of Brooklyn, that in order to disengage Hendrick Remsen from the interest of the town, they gave him a house and lot of land near Coenties Slip, in the City of New York. How far this tradition is correct, the Compiler is unable to say. It appears, however, that he, about that time, became in possession of such property, and the same remained in his family within the memory of some of our inhabitants.

Our two Patents are confirmed by the Constitution of this State, which confirms all grants of land within the State, made by the authority of the King of Great Britain, or his predecessors, prior to the 14th of August, 1775.

The Compiler, thinking it would not be uninteresting to his fellow-citizens to see a statement of the amount received by the Corporation of New York for quit-rent on the water lots claimed by them, has given the following short statement:

The Commissioners of the Sinking Fund of the City of New York have received, from August 23d, 1813, to Dec. 31, 1824,

For water lot rents............	$17,635 24
Commutation for water lot rents.	17,275 41
	$34,910 65

The Corporation of New York during the present year 1824, have received for water lot rents the sum of..................$8,862 97

Within a short time the jurisdiction of the village of Brooklyn has been extended beyond low water mark, leaving the pretended right of soil still in the Corporation of New York.* August term, 1821, in the case of Udall *vs.* the Trustees of Brooklyn, the Supreme Court of this State decided that Kings County, of which the village of

* The jurisdiction of New York by their first charter in 1686, was limited to low water mark around Manhattan Island; but was extended to low water mark on the Brooklyn side by Governor Montgomery's charter in 1730.

Brooklyn is part, includes all the wharves, docks, and other artificial erections in the East River, opposite to the City of New York, though west of the natural low water mark on the Nassau or Long Island shore; and the jurisdiction of the village extends to the actual line of low water, whether formed by natural or artificial means. Same term, in the case of Stryker *vs.* the Mayor, etc., of the City of New York, the Supreme Court decided that the City and County of New York includes the whole of the Rivers and harbour adjacent to actual low water mark, on the opposite shores, as the same may be formed, from time to time, by docks, wharves and other permanent erections; and although the jurisdiction of the city does not extend so as to include such wharves or artificial erections, yet it extends over the ships and vessels floating on the water, though they be fastened to such wharves or docks.

April 9, 1824. The Legislature of the State of New York in the act to amend the act entitled "an Act to incorporate and vest certain powers in the freeholders and inhabitants of the village of Brooklyn in the County of Kings," granted this town concurrent jurisdiction with the City of New York in the service of process, in actions civil and criminal, on board of vessels attached to our wharves; and in the act for the establishment of a Board of Health in the village of Brooklyn, authority is given to the said Board to remove all infected vessels from the wharves within the said village.

The ferries have been unavoidably, in some degree, taken into consideration when speaking of our town rights. The Compiler will therefore confine himself to such historical facts, and laws, and such proceedings, passed and had by the Colonial and State Legislatures as may relate particularly to them.

During the early years of this Colony, the old ferry was from near the foot of Joralemon street, to the Breede Graft, now Broad street, in the City of New York. At that period a creek ran through the middle of Broad street, up which the boats ascended to a ferry-house which is still standing. At this time it is difficult to ascertain the exact period when the old ferry was established at its present situation on the Brooklyn side. In 1697, John Aeresen was ferry master.

It appears from the following order, that the Court of Sessions of Kings County, exercised some authority over the ferry between Brooklyn and New York. October 7, 1690. "Whereas much inconvenience does arise by several negroes coming on this island from New York and other places, and from this island to New York. It is ordered, that the ferrymen shall not bring or set over any negroes or slaves upon the Sabbath day, without a ticket from their masters."

Acts have been passed by the Colonial and State Legislatures for the purpose of regulating the ferries between this town and the City of New York, in the following chronological order:

November 2d, 1717, an act was passed, which was revived in the year 1726, and again in 1727. October 14, 1732, another act was passed for the same purpose. By this act it was provided, "That the ferryman for the time being, shall not impose, exact, demand, or receive any rates or ferriage for any goods or things whatsoever, transported by any of the inhabitants living alongst the River, at or near the Ferry on Nassau Island, in their own boats or canoes," provided that the same be their own goods or commodities. This act continued in force until the 28th of February, 1789, when another act was passed regulating the ferriage, and containing a similar proviso. April 9, 1813. The last mentioned law was re-enacted, with the same provision.

The winter previous to the prosecution of the suit between Hendrick Remsen, and the Corporation of the City of New York, the inhabitants of Brooklyn made an attempt to obtain from the

Colonial Legislature, a further confirmation of some of their rights, particularly relating to the ferry; on which application the following proceedings were had.

January 30, 1745–6. In General Assembly, a petition of the Trustees of the town of Brookland, in Kings County, in behalf of themselves, and the freeholders and inhabitants of the said township, was presented to the House and read, setting forth, That a great number of the inhabitants of the said township, living near the ferry from Nassau Island to New York, and having their chief dependence of supporting their families by trading to the New York markets, are by one act of the General Assembly, entitled, an act to regulate the ferry between the City of New York and the Island of Nassau, and to establish the ferriage thereof, passed in the sixth year of his Majesty's reign, debarred from transporting their goods in their own vessels, to the said markets, which exposes them to very great hardships, difficulties and expenses, and therefore humbly praying that they may have leave to bring in a bill to relieve them from the aforesaid hardships. Upon a motion of Major Van Horne (of New York), ordered that the clerk of this House serve the Corporation of the City of New York, with a copy of the said petition forthwith.

In General Assembly, April 12th, 1746, Mr. Abraham Lott, according to leave, presented to the House, a bill entitled, "an act to repeal an act therein mentioned, so far as it relates to the freeholders and inhabitants of the township of Brooklyn, in Kings County, within this colony;" which was read the first time, and ordered a second reading.—Ordered, that the Corporation of the City of New York be served with a copy of the said bill.

April 18, 1746. In General Assembly. The bill entitled, an act to repeal an act therein mentioned, so far as it relates to the freeholders and inhabitants of the township of Brooklyn, in Kings County, within this colony, being offered to be read a second time, Capt. Richards (of New York) moved, that the second reading of the said bill might be deferred until the next meeting of the House, after the first day of June next; which was agreed to by the House, and ordered accordingly.

June 20, 1746. In General Assembly. A petition of the Mayor, Aldermen and Commonalty, of the City of New York was presented to the House and read, setting forth, That the Corporation having been served with a copy of a bill now before this House, entitled, an act to repeal an act therein mentioned, so far as it relates to the freeholders and inhabitants of the township of Brooklyn, in Kings County, within this colony; do conceive that the passing the said bill into a law may affect their ancient rights and freehold, and therefore humbly praying that they may be heard by their counsel against the said bill, at the bar of this House, on Friday next, ordered that the Trustees of the township of Brooklyn be heard by their counsel in support of the said bill, at the bar of this House, on Friday next, and that Mr. William Smith appear for them. Ordered, that the clerk of this House serve the parties with a copy of these orders forthwith.

June 27, 1746. In General Assembly. The House being informed that the Corporation of the City of New York were attending with their counsel to be heard against the bill; and that the trustees of the township of Brooklyn were also attending with their counsel to be heard in support of the said bill; both parties were called in, and the counsel on both sides having been fully heard, for and against the said bill, they were directed to withdraw; and the bill being read the second time, the question was put,—whether the said bill should be committed, and carried in the affirmative in the manner following:—Affirmative, Messrs. Lott, Chambers, Stillwell, Living ston, Harring, Cornell, Abraham Lott, Lecount, Bradt, Nicoll, Hardenbergh, and Gale, 12.—Negative, Messrs. Richards, Cruger, Clarkson, Van Horne, Philipse, Morris, Verplank, and Thomas, 8.

July 4, 1746. In General Assembly, the engrossed Bill entitled, an act to repeal an act therein mentioned, so far as it relates to the freeholders and inhabitants of the township of Brooklyn, in Kings County, within this colony, was read the third time, and upon Mr. Speaker's putting the question, whether the Bill should pass, a motion was made by Col. Morris in the words following, viz.—As this Bill has been already ordered to be engrossed, by a majority of the House, and the question that now is put, is, whether this Bill shall pass; I must beg leave to give my reasons for opposing its passage. The first is, it is alleged by this bill, that the people of Brooklyn had a right, prior to the act passed in the year 1742, which was not proved, nor attempted upon the hearing before this House; but if we pass this Bill, we allow that right to be proved, and then it becomes our allegation, which I conceive inconsistent with the honor and justice of this House, to allege anything in such a case, but what has been proved. The second is, it implies that the act in 1732, took away unjustly, a right from the people of Brooklyn, that they were entitled to. Thirdly, it implies, that the House have fixed the two points before mentioned, and then it will necessarily follow, that we have considered the rights of the Corporation,* as well as those of the people of Brooklyn; that we have not, I appeal to the House, who must allow that no such right ever appeared to us, at least as a House, and for us to declare certain facts by a bill, which has never been proved, will be doing what I conceive we ought not to do, if we make justice and equity the rule of our conduct. For these reasons, I move, that the Bill may be rejected. The question being put thereon it was carried in the negative, in the manner following, viz.—For the negative, Messrs. Chambers, Lott, Cornell, Hardenberg, A. Lott, Bradt, Lecount, Gale, and Harring, 9. Affirmative, Messrs. Cruger, Morris, Richards, Van Horne, Clarkson, Verplank, Philipse, and Thomas, 8.

Resolved, That the Bill do pass. Ordered, that Colonel Harring, and Mr. Hardenberg do

* For what purpose was it that the Corporation's counsel was heard at the bar of the House, if not to advance and support their rights? If it was not done at that time, the plain inference would be, that they were aware they had no right.

carry the Bill to the Council and desire their concurrence. By which it appears that it was considered by the House, as well as subsequently by the Supreme Court, that the right of the town was sufficiently proved, notwithstanding the assertions of Colonel Morris.

This Bill by *some means* was stifled in the Council,* and never became a law.

During the Revolution the Old ferry was kept by Messrs. Van Winkle and Bukett; at which period the usual charge for crossing was six pence for each passenger.

August 1, 1795. The ferry from the foot of Main street, Brooklyn, to the foot of Catharine street, New York, commonly called the New ferry, was established by Messrs. William Furman and Theodosius Hunt, lessees from the Corporation of the City of New York.

In consequence of the prevalence of the Yellow fever in Brooklyn, in the month of August, 1809, the old ferry was removed to the foot of Joralemon street, and the boats plied from there to Whitehall, New York.

---

* The Council was appointed by the King's mandamus and sign manual, and all their privileges and powers were contained in the Governor's instructions. The tenure of their places was extremely precarious.—See Smith's *History of New York*, p. 364.

On the 4th day of March, 1814, the Legislature of this State passed an act allowing William Cutting and others his associates, to charge four cents for each passenger crossing in the Steam-boat to be by them placed on the Old ferry. Previous to this, the fare was two cents for each passenger. May, 1814, the Steam-boat commenced plying on the old ferry between Brooklyn and New York.

This Ferry Company derive their interest in the old or Fulton ferry, from a lease executed January 24th, 1814, by the Mayor, Aldermen and Commonalty of the City of New York, to Robert Fulton and William Cutting. The rent reserved by the Corporation on this lease is $4,000 per annum for the first 18 years, and $4,500 per annum for the remaining 7 years.* It is a difficult matter to speak correctly of the present income of this ferry. At its first establishment the dividends were made on a capital estimated at $45,-000, divided into shares of $1,000 each, and were made at the rate of 5 per cent. for six months, and what remained after this 5 per cent. taken out, formed the surplus dividend. From May,

* The Corporation of New York, during the year 1824, have received from the ferries the sum of $12,003.75—more than three-fourths of which sum is from the ferries on the East River.

1814, to November, 1815, the regular dividends on one share amounted to \$157.11½, and during the same period the surplus dividend amounted to \$228.21½, making a dividend of \$385.33, on one share for about 18 months, equal to about 25 per cent. per annum.

At the Session of the Legislature in the winter of 1818, the Corporation of New York presented a petition praying that they might have the regulation of the rates of ferriage between this town and the city of New York—against which the Trustees of the village of Brooklyn, and the inhabitants of this town strongly remonstrated, stating that "they had full confidence that the Legislature of this State would never increase the rates of ferriage, nor permit the same to be increased, beyond what is necessary to support the ferries in the best manner; they therefore prayed that the Legislature would not surrender to the Corporation of New York a right which had been reserved by the Legislature, and which the petitioners deemed of the greatest importance to the inhabitants of Nassau Island."

ROADS AND PUBLIC LANDING PLACES.

This town appears to have entered early into the contest respecting roads. There are many instances on record previous to 1683, of the Constable of Brooklyn being ordered to repair the roads, and in case of neglect, fined; and in one instance he was ordered by the Court not to depart until further order.

The main road, or as part of it is now called, Fulton street, in the village of Brooklyn, was laid out March 28th, 1704, by Joseph Hagaman, Peter Cortelyou, and Benjamin Vandewater, Commissioners, appointed by an act of the General Assembly of the colony of New York, for the laying out, regulating, clearing and preserving of public highways in the colony. The record of this road is as follows:—"One publique, common and general highway, to begin ffrom *low water marke* at the ferry in the township of Broockland, in Kings county, and ffrom thence to run ffour rod wide up between the houses and lands of John Aerson, John Coe, and George Jacobs, and soe all along to Broockland towne aforesaid, through the lane that now is, and ffrom thence straight along a certaine lane to the Southward corner of John Van Couwenhoven's land, and ffrom thence straight to Bedfford as it is now staked out, to the lane where the house of Benjamin Vandewater stands, and ffrom thence straight along through Bedfford towne to Bedfford lane, running between the lands of John Garretse, Dorlant and Claes

Barnse, to the rear of the lands of the said Cloyse, and ffrom thence southerly to the old path now in use, and soe all along said path to Philip Volkertses land, taking in a little slip of said Philip's land on the south corner, soe all along said road by Isaack Greg's house to the Fflackbush new lotts ffence, and soe all along said ffence to the eastward, to the north-east corner of Eldert Lucas's land, lying within the New lotts, of Fflattbush aforesaid, being ffour rod wide all along, to be and continue forever."

This road, or "king's highway," as it was then called, leading from the ferry to the old Dutch Church, or Brooklyn parish, was the cause of much contention. At the April term of the General Sessions of the Peace for Kings County, in 1721, indictments were found for encroaching on the "common high way of the King, leading from the ferry to the Church at Brookland," against John Rapalje, Hans Bergen and James Harding, and others.—By which indictments it appears that the road should have been four rods wide.

These indictments appear to have been predicated as well on the following application of John Rapalje and Hans Bergen, as on complaints from several of the inhabitants:

"Fflatbush, April 19, 1721. John Rapalje and

Hans Bergen of the fferry, desires of tne grand jury that the Commissioners now being should be presented for not doing their duty in laying out the king's highway according to ye law, being the King's highway is too narrow from the ferry to one Nicalus Cowenhoven, living at Brooklyn and if all our neighbours will make ye road according to law, then ye said John Rapelje and Hans Bergen is willing to do the same as aforesaid, being they are not willing to suffer more than their neighbours. As witness our hands the day and year first above written.

JAN RAPELJE,
HANS BERGEN."

Some of the persons indicted considering themselves aggrieved, and others who feared being placed in the same situation, applied to the Colonial Legislature, and July 27th, 1721, obtained the passage of a law to "continue the common road or king's highway, from the ferry, towards the town of Breuckland, on the Island of Nassau, in the Province of New-York," with the following preamble: "Whereas several of the inhabitants on the ferry, on the Island of Nassau, by their petition preferred to the General Assembly, by setting forth, that they have been molested prosecutions, occasioned by the contrivance and instigations of ill and disaffected persons to the neighbourhood, who would encroach upon the buildings and fences that have been made many years, alledging the road was not wide enough, to the great damage of several of the old inhabitants, on the said ferry; the said road as it now is, has been so for at least these sixty years past, without any complaint, either of the inhabitants or travellers."

The law then proceeds to establish the road "forever," as it then was, from the ferry upwards to the town of Breuckland, as far as the swinging gate of John Rapalje, just above the house and land belonging to James Harding. These proceedings will readily account for Fulton-street, in the present village of Brooklyn, being so narrow and crooked in many places.

The point, however, to which the Compiler wishes to draw the attention of his fellow citizens, is to the existence and location of several public highways and landing-places in this town which at present are known to very few.

There is a public landing-place at or near the mills of Nehemiah Denton, Esq., and a public highway leading thereto.—The record of which is as follows:—"One common highway to Gawanus mill, to begin ffrom the north-east corner of Leffert Peterses ffence, and soe along the roade westerly, as it is now in use to the lane yt parts the lands of Hendrick Vechte, and Abraham Brower, and Nicholas Brower, and soe all along said lane as it is now in ffence to the house of Jurian Collier, and from thence all along the roade now in use to the said Gowanos mill, being in all four rod wide to the said lane; and that there be a convenient landing place for all persons whatsoever, to begin ffrom the southermost side of said Gowanus mill house, and ffrom said house to run ffour rod to the southward, ffor the transportation of goods and the commodious passing of travellers; and that said highway to said Gowanos mill ffrom said house of said Jurian Collier shall be but two rod only and where it is now in use; said common highway to be and continue forever; and ffurther that the ffence and gate that now stands upon the entrance into said mill neck, ffor the inclosing and securing of said neck, shall soe remaine and be alwayes kept soe inclosed with a ffence and hanging gate; and the way to said mill to be thorow that gate only and to be alwayes shutt or put to by all persons that passes thorow." The Commissioners laid out the above road and landing place, March 28th, 1704.

In 1709, the Commissioners laid out another road and landing place, at or near the mill of

John C. Freeke, Esq. The record of which is as follows:—"One common highway to begin ffrom the house of Jurian Collier to the New mill of Nicholas Brower, now sett up on Gowanos mill neck soe called, as the way is now in use along said neck to said mill to be of two rod wide; and that there shall be a landing place by said mill in the most convenient place ffor the transportation of goods and the commodious passing of travellers; and said highway and landing place to be, remaine and continue forever."

This town has a public landing place seven rods in length, near the foot of what is now called District-street, in the village of Brooklyn.—This landing place is mentioned in the record of a road three rods wide, leading to the same, which record the Compiler omits inserting in consequence of its length and the multitude of entries connected therewith.

It is believed by many, and not without very good reason, that this town has a public landing place a short distance to the North of the Old or Fulton ferry, and which landing place is now in the possession of the Corporation of New-York.

There is a very distinct tradition of a road to near where this landing place is supposed to have been, at the foot of which road was the public slaughter house, where the butchers of Brooklyn dressed their meats. The road referred to, came out where the house of the Fire Engine No. 4 now stands, and the existence of that road gives the town its title to that small piece of ground.

COMMON LANDS, AND THE DIVISION THEREOF.

The town having acquired so great an extent of Common land by the purchase of 1670, from the Indians, the inhabitants thought proper to take some order for the division and defending thereof, together with their other lands--accordingly, "at a town meeting held the 25th day of February, 169$\frac{3}{5}$, att Breuklyn, in Kings County. Then Resolved to divide their common lands and woods into three parts, in manner following to witt.

1. All the lands and woods after Bedford and Cripplebush, over the hills to the path of New-lotts shall belong to the inhabitants and free-holders of the Gowanis, beginning from Jacob Brewer and soe to the uttermost bounds of the limits of New Utrecht.

2. And all the lands and woods that lyes betwixt the abovesaid path and the highway from the ferry towards Flattbush, shall belong to the freeholders and inhabitants of Bedford and Cripplebush.

3. And all the lands that lyes in common after

the Gowanis, betwixt the limits and bounds of Flattbush and New Utrecht shall belong to the freeholders and inhabitants of Brooklyn, fred. neck, the ferry and the Wallabout." This proceeding of the Town meeting was allowed of by the Court of Sessions, held at Flatbush, on the 10th day of May, 1693.

The following will serve to shew the manner in which the inhabitants of this town elected the Trustees of their common lands, and the duties of those Trustees. "Att a towne meeting held this 29th day off Aprill, 1699, at Breucklyn, by order off Justice Machiel Hanssen, ffor to chose townsmen ffor to order all townes business and to deffend theire limitts and bounds and to dispose and lay out sum part thereoff in lotts, to make lawes and orders ffor the best off the inhabitants, and to raise a small tax ffor to defray the towne charges, now being or hereaffter to come, to receive towns revenues and to pay townes debts, and that with the advice off the Justices off this said towne standing the space and time off two years. Chosen ffor that purpose by pluralitie off votes. Benjamin Vande Water, Joores Hanssen, Jan Garretse Dorlant.

By order of inhabitants afforesaid.

J. VANDE WATER, Clarke."

These proceedings were recorded by order of the Court of Sessions, on the 9th day of May, 1699.

The following proceeding is curious, setting forth the ancient practice of tradesmen cutting down timber in the public woods, and the regulations made respecting the same. It appears that directly after the Trustees were chosen by the above meeting they together with the Justices, held the following meeting. "Att a meeting held this 29th day off Aprill (1699) in Breucklyn, Present, Benjamin Vande Water, Jooris Hanssen, Jan Geritse Dorlant, being choisen townsmen in the presence and with the advice off the Justices off this towne.

Considering the greate inconvenience, lose and intrest that the inhabitants off this towne have by reason that the tradesmen here living in this towne doe ffall and cutt the best trees and sully the best of our woods and sell the worke thereoff made the most part to others living withoute the towne, and that the shoemakers and others doe cutt and fall all the best treese ffor the barke, and the wood lyes and rott, and that some persons doe cutt and ffall trees for timber and ffensing stuff, and leave the trees in the woods soe cutt until they are spoilt, and that people off other towns come and cutt and fall trees ffor timber, ffensing stuff, and ffire woods, and transport the same away out off our townes bounds and limitts, and that without leave or consent off the towne, soe that in the time off ffew yeares there shall bee no woods leaved ffor the inhabitants ffor timber or ffensing stuff to the ruine off the said towne. It is thereffore ordered, That ffrom the date hereoff no tradesman shall make any worke ffor to sell to others without thee towne, ffrom wood soe cutt as afforesaid as only ffrom old wood.

That no shoemaker or others shall cutt or ffall any trees ffor to barke in the common woods upon the penaltie off ffive pound ffor every tree soe cutt.

That no men shall leave any timber, ffensing stuffe, or other wood in the woods longer as six weeks affter itt is cutt, uppon the penaltie, that itt shall be ffree ffor others to take and carry the same away as theire owne wood. And that iff any one off other townes shall be ffounden within our townes limitts to cutt or carry away any sorts off woods ffor timber, ffensing stuff or ffire wood, that itt shall bee ffree ffor any one off this towne to take it away and to take out writt to arrest, or to apprehend such offender or offenders presently, and that the Justices off this towne shall answer the action as iff itt were done by theire owneselves.* These proceedings were also recorded by order of the Court of Sessions.

"Towne meeting held this 5th day off May, 1701, by order off Justices Cornelis Sebringh and Machiell Hanssen. We the major part off the ffreeholders off Breucklyn doe hereby nominate, constitute and appoint Capt. Jooris Hanssen, Jacob Hanssen and Cornelis Van Duyn, to bee trustees of our Common and undivided lands, and to deffend and maintaine the rights and privileges off our General pattent, as well within as without."

"Towne meeting held this 2d day off February, 1701–2, by order off Justice Cornelis Sebringh. Purposed iff the order off Bedford, made the 12th day off April, 1697, shall bee conffirmed concerning the lying out of the common or undivided lands or that the said land shall bee lyed out according to the last tax, concerning the deffending off our limitts.

Resolved by the ffreeholders aforesaid, that the chosen townsmen shall ley out the commens according as by the said order off Bedford was concluded, with the ffirst opportunitie, and that all

---

* The idea intended to be conveyed by this regulation, I understand to be, that the justices of the town of Brooklyn shall have cognizance of the offence, as much as if the offenders resided within the town.

the lotts joyning to the common woods shall be surveyed according to their grants."

The following Resolution was passed for defending those inhabitants to whom portions of the Common lands were allotted, in their enjoyment of the same. "Att a Towne meeting held att Brookland, in Kings County, this 14th day of March, 1701–2. Present, Machiel Hanssen, Cornelis Sebringh, and Hendrick Vechten, Esquires, Justices.—Resolved, by the major part of the freeholders of the said towne of Brookland, that every man that has now a right, lott, or lotts laid out in the quondam Common and undivided lands of Brookland aforesaid, shall forever free liberty have for egress and regress to his said lotts for fetching off wood or otherwise, over all or any of the said lott or lotts of the said freeholders in the lands aforesaid. And further, that if any of the said freeholders shall at any time or times hereafter, come by any loss or trouble, cost or charges by lawe or otherwise, of, for or concerning the title of any of their said lott or lotts, by any person or persons, either within the township of Brookland afforesaid, or without, that it shall be defended and made goode, (if lost) att all the proper costs and charges of all the freeholders of said towne equally."

It appears that all the Common lands of this

town had been divided among the freeholders, and a portion annexed to each house in the town. —A deed dated the 17th of April, 1705, after conveying a house and lot of land in this town, conveys "alsoe all the rights and priviledges in the common woodlands of the towne of Broockland aforesaid, to said house, belonging as per record of said towne may appear."*

These lands, in the month of February, 1701–2, were surveyed by Pieter Corteljeu and S. Clowes, two surveyors, and divided by them into three divisions. The first or west division consisted of 62 lots, containing about 5 acres each, about 310 acres. The second or middle division of 62 lots, containing about 10 acres each, about 620 acres; and the third or east division also of 62 lots, containing about 10 acres each, about 620 acres.—Total number of acres about 1550.

DIFFERENCES AS TO BOUNDS.

The difference between this town and the city of New York, having been treated of under the head of Town Rights and Ferries, the compiler will confine himself to the disputes which formerly existed between this town, and the towns

* The records referred to, together with all our other town records, were destroyed during the Revolution.

of Bushwick, Flatbush and New-Utrecht, respecting their bounds.

The following proceeding relates generally to the defence and settling of the limits of this town.

"Towne meeting held this 7th day of February, 1701–2, by order of Hendrick Vechten, Justice. —The Justice Hendrick Vechten, brings in that the towns men were nott well authorised concerninge the lying out and deffending of our bounds by reason that they have no power to compounde or agree with any of the neighbouring townes, &c.—These are thereffore, that the freeholders and inhabitants doe give full power to the said Intrusties, for to agree and compounde with any of the neighbour townes concerning our bounds, and all what our said Intrusties shall doe and agree with them, we shall stand to itt." This proceeding was recorded by order of the Court of Sessions, on the 13th of May, 1702.

DIFFERENCE WITH BUSHWICK.

The difference as to the bounds of these two towns seems generally to have been contested between individuals. The following is the only general order on record respecting the same:

At a Court of Sessions, held at Flatbush for Kings County, May 10, 1699. "Uppon the desire of the inhabitants of Breucklyn, that according to use and order every three yeare the limmitts betweene towne and towne must be runn, that a warrant or order may be given, that upon the 17th off May, the line and bounds betwixt said townes of Breucklyn and Boswyck, shall be runn according to their pattents or agrements." Ordered, "That an order should be past according to theire request."

DIFFERENCE WITH FLATBUSH.

The dispute between this town and Flatbush, respecting their bounds appears to have been of more importance than that with any other place, excepting New-York.

At a Court of Sessions, held for the West Riding of Yorkshire, upon Long-Island, the 18th of December, 1678, the following order was made:

"There being some difference between the townes of Flat Bush and Breucklyn concerning their bounds, the which they are both willing to refer to Captain Jaques Cortelyou and Captain Richard Stillwell to decide. The Court doth approve thereof, and order their Report to be determinative."

Messrs. Cortelyou and Stillwell complied with the requisition of the above order as will appear by the following report: but subsequent disputes shew that the same was not "determinative."

"To the worshipfull Court of Sessions, now sitting at Gravesend, June 21, 1683. These may certiffie that in obedience to an order from said Court, and by consent of both towns of Breucklyn and Flatbush, to runn the line betwixt the said townes which are we underwritten have done and marked the trees betwixt towne and towne, as wittnesse our hands the daye and yeare above written.

JACQUES CORTELYOU,
RICHARD STILLWELL."

It appears by the following Certificate, that a subsequent survey was made in 1684, of the division line between this town and Flatbush.

"To satisffie whom itt may concerne, that I being with Mr. Jacobus Cortland, about the twentyeth day off November, 1684, employed by Breuckland and Fflackbush, to vew and run out the line betweene the two towns to the south of the hills found that the line run fformerly by Capts. Jaques, Cortelyou and Mr. Stillwell, is right and just, which wee both being agreed, gave in our approbation of the same.

PHILIP WELLS, Surveyor."

Staaten-Island, in the County of Richmond, this 4th day of April, 1687."

The above Certificate was recorded by order of several of the inhabitants of Brooklyn.

At a Court of Sessions for Kings County, held the 4th day of October, 1687, the following proceeding was had:

"Complaint off Jan Oake, and Cornelis Barduff, authorised by the inhabitants of Fflackbush being read against Pieter Cronwer, concerning the building uppon the land in question, betwixt Breucklyn and Fflackbush, Itt is ordered, that none off the partys shall meddle themselves with the said land before the question off the said land shall be finished."

December 4, 1689. Jooris Bergen, Jan Dorlant and H. Claes Vechte, Commissioners of this town, together with Jurrian Bries, Constable, granted to Jeronimius Remsen, a piece of land lying at Bedford, in lieu of a piece of land which they had formerly sold him, lying at the Port or entrance, and which was claimed by the town of Flatbush.

At a town meeting, held in this town the 11th day of April, 1702, by order of Justices Machiel Hanssen, and Cornelis Seberingh; it was

"Purposed to choise townsmen in place off George Hanssen, Jacob Hanssen, and Cornelis Van Duyn, by cause theire times being past the 29th off this instant. Resolved to prolong the old townsmen's time to the twenty-fifth of May next, by reason they are in action off lawe with them off Fflackbush, to be tryed this May court."

The differences between these two towns have been amicably settled, and proper monuments placed on the boundary lines, to prevent, if possible, all future disputes.

DIFFERENCE WITH NEW UTRECHT.

February 14, 1702, George Hansen, Jacob Hansen and Cornelius Van Duyn, Trustees on the part of the town of Brooklyn, and Cornelius Van Brunt, Peter Cortelyou, and Aert Van Pelt, Trustees on the part of the town of New Utrecht, entered into an agreement, which, after setting forth the said Trustees' powers to enter into the same, proceeds to say, "that the courses and lines hereafter specified shall be the exact bounds between the said two towns of Brooklyn and New-Utrecht and soe to continue to perpetuity without any alteration; viz. The bounds to begin in the sloott or pond lying and being by and between the house of Argyes Vandyke, of the said towne of Brookland and the house of Thomas Sharax, of the said towne of New Utrecht, where the water runns into the salt water River, by a certaine fence from thence stretching away south-east one degree southerly, two hundred eighty and eight English rod, to a winter white oake tree markt on the south and north-west side; and from thence running east eight and twenty degrees northerly to a white oake tree, being on the east side of the path leading to New-Utrecht, aforesaid, to the Gowanos soe called in the towneship of Brookland abovesaid, said tree being markt on two sides, and being formerly the old markt tree betweene the said towns, &c."

At the time of the execution of the abovementioned agreement, the Trustees of the town of Brookland, gave a bond to the Trustees of the town of New Utrecht, in the sum of one thousand pounds "currant money of New Yorke."—The condition of which Bond or obligation was, "That if the above bounden George Hansen, Jacob Hansen and Cornelius Van Duyn, severally and their severall heires and assigns, doe and shall from time to time and at all times hereafter, well and truly observe, performe and keepe, all and every the covenants, articles of agreements, which on their and every of their parts, are or ought to be observed, performed and kept, contained and specified in and by certain articles of agreements of the date hereof and made betweene the above bounden George Hansen, Jacob Hansen and Cornelius Van Duyn of the one part, and the above-named Cornelius Van Brunt, Peter Cortillyou and Aert Van Pelt of the other part, of, in and concerning the limmitts and bounds of their townes pattents, and that in and by all things according to the true meaning of the said articles of agreement in such wise that no breache be made of the premises in said articles of agreement by the towne of Brookland aforesaid, at any time or times hereafter, then this obligation to be void and of none effect, otherwise to stand and remain in full force, virtue and power in law."

In the year 1797, a survey was made of all the bounds of this town, and a map thereof transmitted to the Surveyor General of this state.

REVOLUTIONARY INCIDENTS.

This town had a full share of the military operations during the Revolutionary war; and was for a long time in the possession of the British army. It is covered with the remains of fortifications which were thrown up by the Americans* and English for their defence against each other. In this town was fought the most san-

* The fortifications at Red Hook were erected by a regiment of Continental troops, the night of April 8, 1776.

guinary part of the battle of Long Island, August 27, 1776; which took place on the retreat of the American army within their lines, and the attempt of a portion of them to ford the mill ponds at Gowanus; in which attempt nearly the whole of a Regiment of young men from Maryland were cut off.

Many of the minor events connected with this battle, and the Revolutionary contest, are fast sinking into the shades of oblivion: the compiler has therefore thought proper to give place to the following piece of history, not with an idea, that he can immortalize any event which he relates; but with a hope, that his efforts will call forth some nobler pen to do justice to the memories of many of the almost forgotten heroes of those hard fought battles and arduous contests. In the battle above-mentioned, part of the British army marched down a lane or road leading from the Brush tavern to Gowanus, pursuing the Americans. Several of the American riflemen, in order to be more secure, and at the same time more effectually to succeed in their designs, had posted themselves in the high trees near the road. One of them, whose name is now partially forgotten, shot the English Major Grant; in this he passed unobserved. Again he loaded his deadly rifle, and fired—another English officer fell. He was then marked, and a platoon ordered to advance, and fire into the tree; which order was immediately carried into execution, and the rifleman fell to the ground, dead. After the battle was over, the two British officers were buried in a field, near where they fell, and their graves fenced in with some posts and rails, where their remains still rest. But "for an example to the rebels," they refused to the American rifleman the rites of sepulture; and his remains were exposed on the ground, till the flesh was rotted and torn off his bones by the fowls of the air. After a considerable length of time, in a heavy gale of wind, a large tree was uprooted; in the cavity formed by which, some friends to the Americans, notwithstanding the prohibition of the English, placed the brave soldier's bones to mingle in peace with their kindred earth.

August 28, 1776. Before day break, in a very thick fog, General Washington retreated with his army from near the old ferry, Brooklyn, to New York. As the last boat of the Americans left the shore, the fog dissipated, and the British made their appearance on the hills above the place of embarkation, when a shot or two from an American Battery on the hill near the house of Col. Henry Rutgers, in New York, compelled the British to desist in their march to the ferry.

A short time after the retreat of the Americans, Captain Hale, of the American army, was dispatched by General Washington, to see if the English had taken possession of his camp at Brooklyn, and what their situation was. This unfortunate young officer was taken by the English and hung as a spy, without even a form of trial; and not allowed a clergyman at his execution. It is believed he was executed somewhere along the Brooklyn shore, to the south-west of the old ferry. In our pity for Major Andre we have almost entirely lost sight of this meritorious officer, whose claims on our gratitude ought ever to be remembered, in proportion as his sufferings were greater than those of the former.

During the stay of the American army on Long Island, the head quarters of General Washington were at the house on Brooklyn Heights, now owned and occupied by Henry Waring, Esq. The house now owned and occupied by Teunis Joralemon, Esq., was used by the English as a Hospital during the Revolution, and in its vicinity hundreds of British soldiers and sailors are buried.

Most of the records of this town were destroyed by the English when they came in possession of it after the battle of Long Island.

In the month of November, 1776, one of the British prison ships, called the Whitby, was moored in the Wallaboght, near Remsen's mills. On board this vessel great mortality prevailed among the prisoners, and many of them died. Those of the prisoners who died from this ship, and from the others, which were afterwards brought to this place, were interred in the hill at the present Navy-Yard; where their remains were found, and in the year 1808, deposited in a vault erected for that purpose. March, 1777, two other prison ships anchored in the Wallaboght, one of which bore the name of Good Hope; which vessel, in the month of October, in the same year, took fire and was burnt. The prisoners were saved and transferred to the other vessels.—The hull of this ship lies under a dock at the Navy-Yard, in this town. In the month of February, 1778, on a Sunday afternoon, another British prison ship was burnt in the Wallaboght. The hull of this vessel lies in the mud in that Bay. 1778, the Jersey ship of the line, having arrived at New York, was condemned as unfit for the service, and converted into a prison ship. As such she anchored in the Wallaboght during the month of April, in the same year, together with the Falmouth and Hope, for Hospital ships; where they remained till the close of the Revolutionary war.

October 22, 1779, An act of attainder was

passed by the Legislature of this State, against John Rapalje, Esq., of this town, by which his property was confiscated to use of the State. That part of his property lying within the bounds of the present village of Brooklyn, was on the 13th of July, 1784, sold by the Commissioners of Forfeitures, to Comfort, and Joshua Sands, Esqrs. for £12,430.

In the year 1780, the British being apprehensive of an attack from the American army under General Washington, commenced fortifying the high grounds about Brooklyn; which works they continued until the peace in 1783. In this town the British had their army yard, where their forage department, and blacksmith's shops, &c. were kept. The entrance to this yard was near the junction of Main-street with Fulton-street, in the present village of Brooklyn.

During the Revolution, this place was much resorted to by the officers of the English army, and the fashionables of the day, as a scene of amusement. In the Royal Gazette of August 8th, 1781, published at New-York, Charles Loosley advertises a Lottery of $12,500, to be drawn at "Brooklyn Hall." The same paper contains the following advertisement: "Pro bono publico. Gentlemen that are fond of fox hunting, are requested to meet at Loosley's Tavern, on Ascot

Heath, on Friday morning next, between the hours of five and six, as a pack of hounds will be there purposely for a trial of their abilities: Breakfasting and Relishes until the Races commence.—At eleven o'clock will be run for, an elegant saddle, &c., value at least twenty pounds, for which upwards of twelve gentlemen will ride their own horses.—At twelve, a match will be rode by two gentlemen, Horse for Horse.—At one, a match for thirty guineas, by two gentlemen, who will also ride their own horses.—Dinner will be ready at two o'clock, after which, and suitable regalements, racing and other diversions, will be calculated to conclude the day with pleasure and harmony. Brooklyn Hall, 6th August, 1781."

Lieutenant Anberry, in a letter from New-York, to a friend in England, dated October 30th, 1781, says, "on crossing the East River from New York, you land at Brooklyn, which is a scattered village, consisting of a few houses. At this place is an excellent Tavern, where parties are made to go and eat fish; the landlord of which has saved an immense fortune this war." The public house referred to in the above advertisements, and letter, was the same house, which after the Revolution, and in the Compiler's recollection, was called the "Corporation House."

It was a large, gloomy, old fashioned stone edifice; and was destroyed by fire, September 23d, 1812.

This town was left by the British troops, the same day that they evacuated New-York.

ANCIENT GOVERNMENT.

The first public officer appointed by the Dutch Government for this town after its settlement in 1625, was a "Superintendant," whose duties were to preserve the peace, and regulate the police of the town. A few years after the office of Superintendant was abolished, and the offices of Schout, Secretary, and Assessor, created; these officers were also appointed by the Governor. In 1646, the town having considerably increased, the inhabitants were permitted to elect two magistrates; subject, however, to the approval or rejection of the Governor. These magistrates had increased powers: they were authorised to give judgment in all cases as they might think proper; provided that the judgment so given be not contrary to the charter of New Netherland. Subsequently this Town Court was new modelled by the Dutch Government, and its power and authority more clearly defined.

The inhabitants suffering very much under the arbitrary exercise of power on the part of the government, frequently remonstrated against the same. Finally a convention of delegates from this, and the other towns under the Dutch government assembled at New Amsterdam, November 26th, 1653, on an invitation from the Governor. Where they, on the 11th of December, following, entered into a remonstrance against the exclusion of the people from their share in legislation, and generally against their mode of government. The Governor and his Council sent them no answer, but entered one on the minutes; in which they denied the right of this town, Flatbush, and Flatlands, to send deputies, and protested against the meeting, notwithstanding the same was held at the Governor's request. Entertaining a just sense of the responsibility attached to them, the deputies made another, but ineffectual attempt, to obtain a recognition of their rights, and on the 13th of the last mentioned month, presented another remonstrance, in which they declared, that if they could not obtain them from the Governor and Council, they would be under the necessity of appealing to their superiors, the States General.—The Governor in a fit of anger dissolved their meeting, and sent them home.

In 1654, it appears that the country was very much infested with robbers; to disperse whom, April 7, 1654, the magistrates of this town, together with those of Midwout and Amersfort, united in forming a company of soldiers to act against "robbers and pirates," and determined that there should be a military officer in each town, called a Sergeant.

In order to prevent the depredations of the Indians, the Governor in 1660, ordered the inhabitants of Brooklyn to put the town in a state of defence; and commanded the farmers to remove within the fortifications, on the pain of forfeiting their estates.*

---

* In 1655, a large body of Northern Indians made a descent on Staten Island, and massacred 67 persons; after which they crossed to Long Island, and invested Gravesend; which place was relieved by a party of soldiers from New Amsterdam. It appears from the records that these Indians were on their way to commence a war against the Indians on the east end of Long Island.

The inhabitants of Flatbush were ordered by Governor Stuyvesant, in 1656, to enclose their village with palisadoes to protect them from the Indians. These fortifications were required to be kept under the English government, as will appear by the following record of the Court of Sessions for the West Riding of Yorkshire upon Long Island, December 15th, 1675. "The towne of Fflatbush having neglected the making of ffortifications, the Court take notis of it, and reffer the censure to ye Governor."

For the first two or three years under the English government, the magistrates of this town were but temporary officers. Nearly all that we know about the government previous to 1669, is, that Town Courts were established in this Colony. The inference would be, that as this town was granted "all the rights and privileges belonging to a town within this government," a Town Court was also organized here.

The Town Clerk of this town was appointed by the Governor, and confirmed by the Court of Sessions, as will appear by the following record: At a Court of Sessions held at Gravesend for the West Riding of Yorkshire upon Long Island, December 15, 1669. "Whereas Derick Storm presented an order from his Hon. the Governor, for the approbation of the Court of Sessions, to allow him to be towne clerk of Breucklen, taking his oath, the Court having allowed thereof, and doe hereby confirme him of Clerke of said towne."

In the year 1669, the first mention is made in the records of the "Constable of Breucklen;" which office at that period was held by Michael Lenell. The duties of constable as laid down in the Duke's laws were, holding town courts with the overseers, and with them making assessments, &c., whipping, or punishing offenders, raising the hue and cry after murderers, manslayers, thieves, robbers, burglars ; and also to apprehend without warrant such as were overtaken with drink, swearing, Sabbath breaking, vagrant persons, or night-walkers ; "provided they bee taken in the manner, either by the sighte of the constable, or by present imformacon from others ; as alsoe to make searche for all such persons either on ye Sabbath daye, or other, when there shall bee occation in all houses licensed to sell beere or wine, or any other suspected or disordered places, and those to apprehend and keepe in safe custody till opportunity serves to bring them before the next Justice of ye Peace for further examinacon." The Constable was chosen out of the number of Overseers, whose term of service had expired.

The following is a list of the Constables of Brooklyn, from 1669 to 1690 :

1669. Michael Lenell.
1671. Lambert Johnson.
1675. Andries Juriaensen.
1676. Cornelius Corsen.
1678. Thomas Lambertse.
1679. John Aeresen.
1680. Andries Juriaensen.
1682. Martin Ryersen.

Brooklyn and Newtown were ordered to make a new choice according to law.

1683. Jan Cornelis Dam.
1684. Thomas Ffardon.
1687. John Aertsen.
1668. Volkert Andriese.
1689. Jacobus Beavois.
1689. Jurian Bries.
1690. Jurian Hendrickse.

Shortly after the conquest of this Colony by the English from the Dutch, the towns of Brooklyn, Bushwyck, Midwout, or Flatbush, Amersfort, or Flatlands, and New Utrecht, were formed into a separate district for certain purposes, by the name of the "Five Dutch towns." A Secretary was specially appointed for these five towns, whose duties appear to have been confined to the taking acknowledgment of transports, and marriage settlements, and proof of wills, &c. This office, in 1674, was held by "Nicasius De Sille, in the absence of Sir Ffrancis De Brugh." This same Mr. De Sille, was in authority under the Dutch government, in the year 1658, as Schout of the city of New-Amsterdam. He was styled, "Heer Nicasius De Sille." There was no uniformity in the title of those acknowledging officers of the

Five Dutch towns. In 1675, Michiel Hainelle exercised that office, and styled himself "Clerk." In the same year the Court of Sessions for this Riding, after setting forth the appointment of Hainell, and calling him "Secretary," said, "It is the opinion of the Court that for what publique or private business he shall doe he ought to have reasonable satisfaction.*

There were also in this town, officers, who were called "Overseers." The Duke's Laws provide for their appointment in the following manner. "Overseers shall be eight in number, men of good fame, and life, chosen by the plurality of voyces of the freeholders in each towne, whereof foure shall remain in their office two yeares successively, and foure shall be changed for new ones every yeare; which election shall preceed the elections of Constables, in point of time, in regard the Constable for the year ensuing, is to bee chosen out of that number which are dismist from their office of Overseers."

* There were also a "Clerk" in most if not in all of these towns, who seems to have been authorised to take proof of the execution of wills; whether he was the Town Clerk does not appear. This officer was differently appointed in the different towns. In Bushwick he was appointed by the Commissioners of the town, and in New Utrecht he was elected by the people, and approved of by the Governor.

The following is a copy of the oath which was administered to the overseers elect.

"Whereas you are chosen and appointed an Overseer for the Towne of Breucklen you doe sweare by the Ever-living God, that you will faithfully and diligently discharge the trust reposed in you, in relation to the publique and towne affaires, according to the present lawes established, without favour, affection or partiality to any person or cause which shall fall under your cognizance; and at time when you shall bee required by your superiors to attend the private differences of neighbours, you will endeavour to reconcile them: and in all causes conscientiously and according to the best of your judgment deliver your voice in the towne meetings of Constable and Overseers. So helpe you God." These officers were commonly sworn by the Court of Sessions; but in the year 1671, the Constable of Newtown objected to the Court's swearing the overseers of that town, "alledginge that accordinge to the amendments of the law iff special occation required, itt is in the power of the Constable to sweare them, otherwise not, which is left to his Honor the Governor to decide." The inhabitants of the town for which the overseers were elected were authorised to determine by a major vote whether the said overseers should, on admission to office, take the oath prescribed as above; and in case the said overseers were not sworn, it was a legal objection against their proceedings on the part of any person prosecuted in their court, unless the overseers immediately on objection being made, took the oath, which the Constable was permitted to administer.

It was the duty of the Overseers, together with the Constable, to hold Town Courts, for the trial of causes under £5. Their other duties are contained in the following summary. On the death of any person, they were to repair with the Constable, to the house of the deceased, and inquire after the manner of his death, and of his will and testament; and if no will was found, the Constable in the presence of the Overseers was, within 48 hours, to search after the estate of the deceased, and to deliver an account of the same in writing, under oath, to the next Justice of the Peace. They, together with the Constable made all assessments. If any Overseer died during his term, the rest of the Overseers by a major vote, made choice of another in his place; and if the person so chosen refused to serve, he forfeited the sum of £10, towards defraying the town charges. They were to settle the bounds of the town, within twelve months after the bounds were granted. They had the power of regulating fences. They were authorised together with the Constable to make choice of two out of the eight overseers of the Church affairs.

They and the Constable, were frequently to admonish the inhabitants "to instruct their children and servants in matters of religion, and the lawes of the country." They, with the Constable, appointed an officer "to record every man's particular marke, and see each man's horse and colt branded." The Constable and two of the Overseers were to pay the value of an Indian coat for each wolf killed; and they were to cause the wolf's head to be "nayled over the door of the Constable, their to remaine, as also to cut of both the eares in token that the head is bought and paid for."

The following is the only list that the Compiler could obtain of the Overseers of this town.

1671. Frederick Lubertse and Peter Perniedeare.

1675. John Peterson Mackhike, and Jerome De Rapostelley.

1676. Tunis Guis Bergen, and Thomas Lambertson.

1679. John Harrill, and Martyn Reyandsen.

1680. Symon Aeresen, and Michael Harsen.

1683. John Aeresen, and Daniel Rapellie.

In the year 1683, the "Overseers" were

changed to "Commissioners." The "act for defraying the publique and necessary charge of each respective citty, towne, and county throughout this province; and for maintaining the poore and preventing vagabonds." Passed by the General Assembly of this colony, November 1st, 1683, provides—"That annually and once in every yeare there shall be elected a certaine number out of each respective citty, towne, and county throughout this province; to be elected and chosen by the major part of all the ffreeholders and ffreemen; which certaine number so duely elected shall have full power and authority to make an assessment or certaine rate within their respective cittys, townes and countys annually, and once in every yeare, which assessment and certain rate so established as aforesaid, shall bee paid into a certaine Treasurer, who shall be chosen by a major part of all the ffreemen of each respective citty, towne, and county; which Treasurer soe duly chosen, shall make such payment for the defraying of all the publique and necessary charges of each respective place above-menconed, as shall bee appointed by the commissioners, or their President, that shall be appointed in each respective citty, towne, and county within this province, for he *supervising the publique affaires and charge* of each respective citty, towne and county aforesaid." And the said act proceeds further to say, "And whereas it is the custome and practice of his Majesties realme of England, and all the adjacent colonyes in America, that every respective county, citty, towne, parrish, and precinct, doth take care and provide for the poore who doe inhabit in their respective precincts aforesaid; Therefore it is enacted, &c., that for the time to come the respective commissioners of every county, citty, towne, parish, precinct aforesaid, shall make provision for the maintainance and support of their poore respectively." *

The following is a list of the Commissioners of this town from 1684, to 1690, inclusive.

1684. Thomas Lambertson, Randolph Emans, and John Aeresen.

1685. Tunis Guis Bergen, and Daniel Rapalie.

---

* This law provides, that any person not having a visible estate, or a manual craft or occupation, coming into any place within this province, should give security, not to become chargeable within two years; and the captains of vessels bringing passengers into this province, were required to report them to the chief magistrate of the place within 24 hours after their arrival. Under the Dutch government the poor were supported out of the fines imposed for offences committed, and by contributions taken up in the Churches.

1686. Michael Hansen, and Jeromus De Rapalie.

The town made choice of Hansen and De Rapalie; and were ordered by the Court of Sessions to make a new selection by the 12th of April, 1686, and return the same to one of the Justices of the Peace for Kings County.

1687. Adriaen Bennet, Thomas Lambertson, and Tunis Guysbert.

The Court of Sessions ordered the town to make choice of a new Commissioner in the place of Tunis Guysbert; which they according did, and elected Jan Gerritsen Dorland.

1688. Simon Aertsen, Michael Hansen, and Claes Barense.

The Court of Sessions refused to swear Michael Hansen.

1690. Joris Hansen, Hendrick Claasen, and Jan Gerbritse.

The office of "Commissioner" continued until 1703, when a "Supervisor" was elected. The Supervisors of Kings County had their first meeting on the first Tuesday of October, 1703; at which meeting Captain Joras Hansen was the Supervisor from Brooklyn. The duty of the Supervisors was, "to compute, ascertaine, examine, oversee, and allow the contingent, publick, and necessary charge of each county." Two assessors were also elected for this town, whose names were, Peter Garabrantse and John E. Bennett; and one Collector. This is not the first mention of the assessors and collectors of this town in our County Records. In 1688, Michael Hansen and Daniel Rapalie were chosen assessors, for the purpose of assessing this town's proportion of a tax of £308 8s 0d, which was imposed on King's County. It is the opinion of the Compiler, that these were distinct officers from the Commissioners, whose duty it was to assess the ordinary rates; and that these assessors were but temporary officers, appointed to assess this particular tax. In 1699, Jan Garretse Dorlant is mentioned as Collector of Brooklyn; and in 1701, John Bybout held the same office.

In 1691, a majority of the freeholders of the town were empowered to make orders for the improvement of their public lands; and annually to elect three surveyors of highways. The duties of these surveyors were to amend and lay out highways and fences. The town meeting at which these orders were made, and officers elected, were held by the direction and under the superintendence of one or more justices of the peace.

November 8, 1692. The court of sessions for Kings County ordered that each town within the county should erect "a good pair of stocks, and a good pound;" and that the clerk of the court should issue a warrant to the constable of every town, requiring them to see this order complied with "at their peril." The following is a list of the constables of this town, from the new organization of the colony in 1691 to 1711, as far as the Compiler has been able to ascertain the same:

1693. Volkert Brier.

1697. Volkert Brier.

1698. Jacob Hansen. [This man was complained of by the last constable for not making his appearance at court; and the sheriff was ordered to summon him to appear at the next court.]

1699. Jacobus Beauvois.

1700. Cornelius Verhoeven.

1701. Jacob Verdon.

1702. Thomas Davies.

1703. Thomas Davies.

1704. William Brower.

1705. Jacob Ffardon. [This constable refused to call a town meeting in 1706, in compliance with the requisitions of a warrant he had received from Justice Ffilkin, for the election of town officers; and the inhabitants complained of him to the court of sessions, who ordered that a town meeting should be held for the election of town officers, and that Ffardon should hold over until a new constable was elected and sworn in his stead.]

1707. Abram Sleghter.
1708. Cornelius Collier.
1709. William Brower.
1711. Thomas Davies.

For some time previous and subsequent to the year 1693, the colony was in a very disordered state, arising probably from its new organization after the Revolution in Great Britain.

At the same period, both the civil and military governments in this town, and also in the county, were very unpopular. In order to support their authority, the justices of the peace resorted to the exercise of very arbitrary measures: arresting and confining many persons under the pretence of their having uttered scandalous words against them and the government; by which proceedings they completely alienated the people's affections, and exasperated them to such a degree that they committed many excesses: all which will appear by the following extracts from the records:

"October 11, 1693. At a meeting of the justices of Kings County, at the county hall. Present, Roeleff Martense, Nicholas Stillwell, Joseph Hegeman, and Henry Ffilkin, esqrs., justices. John Bibout, of Broockland, in the county aforesaid, we aver, being committed by the said justices to the common jail of Kings County, for divers scandalous and abusive words spoken by the said John against their majesties justices of the peace for the county aforesaid, to the contempt of their majesties authority and breach of the peace; the said John having now humbly submitted himself, and craves pardon and mercy of the said justices for his misdemeanour, is discharged, paying the officer's fees, and being on his good behaviour till the next court of sessions, in November next ensuing the date hereof."

In another instance, during the same year, in the month of October, in the town of Bushwyck, a man named Urian Hagell, was imprisoned for having said on a training day, speaking jestingly of the soldiers, "Let us knock them down, we are three to their one." The justices called these "mutinous, factious, and seditious words;" which, with the like, appear to have been favourite terms with them. Again, in the same month and year, Hendrick Claes Vechte, of the town of Brooklyn, was imprisoned by the justices, on a charge of "raising of dissension, strife, and mutiny, among their majesties subjects." And May 8, 1694, two women of Bushwick were indicted at the sessions, for having beat and pulled the hair of Captain Peter Praa, whilst at the head of his company of soldiers on parade. One of them was fined £3, and the cost, £1 19*s.* 9*d.*; and the other 40*s.* and the cost, £1 19*s.* 9*d.* In the last mentioned year (1694) Volkert Brier, constable of Brooklyn, was fined £5, and the costs of court amounting to £1, by the sessions, "for tearing and burning an execution directed to him as constable."* Brier afterwards petitioned the governor to have the fine remitted; a copy of which petition is in the appendix, marked C.

This town with respect to legal matters was under the jurisdiction of the court of sessions held at Gravesend, for the West Riding of Yorkshire, upon Long Island,† until the year 1683; when an act was passed by the first legislative assembly of this colony, dividing the province into counties by which the ridings were abolished. The court however, continued to be held at Gravesend until 1686, when it was removed to Flatbush, in conformity to an act of the colonial assembly, passed

* Sept. 14, 1696, about 8 o'clock in the evening, John Rapale, Isaac Remsen, Joras Yannester, Joras Danielse Rapale, Jacob Reyersen, Aert Aersen, Tunis Buys, Garret Cowenhoven, Gabriel Sprong, Urian Andriese, John Williamse Bennet, Jacob Bennet and John Meserole, Jr. met armed at the court-house of Kings, where they destroyed and defaced the king's arms which were hanging up there.

† The West Riding was composed of the towns of Brooklyn, Bushwick, Flatbush, Flatlands, New-Utrecht, and Gravesend, together with Staten Island and Newtown.

in the year 1685. This town continued under the jurisdiction of that court and the court of common pleas, which was afterwards established, until the close of the revolutionary war. At the close of the war the courts were re-organized, and this town still continues under their jurisdiction.

PRESENT GOVERNMENT.

In 1816 the village of Brooklyn was erected out of the town, and constituted a distinct government; thereby forming an *imperium in imperio.*

The present government both of the town and village, approach as near a pure democracy as that of any other place in this State. No business of importance is undertaken without first having the sanction of a public meeting. Here these sterling principles, that all power emanates from the people, and that public officers are but public servants, are fully recognized and acted upon.

This head the Compiler will divide into two divisions, in order to avoid confusion: First, the Town Government, and second, the Village Government.

First—the Town Government.

The government of the town is administered by

A *Supervisor*, elected by the people, at the annual town-meeting, on the first Tuesday of April.

The duties of this officer are principally confined to the apportionment of taxes, presiding at elections, &c. He is also ex-officio a commissioner of excise for granting tavern licenses in the town, and the general guardian of the town rights. There is no salary attached to this office: the supervisor receives a compensation of two dollars per day, for attending the general meeting of the supervisors of the different towns in the county, and a trifling amount for granting licenses. The present supervisor is William Furman, esq.

A *Town Clerk*, also elected by the people. The duties of this officer are to call special town-meetings on the request of twelve freeholders, record the proceedings of town-meetings, and preserve the records of the town. In 1698, Jacob Vandewater, town clerk of this town, received the sum of £6 5*s*. for two years and six months salary.* In 1822, in order to make the town clerk's salary in some degree proportionate to the increase of business, the town voted him a salary of $50. In 1824, the town clerk's salary was increased to $75. The office is at present held by John Doughty, Esq., who has been successively elected since the year 1796.

---

* At the same period, the salary of the clerk of the county was £10 per annum.

Five *Assessors*, also elected by the people—whose duties are to assess all real and personal estate liable to taxation within the town, and to forward such assessment to the supervisors, that they may apportion the amount of tax on the same. The present assessors are Messrs. John S. Bergen, Richard Stanton, John Spader, Joseph Moser, and Andrew Demarest. Their compensation is one dollar and twenty-five cents per day during the time they are employed in making and completing the assessment.

There are also elected two *overseers of the poor*, Messrs. William Cornwell and Isaac Moser; one *constable and collector*, Mr. John McKenney; two *constables*, Messrs. John Lawrence and Samuel Doxsey; and several other officers, whose names and duties will be set forth in the subsequent parts of this work.

The judicial business of this town is at present transacted by three *justices of the peace*, viz., John Garrison, John C. Murphy, and Samuel Smith, Esqs. These magistrates are appointed by the judges of the common pleas and the supervisors of the county.

Second—the Village Government.

April 12, 1816, the village of Brooklyn was incorporated by an act of the legislature of this state. By this act the freeholders and inhabitants are authorized annually to elect, on the first Monday of May, "Five discreet freeholders, resident within the said village, Trustees thereof;" and these trustees are authorized to appoint a president and clerk. The first trustees, Messrs. Andrew Mercein, John Garrison, John Doughty, John Seaman, and John Dean, were appointed by the legislature, and continued in office until the first Monday of May, 1817; when the first election was made by the people, and they made choice of Messrs. William Furman, Henry Stanton, William Henry, Tunis Joralemon, and Noah Waterbury. The present trustees are Messrs. Joshua Sands, John Doughty, Joseph Moser, John Moon, and Samuel James. Joshua Sands, Esq., president, and John Dikeman, Esq., clerk of the board. The president, previous to 1824, received no salary; at present, his salary is $300. The clerk formerly received a salary of $100, which, in consequence of the great increase of business, is now raised to $200. The powers of the trustees are principally "to make, ordain, constitute, and publish, such prudential by-laws, rules and regulations, as they from time to time shall deem meet and proper; and such in particular as relate to the public markets, streets, alleys, and highways of the said village; to draining, filling up, levelling, paving, improving, and keeping in order the same; relative to slaughter-houses, houses of ill-fame, and nuisances generally; relative to a village watch, and lighting the streets of said village; relative to restraining geese, swine, or cattle of any kind; relative to the better improvement of their common lands; relative to the inspection of weights and measures, and the assize of bread; relative to erecting and regulating hay-scales; relative to the licensing of public porters, cartmen, hackney-coachmen, gaugers, weigh-masters, measurers, inspectors of beef and pork, of wood, of staves and heading, and of lumber; relative to public wells, pumps, and reservoirs or cisterns of water to be kept filled for the extinguishment of fires; relative to the number of taverns or inns to be licensed in said village; and relative to any thing whatsoever that may concern the public and good government of the said village; but no such by-laws shall extend to the regulating or fixing the prices of any commodities or articles of provision, except the article of bread, that may be offered for sale." The powers of the trustees in opening, regulating, and widening streets, are enlarged and defined by an act passed by the legislature of this state, April 9, 1824.

The board of trustees have the appointment of several officers. The following is a list of the names of the officers at present holding under them.

John Lawrence, Collector.
Samuel Watts,
John Titus,
Andrew Tombs,
Robert W. Doughty, } Weighers.
Burdet Striker, Measurer.
William A. Sale, Measurer of Lime.

Three village Assessors are also elected by the people, for the purpose of making an assessment on which to apportion the village tax. The present assessors are Losee Van Nostrand, Gamaliel King, and John D. Conklin.

The Trustees, by an act passed April 9th, 1824, are constituted a Board of Health. The President and Clerk of the Trustees are ex-officio President and Clerk of the Board of Health. The salary of the President of this Board is $150.

A Health Physician is appointed by the Board of Health; which office is at present held by Dr. J. G. T. Hunt, with a salary of $200.

The duties of the Board relate to the general conservation of the health of the village.

As early as 1809, during the prevalence of the

yellow fever in this town, the inhabitants met together in consequence of repeated solicitations from the Common Council of New York, and after stating in their proceedings that, "reports prevailed, that disease exists to an alarming extent in the town of Brooklyn," they appointed the following gentlemen a committee "for the purpose of inquiring into the state of the health of the inhabitants of said town, and to act as the case in their opinion may require," viz., William Furman, John Garrison, Burdet Stryker, Henry Stanton, and Andrew Mercein. A sum of money was raised by subscription to meet the expense of this Committee.

In the year 1819, the Trustees, although not strictly invested with power, yet feeling the necessity of acting with some degree of energy, in order to quiet the fears of the inhabitants, arising from reports of the existence of a pestilential disease in New York, published an address, in which they state, "that during this season of alarm, they have not been unmindful of that part of their duty incumbent on them as a *Board of Health* for the village," and that "measures have been taken to obtain from time to time a report of the state of health throughout the village, that the inhabitants may be early apprised of any change affecting their welfare."

PUBLIC BUILDINGS AND INSTITUTIONS.

This head will be divided into three divisions —first, Churches; second, Markets; and third Public Institutions.

First, Churches.

The first Church established in Kings County, was, October 13, 1654, when the Rev. Joannes Theodorus Polhemus, a minister of the Dutch Reformed Church, was *permitted* by Governor Stuyvesant, to preach at Midwout (Flatbush) and Amersfort (Flatlands).* The congregation was gathered at this time; but the order of Governor Stuyvesant for building the Church is dated December 15, 1654. February 9, 1655, the Governor ordered the inhabitants of Brooklyn and Amersfort, which at that period, together with Gravesend, were one congregation, to cut timber for the erection of the Church at Midwout; which building was to be 60 feet in length, 28 feet in breadth, and 14 feet in height below the beams.

In order to accommodate the four towns of Gravesend, Amersfort, Midwout, and Brooklyn, the Governor ordered that Mr. Polhemus should preach every Sunday morning at Midwout, and

* This minister died in the month of June, 1676.

Sunday afternoons alternately at Amersfort and Brooklyn.

In the year 1659, the inhabitants of this town applied to Governor Stuyvesant for permission to call a minister for their congregation, assigning as their reason for their application, the badness of the road to Flatbush, the difficulty of attending divine service at New York, and the extreme old age and inability of the Rev. Mr. Polhemus to perform his services at Brooklyn.

The Governor deemed the request reasonable, and sent Nicasius de Sille, Fiscal of New Netherland, and Martin Kregier, Burgomaster, of New Amsterdam, to this town, as a committee of inquiry, who reported in favor of the application; whereupon the request of the inhabitants was granted. The inhabitants prepared a call for the Rev. Henry Solinus, alias Henricus Selwyn, from Holland, who was approved of by the classis of Amsterdam, on the 16th of February, 1660, when the classis also gave the Rev. Mr. Solinus a dismission, wishing him a safe and prosperous journey by land and by water to his congregation in the New Netherland. The time of the arrival of this minister is not known. He was installed in his church on the 3d of September, 1660, in the presence of the Fiscal, and Burgomaster Kregier, by the order of Governor Stuyvesant, who appears to have been at the head of the ecclesiastical, as well as the civil and military government of the colony.

On the 7th of September, 1660, a letter was written to the Rev. Mr. Polhemus, informing him of the installation of the Rev. Mr. Solinus in the Church of Brooklyn, and thanking him for his labours and attention to the Congregation. The letter was sent by a respectable person, to whom the Rev. Mr. Polhemus returned his thanks for the attention which the Church at Brooklyn had paid him, and furnished the messenger with a list of the names of the Church members, twenty-five in number.

Mr. Solinus' salary was 600 guilders per annum, equal to $200. Three hundred guilders of which was to be paid by Brooklyn, and three hundred by Fatherland (Holland). Some time after, the inhabitants of Brooklyn objected to raising their proportion of the salary; and May 25, 1662, petitioned the Governor that Mr. Solinus should reside among them; setting forth as a reason, that if their minister resided with them more people would go to church, and they would be better able to raise the salary. Governor Stuyvesant, in order to accommodate this dispute, proposed to pay 250 guilders towards Mr. Solinus' salary, on condition that he would preach in the Bouwery on Sunday afternoons.—This arrangement appears to have been entered into, for a short time after Mr. Solinus preached at the Bouwery half the time.

The Indians having on the 7th of June, 1663, attacked the town of Esopus, burnt the same, and destroyed many of the inhabitants, and took many prisoners; the event was communicated by Governor Stuyvesant to the church at Brooklyn, in the following manner.

"As a sorrowfull accident and willfull massacre has been committed by the Esopus Indians, who have with deliberate design under the insidious cover of friendship, determined to destroy Esopus, which they effected on the 7th instant, killing and wounding a number of the inhabitants, and taking many prisoners, burning the new town, and desolating the place. Whereupon the congregation is directed and desired by his Excellency the Governor General to observe and keep the ensuing Wednesday as a day of fasting, humiliation and prayer to the Almighty, hoping that he may avert further calamities from the New Netherlands, and extend his fatherly protection and care to the country. And it is further ordered, that the first Wednesday in every month be observed in like manner. By order of the Director-General, and Council, &c. Dated at

Fort Orange, June 26, 1663." Wednesday the 4th of July, 1663, was observed as a day of thanksgiving on account of a treaty of peace having been made with the Esopus Indians, and the release of the inhabitants who had been taken prisoners; and also for the success obtained over the British, who attempted with flying colours to take possession of all Long Island for the King of England, which was prevented by the timely arrival of the Dutch fleet.

On the 23d of July, 1664, the Rev. Henry Solinus took leave of his congregation and sailed in the ship Beaver for Holland. After his departure, Charles Debevoise, the schoolmaster of the town, and sexton of the church, was directed to read prayers, and a sermon from an approved author, every Sabbath day in the church for the improvement of the congregation, until another minister was called.

The first Dutch church in Brooklyn was built in the year 1666, although a minister had been settled to preach here for some years previous. —A second church was erected on the site of that built in 1666; which second church continued standing until about 1810, when a new and substantial church was erected on Joralemon street, and the old one taken down. This old church was a very gloomy looking building, with small windows, and stood in the middle of the highway, about a mile from Brooklyn ferry. In removing it the workmen found the remains of a Hessian officer, who had been buried there in his uniform, during the Revolutionary war.

The Dutch congregations on this island formed but one church, although they had different consistories.

The ministers under the Dutch government were not permitted to marry any persons without making the marriage proclamation on three succeeding Sabbaths in their churches. The same practice was observed after the Colony came under the British government. The last mentioned government however sold marriage licenses, which were granted by the Governor's Secretary in New York, for the sum of eight dollars each. The inhabitants generally preferred purchasing a marriage license, and thus contributed to the revenue of the Governor and Secretary.

During the ministry of the Rev. Mr. Solinus, the marriage fees were not the perquisite of the Minister, as appears by his account rendered by him to the Consistory, on the 29th of October, 1662, when he paid over to the consistory the sum of seventy-eight guilders and ten stivers, for fourteen marriage fees received by him.

The following is a list of ministers of the Dutch

Reformed Church, who officiated in the church on this island (with the exception of Polhemus and Solinus), taken from a manuscript of the Rev. Peter Lowe.

Joannes Magapolensis, probably died. 1668
Casperus Van Zuren " " . 1677
Clark " " . 1695
William Lupardus " " . 1709
Bernardus Freeman,* from 1702 to... 1741
Vincintius Antonides, from 1715 to... 1744
Joannes Arondeus, probably died.... 1742
Anthony Curtenius, from 1730 to..... 1756
Ulpianus Van Sinderin, from 1747 to. 1796
John Casper Rubel, from 1760 to.... 1797
Martinus Schoonmaker, from 1785 to 1824

[This venerable pastor was eighty-eight years of age at his death ; and a short time previous officiated in four congregations.]

Peter Lowe, from 1787 to........... 1818

In the month of April, 1708, fifty-seven of the inhabitants of Brooklyn entered into an agreement (which is written in Dutch) to call a minister from Holland to preach in the church of this town. The elders of the church at that time were Daniel Rapalie and Jores Hanse.

---

* This minister was naturalized in the Court of Sessions for Kings County, November 8, 1715.

The salary of the Clerk of the Church in this town was formerly raised by a tax on the whole town. At a town meeting, held February 1, 1568, It was resolved, that the sum of £20 10s. should be raised and paid into the hands of the "church masters" for "the widow of Hendrick Sleght, ffor 1 year and 8 months salary, and being Clarke off the churche."

The following singular proceeding may be amusing to some readers, and will serve to show to what extremes both the people and the magistrates carried themselves in former times. Hendrick Vechte, Esq., a Justice of the Peace, was presented at the Kings County Sessions, May 14, 1710, for coming into the Brooklyn Church, on Sunday, August 10, 1709, " with his pen and ink in his hand, taking of peoples names, and taking up one particular mans hatt up, and in disturbance of the minister and people in the service of God, &c." Vechte's plea was that in obedience to an order of the Governor he did go into the church as alledged, " to take notice of the persons that were guilty of the forcible entry made into the Church, that by Abrom Brower, and others, by breaking of said Church doore with force and arms, forcibly entering into said Church, notwithstanding the forewarning of Mr. Freeman the minister, and his people to the contrary."

The Court found that Justice Vechte was not guilty of a breach of the peace, and discharged him. It must be remembered that Justice Vechte was a member of the Court. There was a considerable difference of opinion and many disputes among the inhabitants of this town, and of the County, as to the right of the Rev. Mr. Freeman to preach; into the merits of which controversy it is not to be expected that the Compiler can enter at this distant day. Excepting the above proceeding of the Court, the only document which the Compiler has been able to obtain relative to this controversy is a letter from Henry Ffilkin, Esq., to the Secretary at New York, which will be found in the Appendix marked with the letter D.

December 18, 1814, the Trustees of the Dutch Reformed Church of the town of Brooklyn were incorporated. At which time the following gentlemen were officers of the Church.

Martinas Schoonmaker, } Ministers.
Peter Lowe, }

Elders.

Fernandus Suydam,	Walter Berry,
Jeremiah Johnson,	John Lefferts.

Deacons.

Jeremiah Brower,	Lambert Schenck,
Abraham De Bevoise,	Abraham Remsen.

The present officers of this Church are,
Rev. S. S. Woodhull, D.D., Pastor.

Elders.

Leffert Lefferts,	Tunis Joralemon,
David Anderson,	Nehemiah Denton.

Deacons.

Theodorus Polhemus,	James De Bevoise,
Adrian Hegeman,	Adriance Van Brunt.

September 18, 1785, an "Independent Meeting House" was incorporated at this place. The officers of which were:

John Matlock, Pastor,
George Wall, Assistant,
John Carpenter, Treasurer,
George Powers, Secretary.

Trustees.

William Bunton,	John Emery,
Robert Steath,	William Hinson.
Barnard Cordman,	

Their place of worship was a frame building on what is now the Episcopalian burying ground in Fulton street. This congregation continued but a short time, in consequence of the seceding of its members to the Episcopalian Church, which was soon after established in this place.

The first celebration of Divine Service after the manner of the Protestant Episcopal Church, in this town, subsequent to the Revolution, was at the old brick house known as No. 40 Fulton street, and now owned by Mr. Abiel Titus.

About the year 1787, the Episcopal Church was established in Brooklyn, under the pastoral care of the Rev. Mr. Wright, at the house on the north-east corner of Fulton and Middagh streets; which house was fitted up with pews, etc.

April 23, 1787. "The Episcopal Church of Brooklyn" was incorporated. The following are the names of the first

Trustees.

Whitehead Cornell,	Joshua Sands,
Joseph Sealy,	Aquila Giles,
Mathew Gleaves,	Henry Stanton,
John Van Nostrand.	

This congregation afterwards came into possession of the place of worship before used by the

Independent Congregation, and continued to worship in that edifice until they erected the Stone Church called "St. Ann's Church," Sands street.

June 22, 1795. The Episcopal Church in this town was re-organized and incorporated by the name of "St. Ann's Church."

Church Wardens.

John Van Nostrand, and George Powers.

Vestrymen.

Joshua Sands,	Aquila Giles,
Paul Durel,	John Cornell,
Joseph Fox,	Gilbert Van Mater,
William Carpenter,	Robert Stoddard.

The congregation at the same time resolved that Monday in Easter week should be the time of their future elections for Church officers.

The stone church which was erected on Sands street, has continued to the present time; but is now in bad repair, in consequence of the walls not having been properly erected. The Vestry passed a vote for erecting a new church to front on Washington street, the corner stone of which was laid March 31, 1824. The new edifice is fast progressing, and promises to be a great ornament to the place.

The present officers of St. Ann's Church are,

Rev. Henry U. Onderdonk, Rector.

Church Wardens.

William Cornwell, and Joshua Sands.

Vestrymen.

James B. Clarke,	John H. Moore,
Robert Bach,	Robert Carter,
Adam Tredwell,	Losee Van Nostrand,
Fanning C. Tucker,	A. H. Van Bokkelen.

William Cornwell, Treasurer.

May 19, 1794, the "First Methodist Episcopal Church" in this town was incorporated. The Trustees at which period were,

John Garrison,	Stephen Hendrickson,
Thomas Van Pelt,	Richard Everit,
Burdet Stryker,	Isaac Moser.

The present Meeting-house of this denomination is erected on the site of their first place of worship, on Sands street; and is a neat, plain edifice. The present officers are,

Rev. William Ross, Pastor in charge.

Trustees.

John Garrison,	George Smith,
Isaac Moser,	Isaac Nostrand,
William Foster,	John G. Murphy,
Jacob Brown,	R. Van Voris.
Andrew Mercein,	

Isaac Moser, Treasurer.

January 12, 1818, the "African Wesleyan Methodist Episcopal Church in the village of Brooklyn," incorporated.

First Trustees.

Peter Croger,	Benjamin Croger,
Israel Jemison,	John E. Jackson,
Ceasar Sprong.	

The place of worship of this congregation is a frame meeting house situate on High street.

March 13, 1822. The "First Presbyterian Church of Brooklyn" was incorporated.

First Trustees.

Jehiel Jaggar,	Elkanah Doolittle,
Nathaniel Howland,	Joseph Sprague,
Silas Butler,	Alden Spooner,
John B. Graham,	George Hall,
Charles H. Richards.	

The corner stone of this church was laid, April 15, 1822. The Church is situate on Cranberry street; and is a very handsome brick building, something in the Gothic style. The present officers are:

Rev. Joseph Sanford, Pastor.

Elders.

Zechariah Smith, Selden Gates,
Ezra C. Woodhull.

Trustees.

Alden Spooner, George Hall,
Edward Coope, Nathaniel Howland,
Henry W. Warner, Benjamin Meeker,
Elkanah Doolittle, Joseph Sprague,
Silas Butler.

Elkanah Doolittle, President of the Board,
Silas Butler, Clerk, do
Nathaniel W. Sandford, Treasurer.

November 20, 1822. "St. James Roman Catholic Church," incorporated.

First Trustees.

George S. Wise, Jr. William Purcell,
Peter Turner, James Rose,
Patrick Scanlan, Darby Dawson,
William M'Laughlin.

The corner stone of this Church was laid, June 25, 1822. The edifice is of brick, and approaches nearer to the Gothic architecture than any other building in this town. It is yet unfinished. This is the first Roman Catholic Church erected on Long Island. The present Trustees are:

—— ——, President,*
Peter Turner, Secretary,
William Purcell, Treasurer,
James Rose,
Darby Dawson,
William M'Laughlin,
Patrick Scanlan.

October 15, 1823. The "First Baptist Church in Brooklyn," incorporated.

Trustees.

Eliakim Raymond,	Elijah Lewis,
John Brown,	Richard Poland,
Charles P. Jacobs.	

March 24, 1824. Rev. William C. Hawley was ordained Pastor of this Church. This congregation have, as yet, erected no building for

* This office was held by George S. Wise, Jun., Esq., until his death in November, 1824.

public worship; but assemble for that purpose in the District School room, No. 1.

There are also in this town some of the denomination of Friends, and a small congregation of Universalists; neither of which have established places of public worship. The Universalists are under the pastoral care of the Rev. William Mitchell, and assemble for Divine service in the District School-room, No. 1.

In the present year, this town purchased of Leffert Lefferts, Esq., a small farm situate at the Wallaboght; a portion of which was set off for a burying ground, and divided into convenient parcels; which were allotted in the following manner to the different congregations worshipping in the town, viz.

No. 1. Dutch Reformed,
2. Friends,
3. Presbyterian,
4. Roman Catholic,
5. Methodist Episcopalian,
6. Universalist,
7. Episcopalian,
8. Baptist,
9. Common.

Second, Markets.

A market was established in this town as early as the year 1676, which will appear from the following order of the General Court of Assizes, made in the month of October, 1675. "Upon proposall of having a fayre and Markett in or neare this City (New York), It is ordered, That after this season, there shall yearely bee kept a fayre and markett at Breucklen near the ferry, for all grayne, cattle, or other produce of the countrey, to be held the first Munday, Tuesday, and Wednesday, in November; and in the City of New York, the Thursday, Friday, and Saturday following."

Previous to the year 1814, there were two markets in this place; one of which was situate at the foot of the old ferry street; and the other at the foot of Main street. Both these markets were taken down in 1814.

At present we have no public market; the inhabitants are supplied from several butchers' shops for the sale of meat, and stands for vegetables, scattered about in different parts of the village. The people have been for some time past endeavouring to obtain a public market, and the great difficulty appears to be the location of a proper site. At a village meeting, held June 26, 1824, the sum of $10,000 was voted to erect a brick market house and Village Hall, with other offices. This amount it was resolved, should be raised by a loan for not less than ten years, at six per cent; that the proceeds of the market arising from the letting of stalls, etc., should be appropriated to paying the interest of said loan; and that if in process of time there should be a surplus, after paying the interest, the same should be converted into a sinking fund for extinguishing the principal. These resolutions have not as yet been carried into effect.

Third, Public Institutions.

Of public institutions we have not many to boast—they may be strictly confined to one Bank, a Fire Insurance Company, and an Apprentices' Library.

The "Long Island Bank" was incorporated, April 1st, 1824, with a capital of $300,000, divided into six thousand shares of $50 each. The present officers are, Leffert Lefferts, Esq., President, and D. Embury, Cashier.

The "Brooklyn Fire Insurance Company" was incorporated, April 3, 1824, with a capital of $150,000, divided into six thousand shares of $25 each. The present officers of this institution are William Furman, President, and Freeman Hopkins, Secretary.

There is also in this village a branch of the "Equitable Fire Insurance Company;" of which Abraham Vanderveer, Esq., is Agent.

The Apprentice's Library Association, which has been formed but a short time, promises to be of great benefit to the apprentices of the place, by introducing among them habits of reading and reflection, which, if properly attended to, will enable them to support the honourable character of good citizens.

The Library at present consists of about twelve hundred volumes, which have been presented by different individuals. About one hundred apprentices take books from it, regularly once a week. This institution was incorporated by an act of the Legislature, passed in November, 1824. The present officers are:

Robert Snow, President; Thomas Kirk, Vice-President; Andrew Mercein, Treasurer; Robert Nicholls, Secretary.

Under this head it may be proper to notice, that there are two Masonic Lodges in this town, and a Post office.

Fortitude Lodge, No. 81.—W. Levi Porter, Master.

Hohenlinden Lodge, No. 338.—W. Abiathar Young, Master.

The Post office is kept at No. 97 Fulton street, by George L. Birch, Esq., Post Master. The mail is carried daily (Sundays excepted) between

Brooklyn and New York, and closes at Brooklyn at 8 A. M. and arrives at 4 P. M.

POPULATION AND INCREASE.

Within a few years this town, and particularly the village has increased very rapidly. In 1814, the town of Brooklyn contained 3805 inhabitants; and in 1816, the town contained 4402 inhabitants. In 1820, the census was as follows (being almost two-thirds of the population of the County).

White males,	under 10 years of age,	876	
do.	between 10 and 16	376	
do.	between 16 and 26	717	
do.	between 26 and 45	961	
do.	between 45 and upwards,	379	
			3309
White females,	under 10 years of age,	876	
do.	between 10 and 16	398	
do.	between 16 and 26	705	
do.	between 26 and 45	961	
do.	between 45 and upwards,	379	
			3319
Free blacks,	- - - -		657
Slaves,	- - - - - -		190
			7475

Foreigners not naturalized - - -	252
Persons engaged in Agriculture, - -	264
do. in Commerce, - -	67
do. in Manufactures, - -	497

The following account of the population of Kings County at different periods, may not be uninteresting to many readers.

The population of Kings County in		
	1731 was	2150
	1756	2707
	1771	3623
	1786	3966
	1790	4495
	1800	5740
	1810	8303
	1820	11187 *

* Governor Nicolls, in a letter to the Duke of York, November, 1665, informed him "that such is the mean condition of this town (New York), that not one soldier to this day has lain in sheets, or upon any other bed than canvas and straw."

1678. New York contained 343 houses, and 3430 inhabitants; and there were owned in the city three ships, eight sloops and seven boats.

1686. The City of New York contained 594 houses, and 6000 inhabitants; and there were owned in it 10 three-masted vessels of between 80 and 100 tons; 3 ketches or barques, of about 40 tons; and about 20 sloops, of 25 tons. In the same year the militia of the colony consisted of 4000 foot, 300 horse, and one company of dragoons.

In 1706, there were 64 feeholders in the town of Brooklyn. In 1802 their number had only increased to 86, as appears from the list of Jurors

---

1696. There were owned in the City of New York, 40 ships, 62 sloops, and 62 boats.

In 1697, the population of New York has considerably decreased, from what it was in 1686; the census taken this year was as follows:

Whites	Men, - - -	946	
	Women, - -	1018	
	Young men and boys,	864	
	Young women and girls	899	
			3727
Blacks	Men, - - -	209	
	Women, - - -	205	
	Boys and girls, - -	161	575
		Total,	4302

1731. The City of New York contained

White males, - - -	3771	
White females, - - -	3274	7045
Black males, - - -	785	
Black females, - - -	792	1577
	Total,	8622

1756. The City contained 10,881 inhabitants.
1771. It contained 21,863 inhabitants.
1736. It contained 3,340 houses, and 23,614 inhabitants.
1790. It contained 33,131 inhabitants
1800. 60,489
1810. 96,373
1820. 139,000

at that period. In the year 1800, there were 253 votes given in this town, at a contested election for assemblyman. In 1824, on the same occasion 1013 votes were taken.

At the close of the Revolutionary war, the town of Brooklyn within the bounds of the present village contained 56 buildings. In 1821, the village contained 867 buildings; of which 96 were Groceries and Taverns, and several store-houses. These store-houses depend principally, on the operations of the Quarantine laws, in the months of June, July and August, for business. On the 23d of July in the same year, there were lying at the wharves in this village, 13 ships, 9 brigs, 8 schooners, and 14 sloops. July 1, 1824, there were lying at the wharves in this village, 8 ships, 16 brigs, 20 schooners, and 12 sloops.

In 1822, 50 dwelling-houses were erected in this village. In 1823, 122 frame dwellings and 32 brick and brick front buildings were erected. January 1, 1824, the village of Brooklyn contained 113 stone, brick and brick front buildings. During the present year 143 frame dwelling-houses have been built in this village.

The town contains 8 Ropewalks, which manufacture 1130 tons of cordage annually; 4 Distilleries; 2 Spirits of Turpentine Distilleries; 1 Glue factory; 1 Chain cable manufactory; 2

Tanneries; 2 White lead works; 1 Whiting manufactory; 1 Glass factory and 1 Furnace for casting iron. The manufacture of Hats is conducted on a large scale in this place.

In the year 1703, a survey was made of "Broocklands improveable lands and meadows within fence," and the same was found to amount to 5177 acres. At that period the greatest holder of that description of land was Simon Aersen, who owned 200 acres. In 1706, all the real and personal estates of the town of Brooklyn were assessed at £3122 12s. 0d. The tax on which was £41 3s. 7½d., and the whole tax of the county £201 16s. 1½d. In 1707, the real and personal estates of this town assessed at £3091 11s. 0d., the government tax on which was for the same year £116 7s. 3d., payable in two payments; and the whole tax of the county £448 3s. 7d. The present year the real estate in this town was assessed at $2,111,390. And the personal estate at $488,690; being considerably more than one half of the whole value of the county. The State, county and town tax on which amounts to $6,497.71. At this period there are in the village 1149 taxable persons, and the village tax amounts to $2,625.76, averaging about $2.29, each taxable person. This village tax includes $450 raised to meet the expenses of the Board of Health, and is exclusive of all local assessments for opening and improving streets, &c.

The receipts of the overseers of the poor of this town for the year 1823, amounted to $3108.-77, and their expenditures to $3469.49, leaving a balance of $360.72 against the town.

On the 22d of March, 1823, there were 54 persons in the Almshouse; 51 persons were admitted during the year ending March 30, 1824. During the same period 34 were discharged, and 10 died. March 30, 1824, there were in the almshouse 40 persons, viz., 11 men, 16 women, 5 girls, and 8 boys. In the winter of 1823–4, 93 loads of wood were distributed from this institution among the poor of the town.*

April 21, 1701, a piece of land about 100 feet square, lying within the present bounds of the village of Brooklyn, was sold for £75, "current money of the Province of New York." 1720, a dwelling-house and lot of ground, containing 62 feet front, 61 feet rear, and 111 feet deep, near the ferry, on the north-east side of what is now called Fulton street, sold for £260, "current money of New York." In the year 1784, all the property owned by the Corporation of the City of

* The town is now erecting a very neat building for an almshouse, on the property lately purchased from Leffert Lefferts, Esq.

New York in this town was assessed at £365, New York currency, which property is now worth $50,000 at the lowest calculation.

August 30, 1701, John Bybon sold to Cornelius Vanderhove, for £37 10s, the one equal half-part of a brew-house, situate at Bedford, in the town of Brookland, fronting the highway leading from Bedford to Cripplebush; together with one equal half-part of all the brewing vessels, &c.

In 1685, a windmill was erected in this town by John Vannise and Peter Hendricks, for Michael Hainell. There is a great reason to believe that this was the first mill erected in this town. August 19, 1689, an agreement was entered into between Cornelius Seberingh, of Brookland, and John Marsh, of East Jersey, relative to building a watermill on Graver's kill, in this town. At present there are in this town seven watermills and two windmills. From February 16, 1823, to February 15, 1824, 5,825 barrels of superfine flour, 260 barrels of fine flour, and 124 hogsheads of cornmeal were inspected in this county. The most, if not all, of which flour and meal was manufactured at the mills in this place.

SCHOOLS, NEWSPAPERS, AND MORAL CHARACTER.

May, 1661, Charles Debevoise was recommended by Governor Stuyvesant as a suitable person for schoolmaster of this town, and also for clerk and sexton of the church, who was employed and received a good salary.

Immediately previous to the Revolutionary war, that part of the town of Brooklyn which is now comprised in the bounds of the village, and for some distance without those bounds, supported but one school of nineteen scholars, five of whom were out of the family of Mr. Andrew Patchen. The school-house was situated on the hill, on property which was then owned by Israel Horsfield, but now belongs to the heirs of Carey Ludlow, deceased. The teacher was Benjamin Brown, a staunch whig from Connecticut.

District School, No. 1.—This school was organized at a public meeting held January 2, 1816, at which meeting Andrew Mercein, John Seaman and Robert Snow were elected trustees, and John Doughty clerk of the school. The trustees were appointed a committee to ascertain a proper site for building a school-house, and report the probable expense thereof. At a meeting held January 12, 1816, the trustees reported that they could purchase four lots of ground on Concord street, of Mr. Noah Waterbury, for $550. The meeting thereupon resolved, that "the sum of $2,000 should be raised by tax on the inhabitants of the said district, to purchase said lots and to build a school-house thereon;" and that in the meantime the "Loisian school be the common school of the said district;" and that "the trustees of the district be authorized to exonerate from payment of teacher's wages all such poor and indigent persons as they shall think proper, pursuant to the act of the legislature;" and that "it be recommended by this meeting, that the common school to be taught in this district, be on the Lancastrian plan of instruction."

In the school of this district, which includes the village of Brooklyn, upwards of 200 children are taught. The price of tuition does not exceed four dollars per annum, and from that amount down to nothing, in proportion to the abilities of the parent. The School District No. 1, at present contains 1,607 children between the ages of five and fifteen years, of whom 1,157 go to the public or private schools.

In 1821 there were eight private schools in the village of Brooklyn.

In 1823 the town received from the State $418.13 for the support of common schools.

The present officers connected with the common schools of the town are:

Commissioners: Jordan Coles, Robert Nichols, Josiah Noyes.

Inspectors: Charles I. Doughty, Evan Beynon, Robert Snow.

Trustees of District School No. 1: William Cornwell, Joseph Sprague, Charles I. Doughty. *Clerk:* Ralph Malbone.

Newspapers.

Four newspapers have been published in this town in the following chronological order:

June 26, 1799. The first number of *The Courier and New York and Long Island Advertiser*, published by Thomas Kirk, Esq. This was the first newspaper established on Long Island.

May 26, 1806. The first number of *The Long Island Weekly Intelligencer*, published by Messrs. Robinson and Little.

June 1, 1809. The first number of *The Long Island Star*, published by Thomas Kirk, Esq.

March 7, 1821. The first number of *The Long Island Patriot*, published by Geo. L. Birch, Esq.

In the month of November, 1810, proposals were issued by Benjamin F. Cowdrey & Co. for establishing in Brooklyn a weekly newspaper, to be entitled *The Long Island Journal and American Freeman.* For some reason unknown to the Compiler this paper was not published.

During the month of May, 1820, Brockholst Livingston, Jun., issued proposals for publishing a weekly newspaper in this village, to be entitled *The Long Island Republican.* Not meeting with sufficient encouragement, this attempt was abandoned.

The only two papers now in existence in this town are *The Star*, published by Alden Spooner, Esq., and *The Long Island Patriot*, by George L. Birch, Esq.

Moral Character.

It is a delicate subject for a writer to treat of the morals of a people among whom he is a resident, lest by telling the truth too plainly, he awaken unpleasant feelings in the breasts of some whom perhaps he would not wish to offend. On the other hand, if glaring faults are slightly passed over, or palliated, it calls down on his devoted head all the envenomed attacks of malicious criticism. The Compiler, however, flatters himself that neither will be the case in this instance.

The people of Brooklyn, it is true, cannot be considered as rigid in religious matters as the saints of Oliver Cromwell's army, whose very cannon had on the inscription of "O Lord, open thou our lips, and our mouth shall show forth thy praise!" But they are far from being irreligious; the churches are well filled, religious societies are liberally supported, vice discountenanced; and for the more effectual suppression thereof, in 1815, a society for the suppression of vice and immorality was formed, consisting of many of the most respectable inhabitants of the town. By the exertions of our Sunday-school societies, attached to the different congregations, the morals of the younger part of the community have been greatly reformed; and it is highly gratifying to observe the improvement made in the general morals of the town, in consequence of their benevolent exertions.

FIRE DEPARTMENT.

Although this might with some propriety be placed under the head of *Public Institutions*, the Compiler has thought proper to make it a head of itself; and he hopes that the following few historical facts relative to this valuable department, may be useful to such as feel an interest in its progression and improvement.

By an act passed by the Legislature of this State, March 15, 1788, "for the better extinguishing of fires in the town of Brooklyn," the number of firemen was limited to eight, who were nominated and appointed by the freeholders and inhabitants of the fire district, which was comprised within nearly the same bounds with the present village.

In the year 1794 the sum of £188 19*s.* 10*d.* was raised by subscription in this town, for purchasing a fire engine. On the 24th March in the following year, an act was passed by the legislature "for the better extinguishing of fires" in this town; by which act the number of firemen was increased to thirty.

1796. The sum of £49 4*s.* was raised by subscription for purchasing "a suitable bell for the use of the town of Brooklyn." This is the present fire bell.

March 21, 1797, an act was passed by the legislature "for the prevention of fires, and for regulating the assize of bread in the town of Brooklyn." This act authorized the inhabitants to choose not less than three, nor more than five freeholders, who might from time to time make such prudential by-laws as they judged necessary for the prevention of fires by the burning of chimneys, and for sweeping and otherwise cleansing the same. The inhabitants accordingly met on the second Tuesday of May, in the same year, and appointed Messrs. Henry Stanton, John

Doughty, Martin Boerum, John Van Nostrand, and John Fisher, to carry into effect the provisions of the above act. In the execution of which duty the persons so appointed ordained, that from and after the 11th day of July, 1797, a fine of ten shillings should be levied on each person whose chimney should take fire through carelessness, or be set on fire for the purpose of cleansing; and that "all penalties shall be received and recovered by the clerk of the fire company for the time being, if he be one of the persons so chosen; if not, the said persons elected shall nominate and appoint one of their number to serve for and receive in the same manner that the clerk is at present authorized." From 1798 to August 6, 1806, the sum of £20 7s. was received for chimney fines.

For a considerable length of time this town had but one small fire engine; they subsequently purchased another, which was called No. 2. About 1810, No. 3, now styled the "Franklin," was purchased by the inhabitants of the Fire District. The Fire Department of the village at present consists of four Fire Engines (of which three are new, namely, Nos. 1, 2, and 4), and a Hook and Ladder Company, viz.:

No. 1. "Washington," full complement 30 men. Foreman, Joshua Sutton.

No. 2. "Neptune," full complement 30 men, Foreman, Gamaliel King.

No. 3, "Franklin," full complement 30 men, Foreman, Jeremiah Wells.

No. 4, "Eagle," full complement 30 men, Foreman, George Fricke.

Hook and Ladder Company, full complement 30 men, Foreman, John Smith.

There are also in the Navy Yard, two excellent fire engines, well manned, and which, together with those from New York, generously come to our assistance whenever our place is visited by that dreadful calamity, fire.

The receipts of the Fire Department, from 1794 to 1815, amounted to £898 10s. 1d. and the expenditures from July 7, 1795, to November 15, 1816, amounted to £964 3s. 3d.

The office of Clerk and Treasurer of the Fire Department of this town, was held by John Hicks, Esq., until 1796; at which time John Doughty, Esq., was appointed, and held that office until the incorporation of the village in 1816, when he was appointed Chief Engineer of the Fire Department of the village, which office he held for one year. In 1817, William Furman, Esq., was appointed Chief Engineer, and officiated in that capacity until 1821, when, on the resignation of Mr. Furman, John Doughty, Esq., was again appointed, and continues to hold the office. The present officers of the Fire Department are:

John Doughty, Chief Engineer.

Fire Wardens, Joseph Moser, Edward Coope, Joseph Sprague.

April 16, 1823, an act was passed by the Legislature of this State to incorporate the firemen of this village, by the name of the "Fire Department of the Village of Brooklyn." The act allows this corporation to hold, purchase, and convey any estate, real or personal, for the use of the corporation, provided such real or personal estate shall not at any time exceed the yearly value of $1,000. The following officers were appointed by the act of incorporation, viz.:

John Doughty, President.

Joshua Sutton, Vice-President.

Richard Cornwell, Secretary.

Trustees: Jeremiah Wells, Morris Simonson, Michael Trapple, Joseph Moser, George Fricke, Gamaliel King, Simeon Back,. Parshall Wells, George L. Birch.

The laudable object proposed by this institution is to raise a fund for the relief of widows and children of deceased firemen.

By an amendment to the act of Incorporation of the village of Brooklyn, passed April 9, 1824, it is provided, " That all fines and penalties under any by-law of the said village, in relation to the burning of chimneys, and for the preventing and extinguishing of fires, and also, all fines and penalties, either under such by-laws, or under any statute of this State, in relation to the manner of keeping and transporting gun-powder within the said village, shall be sued for in the name of the said Trustees (of the village of Brooklyn) by the fire department of the said village, and when recovered shall be paid to the said fire department, for their own use.

MISCELLANEOUS.

June 7, 1625, Sarah De Rapalje, born in this town. Tradition says that she was the first white child born in the colony. Her parents were Walloons; from whence is derived the name of Wallaboght, or Walloons Bay, where they lived.* She was twice married. Her first husband was Hans Hanse Bergen, by whom she had six children, viz. Michael Hanse, Joris Hanse, Jan

* The first settlement in this town was made by George Jansen De Rapalje, the father of Sarah, in 1625, on the farm which is now owned by the family of the Schencks at the Wallaboght.

Hanse, Jacob Hanse, Brechje Hanse, and Marytje Hanse. Her second husband was Teunis Guysbertse Bogart, by whom she also had six children, viz. Aurtie Bogart, Antje Bogart, Neeltje Bogart, Aultje Bogart, Catelyntje Bogart, and Guysbert Bogart. The account of Sarah De Rapelje, in the archives of the New York Historical Society, contains the names of the persons to whom eleven of her children were married, and tells the places where they settled. The twelfth, Brechje Hanse, went to Holland.

March 1, 1665, Hendrick Lubbertson and John Evertsen, appeared as deputies from the town of Brooklyn, at the Assembly convened at Hempstead, by order of Richard Nicolls, Deputy Governor under the Duke of York; at which assembly the code of laws called the "Duke's laws" were adopted and published. In the appendix marked E. will be found the address which these deputies, together with the others, sent to the Duke of York; and which occasioned so much excitement in the Colony at that period.

1671, This town, with five other towns in the West Riding of Yorkshire upon Long Island, petitioned the Court of Sessions "for liberty to transporte wheate," which petition was referred to the Governor.

1687. The Clerk's office of Kings County was kept in this town, by the Deputy Register, Jacob Vandewater, who was also a Notary Public in this town at the same period. The Register, Samuel Bayard, Esq., resided in the city of New York.

About the year 1691, there was a custom prevalent in this town of calling a widow the "last wife of her deceased husband," and a widower "the last man" of his deceased wife.

The following is an Inventory of the estate which a bride in this town brought with her to her husband in the year 1691. The husband by various records appears to have been a man of considerable wealth; notwithstanding which, the following inventory was thought by both of them of sufficient importance to merit being recorded, viz.

"A half worn bed, pillow, 2 cushions of ticking with feathers, one rug, 4 sheets, 4 cushion covers, 2 iron pots, 3 pewter dishes, 1 pewter bason, 1 iron roaster, 1 schuryn spoon, 2 cowes about five yeares old, 1 case or cupboard, 1 table."

November 12, 1695, the Court of Sessions for Kings County, ordered that the Constable of this town, "shall on Sunday or Sabbathday take law for the apprehending of all Sabbath breakers," and "search all ale houses, taverns, and other suspected places for all prophaners and breakers of the Sabbath daye," and bring them before a Justice of the Peace to be dealt with according to law. This was to be done by the Constable under the penalty of six shillings for each neglect or default.

The same Court also made an order, "that Mad James be kept by Kings County in general, and that the deacons of each towne within the said county doe forthwith meet together and consider about their propercons for maintainence of said James." This is the first instance which has come to the Compiler's knowledge of the Court making an order for the county generally to support a pauper.

In the year 1758, the sum of £122 18s. 7d. was assessed in two assessments, by the Justices of the Peace, on this town, towards building "a new Court house and gaol" for Kings County. The whole amount assessed on the County was £448 4s. 1d.

The present Court house of Kings County, was built by contract in the year 1792, at an expense of $2944.71, under the superintendance of John Vanderbilt, Johannes E. Lott, and Charles Doughty, Esq'rs. The contractor was Thomas

Fardon, and plans were furnished for the building by Messrs. Stanton and Newton, and James Robertson.*

---

* In 1700 the Court House was let to James Simson for one year, at £3 "in money." In this agreement, "the Justices reserved for themselves the Chamber in the said house, called the Court Chamber, at the time of their publique Sessions, Courts of Common Pleas, and private meetings; as also the room called the prison for the use of the Sheriff if he hath occasion for it."

APPENDIX.

A.

Deed from William Morris and wife to the Corporation of New-York.

This Indenture made the twelfth day of October, in the sixth year of the reign of our Sovereign Lord and Lady William and Mary, by the grace of God, of England, Scotland, France and Ireland, King and Queen, defenders of the faith, &c. and in the year of our Lord one thousand six hundred and ninety-four, between William Morris, now of the ferry, in the bounds of the town of Breuchlen, in Kings County, on Long-Island, Gentleman, and Rebecca his wife of the one part, and the Mayor, Aldermen, and Commonalty of the City of New York, of the other part, Witnesseth, that the said William Morris, by and with the consent of Rebecca his said wife, testified by her being a party to the sealing and delivery of these presents, for, and in consideration of a certain sum of good and lawful money to him, at and before the sealing and delivery hereof, by the said Mayor, Aldermen, and Commonalty, in hand well and truly paid, the receipt whereof he the said William Morris doth hereby acknowledge, and thereof and therefrom and of and from all and every part thereof, he doth hereby, acquit, exonerate and discharge the said Mayor, Aldermen, and Commonalty, and their successors forever, hath granted, bargained, sold, assigned, conveyed and confirmed, and by these presents doth grant, bargain, sell, assign, convey and confirm unto the said Mayor, Aldermen and Commonalty of the said city of New York, and their successors forever, All that messuage or dwelling house and lot of ground thereunto adjoining and belonging, with the appurtenances, situate, lying and being at the ferry, in the bounds of the town of Breucklen, in Kings County aforesaid, now and late in the possession of him, the said William Morris; as also one small house, now in the possession of one Thomas Hock, lying in the said City of New York, over against the ferry aforesaid, Together with all and singular houses, barns, stables, yards, backsides, wharfs, easements, benefits, emoluments, hereditaments, and appurtenances to the same messuage or dwelling house and premises belonging, or in any wise appertaining, and the reversion and reversions, remainder and remainders, rents, issues, and profits of all and singular the premisses and the appurtenances, and all the estate, right, title, interest, property, possession, claim and demand of him the said William Morris and Rebecca his said wife, of, in, unto or out of, the said messuage or dwelling house and premises, or, of, in, unto, or out of, all or any part or parcel thereof, and all and singular grants, deeds, escripts, minuments, writings and evidences, touching, relating to or concerning the above-mentioned, to be bargained, messuage or dwelling house and all and singular, the premises with the hereditaments and appurtenances to the same belonging, or any part thereof, unto the said Mayor, Aldermen and Commonalty of the city of New York, aforesaid, and their successors unto the only proper use, benefit and behoof of the said Mayor, Aldermen and Commonalty of the City of New York aforesaid, their successors and assigns forever. In witness, &c.*

* The above deed to the Corporation of New York did not extend to the River. January 15, 1717, Samuel Garritsen, of Gravesend, quit-claimed to David Aersen of Brooklyn, all his right and title to a piece of land, "lying next to the house and land belonging to the City of New York, bounded north-west by the River, south-east by the highway that goes to the ferry, south-west by the house and land belonging to the City of New York, and north-east by the house

A Warrant for enforcing the payment of a town tax in the town of Brooklyn.

Whereas there was an order or towne lawe by the ffreeholders of the towne of Brooklyn, in Kings County aforesaid, the 5th day of May, 1701, ffor constituting and appointing of Trustees to defend the rights of their quondam common wood lands, and to raise a tax ffor the same to defray the charge of that and theire towne debts, &c. which said lawe has bin since ffurther confirmed by said ffreeholders at a towne meeting at Bedford, the 11th of April, 1702, and since approved of and confirmed by a Court of Sessions, held at Fflatbush, in said County the 13th day of May, 1702. And whereas by virtue of said lawe, a certaine small tax was raised on the ffreeholders in said towne proportionably to defray the charges aforsaid: And now upon complaint of the said Trustees to us made, that A. B. has refused to pay his juste and due proporcon of said tax wch amounts to *L*1 16s 0d, current money of New-York. These are there-

---

and land belonging to the said John Rapalje, containing one acre be the same more or less." On the 16th day of the same month, David Aersen sold this property to Gerrit Harsum of New York, Gunsmith, for the sum of *L*108 current money of New York.

fore in her Majesty's name, to command you to summons A. B. personally to be and appeare before us, &c., then and there to answer C. D. E. F. Trustees of said towne of Brooklin, in an action of tresspass on the case, to the damage of the said C. D. E. F. £1 16s 0d, current money as aforesaid, as it is said, and have with you then there this precept. Given, &c.

B.

Brookland, November 14, 1753. A Town meeting called by warrant of Carel Debevois, Esq. and Jacobus Debevois, Esq. two of his Majesty's Justices for the township of Brookland, in the County of Kings, to elect and chuse Trustees to defend our Patent of Brookland against the Commonalty of the City of New York.—And the Trustees so elected and chosen by the freeholders and inhabitants of the township of Brookland aforesaid, are as follows: Jacobus Lefferts, Peter Vandervoort, Jacob Remsen, Rem Remsen, and Nicholas Vechte. And we the hereunder subscribers being freeholders and inhabitants of the township of Brookland, by these presents do fully empower and authorize the abovesaid Trustees, Jacobus Lefferts, Peter Vandervoort, Jacob Remsen, Rem Remsen, and Nicholas Vechte, elected and chosen by the freeholders and inhabitants of the township of Brookland aforesaid, to defend our patent where in any manner our liberties, privileges and rights in our patent specified is incroached, lessened or taken away by the Commonalty of the City of New-York. And that we hereunder subscribers of the township of Brookland, oblige ourselves, our heirs, executors and administrators to pay to the abovesaid Trustees, all cost that they are at in protecting of the profits of our patent, and that money shall be collected in by the constable of our town. And that the abovesaid Trustees do oblige themselves to render upon oath a true account of all such moneys they have expended in protecting or defending our patent, to any person or persons, as the hereunder subscribers shall appoint for that purpose. And in defending our patent so that verdict shall come in our favour, where income of money or other profits should arise concerning the premises, all such profits or income should be kept towards defraying of all the necessary cost and charge of our township of Brookland, till such time as it is altered by the majority. And that the Trustees should have three shillings per day for their service and no more.

C.

The Petition of Volkert Brier.

To his Excellency.—The humble peticon of Volkert Brier, inhabitant of the towne of Broockland, on the island of Nassau.

May it please your Excellency your peticoner being fined five pounds last Court of Sessions, in Kings County for tearing an execucon directed to him as Constable. Your peticoner being ignorant of the crime, and not thinking it was of force when he was out of his office, or that he should have made returne of it as the lawe directs, he being an illiterate man could not read said execucon nor understand any thing of lawe: humbly prays yr Excellency yt you would be pleased to remit said fine of five pounds, yr peticoner being a poore man and not capaciated to pay said fine without great damage to himself and family. And for yr Excellecy yr peticoner will ever pray, &c.

D.

A Letter from Justice Ffilkin to the Secretary at New York.

Sir,—I am in expectation of a complaint coming to his Excellency by Coll. Beeckman against me, and that his Excellency may be rightly informed of the matter, my humble request to you is, that if such a thing happen, be pleased to give his Excellency an account thereof, which is as follows: A Ffriday night last, the Justices of the County and I came from his Excellency's; Coll. Beeckman happened to come over in the fferry boat along with us, and as we came over the fferry, Coll. Beeckman and we went into the fferry house to drink a glass of wine, and being soe in company, there happened a dispute between Coll. Beeckman and myself, about his particular order that he lately made to Mr. Ffreeman, when he was President of the Councill, without the consent of the Councill; Coll. Beeckman stood to affirm there, before most of the Justices of Kings County, that said order, that he made then to Mr. Ffreeman as President only, was still in fforce, and that Mr. Ffreeman should preach at Broockland next Sunday according to that order; whereupon I said it was not in fforce, but void and of noe effect, and he had not in this County, any more power now than I have, being equall in commission with him in the general commission of the peace and one of the quorum as well as he; upon which he gave me affronting words, giving me the lie and calling me pittifull fellow, dog, rogue, rascall,

&c. which caused me, being overcome with passion, to tell him that I had a good mind to knock him off his horse, we being both at that time getting upon our horses to goe home, but that I would not goe, I would fight him at any time with a sword. I could wish that these last words had bin kept in, and I am troubled that I was soe overcome with passion and inflamed with wine. The works of these Dutch ministers is the occasion of all our quarrells.* And this is the truth of the matter, there was no blows offerred, nor noe more done. Mr. Ffreeman has preached at Broockland yesterday accordingly, and the church doore was broke open, by whom it is not yet knowne. Soe I beg your pardon ffor this trouble, crave your favour in this matter, and shall alwayes remaine.

Sir, your ffaithful and humble servant,

H. FFILKIN.

---

* The Compiler congratulates his fellow citizens on the extinction of those national animosities which in former times existed between the Dutch and English in this our happy country. We may now truly ask, with Sterne, "are we not all relations?"

E.

The Address of the Deputies, assembled at Hempstead.

We the deputies duly elected from the several towns upon Long-Island, being assembled at Hempstead, in general meeting, by authority derived from your royal highness unto the honorable Colonel Nicolls, as deputy governor, do most humbly and thankfully acknowledge to your royal highness, the great honor and satisfaction we receive in our dependence upon your royal highness according to the tenor of his sacred majesty's patent, granted the 12th day of March, 1664; wherein we acknowledge ourselves, our heirs and successors forever, to be comprized to all intents and purposes, as therein is more at large expressed. And we do publickly and unanimously declare our cheerful submission to all such laws, statutes and ordinances, which are or shall be made by virtue of authority from your royal highness, your heirs and successors forever: As also, that we will maintain, uphold, and defend, to the utmost of our power, and peril of us, our heirs and successors forever, all the rights, title, and interest, granted by his sacred majesty to your royal highness, against all pretensions or invasions, foreign or domestic; we being already well assured, that, in so doing, we perform our duty of allegiance to his majesty, as freeborn subjects of the kingdom of England inhabiting in these his majesty's dominions. We do farther beseech your royal highness to accept of this address, as the first fruits in this general meeting, for a memorial and record against us, our heirs and successors, when we or any of them shall fail in our duties. Lastly we beseech your royal highness to take our poverties and necessities, in this wilderness country, into speedy consideration; that, by constant supplies of trade, and your royal highnesses more particular countenance of grace to us, and protection of us, we may daily more and more be encouraged to bestow our labors to the improvement of these his majesty's western dominions, under your royal highness; for whose health, long life, and eternal happiness, we shall ever pray, as in duty bound.

List of the Deputies.

New Utrecht	Jaques Cortelleau	Younger Hope
Gravesend	James Hubbard	John Bowne
Flatlands	Elbert Elbertsen	Roeloffe Martense
Flatbush	John Striker	Hendrick Gucksen
Bushwick	John Stealman	Gisbert Tunis
Brooklyn	Hendrick Lubbersten	John Evertsen
Newtown	Richard Betts	John Coe

Flushing	Elias Doughty	Richard Cornhill
Jamaica	Daniel Denton	Thomas Benedict
Hempstead	John Hicks	Robert Jackson
Oysterbay	John Underhill	Matthias Harvey
Huntington	Jonas Wood	John Ketcham
Brookhaven	Daniel Lane	Roger Barton
Southold	William Wells	John Youngs
Southampton	Thomas Topping	John Howell
Easthampton	Thomas Baker	John Stratton
Westchester	Edward Jessup	—— Quinby

The people of Long Island considered the language of this address as too servile for freemen; and were exasperated against the makers of it to such a degree that the court of assizes, in order to save the deputies from abuse, if not from personal violence, thought it expedient, at their meeting in October 1666, to declare that "whosoever hereafter shall any wayes detract or speake against any of the deputies signing the address to his royall highnes, at the general meeting at Hempstead, they shall bee presented to the next court of sessions, and if the justices shall see cause, they shall from thence bee bound over, to the assizes, there to answer for the slander upon plaint or information.

The deputies subsequently to the address made to the duke of York, made one to the people, in which they set forth their reasons for agreeing to the code styled the duke's laws.

APPENDIX, No. 2.

The following is a copy of the first charter by which the corporation obtained any color of title to the land between high and low water mark, on the Brooklyn side.

"Anne, by the grace of God, of England, Scotland, France and Ireland, Queen, defender of the Faith, &c. To all whom these presents may in any wise concern, sendeth greeting. Whereas the Mayor, Aldermen, and Commonalty of the city of New York, by their petition to our trusty and well-beloved cousin Edward, Viscount Cornbury,* our captain-general and governor-in-chief in and over our province of New York, and territories depending thereon in America, and Vice

* "Lord Cornbury came to this province in very indigent circumstances; hunted out of England by a host of hungry creditors, he was bent on getting as much money as he could squeeze out of the purses of an impoverished people." He was infamous for his "excessive avarice, his embezzlement of the public money, and his sordid refusal to pay his private debts." Cornbury became so obnoxious to the inhabitants of this province, that they sent a complaint to England against him. The Queen, in consequence of this complaint displaced him. "As soon as his lordship was superseded, his creditors threw him into the custody of the sheriff of New York." See Smith's *History of New York*. Such was the man from whom the corporation of New York obtained the rights of the town of Brooklyn.

Admiral of the same, &c., preferred in council; therein setting forth, that they having a right and interest, under divers autient charters and grants, by divers former governors and commanders in chief of our said province of New York,* under our noble progenitors in a certain ferry from the said city of New York, over the East River, to Nassau Island (alias Long Island), and from the said island to the said city again, and have possessed the same, and received all the profits, benefits, and advantages thereof for the space of fifty years and upwards; and perceiving the profits, advantages, and benefits usually issuing out of the same, to diminish, decrease, and fall short of what might be reasona-

* These "divers former governors," &c., are limited to two, viz.: Nicolls, who in 1665 granted them a charter, if that may be strictly called so, which only altered their form of government from scout, burgomasters, and schepens, to Mayor and Aldermen, without a word about ferries or water rights, or indeed any other matter—the original of which paper is not in existence. There is nothing to warrant a belief that there was a charter of any kind granted to the corporation between Nicolls and Dongan, who is the second of these "divers former governors," &c., and who in 1636 granted them the ferry (as is mentioned in a former part of this work) with an express reservation as to the rights of all others. The charter of Dongan notwithstanding all their pompous recitals, is the oldest they can produce, which in any manner affects the interest of this town.

bly made of the same, for the want of the bounds and limits to be extended and enlarged on the said Island side, whereby to prevent divers persons transporting themselves and goods to and from the said Island Nassau (alias Long Island) over the said river, without coming or landing at the usual and accustomed places, where the ferryboats are usually kept and appointed, to the great loss and damage of the said city of New York; have humbly prayed our grant and confirmation under the great seal of our said province of New York, of the said ferry, called the Old Ferry, on both sides of the East River for the transporting of passengers, goods, horses and cattle, to and from the said city, as the same is now held and enjoyed by the said mayor, aldermen and commonalty of the said city of New York, or their under tenant, or under tenants; and also of all that vacant and unappropriated land, from high water mark to low water mark, on the said Nassau Island (alias Long Island), lying contiguous and fronting the said city of New York, from a certain place called the Wallabout, unto the Red Hook, over against Nutten Island, for the better improvement and accommodation of the said ferry; with full power, leave and license to set up, establish, maintain, and keep one or more ferry, or ferries, for the ease and accommodation of all passengers and travellers, for the transportation of themselves, goods, horses and cattle, over the said river, within the bounds aforesaid, as they shall see meet and convenient, and occasion require; and to establish, ordain, and make bye laws, orders, and ordinances for the due and orderly regulations of the same: The which petition we being minded to grant, Know Ye, That of our especial grace, certain knowledge and meer motion, we have given, granted, ratified and confirmed, and in and by these presents, for us, our heirs and successors, we do give, grant, ratify and confirm, unto the said mayor, aldermen and commonalty of the city of New York, and to their successors and assigns, all that the said ferry, called Old Ferry, on both sides of the East River, for the transportation of passengers, goods, horses and cattle, over the said river, to and from the said city and island, as the same is now used, held and enjoyed, by the said mayor, aldermen and commonalty of the city of New York, or their under tenant or under tenants, with all and singular the usual and accustomed ferriage, fees, perquisites, rents, issues, profits, and other benefits, and advantages whatsoever, to the said Old Ferry belonging, or therewith used, or thereout arising; and also all that the aforesaid vacant and unappropriated ground, lying and being on the said Nassau Island (alias Long Island), from high water mark to low water mark aforesaid, contiguous and fronting the said city of New York, from the aforesaid place called the Wall-about to Red Hook aforesaid; that is to say, from the east side of the Wallabout, opposite the new dwelling house of James Bobine, to the west side of the Red Hook, commonly called the Fishing place, with all and singular the appurtenances and hereditaments to the same belonging, or in any wise of right appertaining; together with all and singular the rents, issues, profits, advantages, and appurtenances, which heretofore have, now are, and which hereafter shall belong to the said ferry, vacant land and premises, herein before granted and confirmed, or to any or either of them, in any wise appertaining, or which heretofore have been, now are, and which hereafter shall belong, be used, held, received, and enjoyed; and all our estate, right, title and interest, benefit and advantage, claim and demand of, in or to the said ferry, vacant land and premises, or any part or parcel thereof, and the reversion and reversions, remainder and remainders; together with the yearly, and other rents, revenues and profits of the premises, and of every part and parcel thereof, except and always reserved out of this our present grant and confirmation, free liberty, leave and license to and for all and every person or persons, inhabiting or having plantations near the said river, by the water side, within the limits and bounds above mentioned, to transport themselves, goods, horses and cattle, over the said river, to and from the said city of New York, and Nassau Island (alias Long Island) to and from their respective dwellings or plantations, without any ferriage, or other account to the said ferry, hereby granted and con firmed, to be paid or given; so always as the said person or persons do transport themselves only, and their own goods, in their own boats only, and not any stranger or their goods, horses or cattle, or in any other boat. To have and to hold, all and singular the said ferry, vacant land and premises, hereinbefore granted and confirmed, or meant, mentioned or intended to be hereby granted and confirmed (except as is herein before excepted) and all and singular the rents, issues, profits, rights, members and appurtenances, to the same belonging, or in any wise of right appertaining, unto the said mayor, aldermen and commonalty of the city of New York, and their successors and assigns forever; to the only proper use and behoof of the said mayor, aldermen, and commonalty of the city of New York, and their successors and assigns forever; to be holden of us, our heirs and successors, in free and common soccage, as of our manour of East Greenwich, in the county of Kent, within our kingdom of England; yielding, rendering, and paying unto us, our heirs and successors, for the same, yearly, at our custom house of New York, to our collector and receiver general there for the time being, at or upon the feast of the nativity of St. John the Baptist, the yearly rent or sum of five shillings, current money, of New York. And we do further, of our especial grace, certain knowledge and meer motion, for us, our heirs and successors, give and grant unto the said mayor, aldermen and commonalty, and their successors, full and free leave and license to set up, establish, keep, and maintain one or more ferry or ferries, as they shall from time to time think fit and convenient, within the limits and bounds aforesaid, for the ease and accommodation of transporting of passengers, goods, horses and cattle, between the said city of New York and the said island (except as is herein before excepted) under such reasonable rates and payments as have been usually paid and received for the same; or which at any time hereafter, shall be by them established, by and with the consent and approbation of our governor and council of our said province, for the time being.* And we do further, of our especial grace, certain knowledge and meer motion, give and grant unto the said mayor, aldermen and commonalty of the city of New York, and their successors, full and absolute power and authority, to make, ordain, establish, constitute and confirm, all manner of by-laws, orders, rules, ordinances and directions, for the more orderly keeping, and regularly maintaining the aforesaid ferry that now is kept, or any ferry or ferries which shall at any time or times hereafter be set up, established, or kept within the bounds aforesaid, by virtue hereof, or of, for, touching or concerning the same (so always as the same be not contrary to our laws of England, and of our province of New York) and the same at all times hereafter to put in execution, or abrogate, revoke, or change, as they in their good discretion shall think fit and most convenient, for the due and orderly keeping, regulating and governing the said ferry or ferries herein before mentioned. And lastly, our will and pleasure is, and we do hereby declare and grant, that these our let-

* The corporation of New York appear to have abandoned the right of regulating the rate of ferriage very early; for in 1717, nine years after the date of this charter, an act was passed by the colonial legislature for that purpose.

ters patent, or the record thereof, in the secretary's office of our said province of New York, shall be good and effectual in the law, to all intents and purposes whatsoever, notwithstanding the not true and well reciting or mentioning of the premises, or any part thereof, or the limits and bounds thereof, or of any former or other letters patents or grants whatsoever, made or granted; or of any part thereof, by us, or any of our progenitors, unto any person or persons whatsoever, bodies politic or corporate,* or any law or other restraint, incertainty or imperfection whatsoever, to the contrary in any wise notwithstanding and although express mention of the true yearly value, or certainty of the premises, or any of them, or of any other gifts or grants by us or by any of our progenitors, heretofore made to the said mayor, aldermen, commonalty of the city of New York, in these presents is not made, or any other matter, cause or thing whatsoever, to the contrary thereof in any wise notwithstanding. In testimony whereof we have caused these our letters to be made patent, and the seal of our said province of New York, to our said letters patent to be af-

* This clause was undoubtedly inserted to obviate if possible the claim under the two Brooklyn patents, both of which were many years older than this charter.

fixed, and the same to be recorded in the secretary's office of our said province. Witness our right trusty and well beloved cousin, Edward Viscount Cornbury, captain-general and governor-in-chief in and over our province of New York, aforesaid, and territories thereon depending in America, and vice admiral of the same, &c., in council, at our Fort in New York, the nineteenth day of April, in the seventh year of our reign, Annoq. Domina, one thousand seven hundred and eight.

CORNBURY.

At the time of printing that part of this work under the head of "Common lands and the division thereof," the Compiler was not aware of the existence of the following proceeding relating to the division of said lands, he has therefore placed the same in this appendix.

"At a towne meeting held this twentieth day of Aprill, 1697, at Bedford, within the jurisdiction of Brookland, in Kings County, upon the Island of Nassau, Resolved by all the ffreeholders of the townes of Brookland, aforesaid, that all their common land not yet laid out or divided, belonging to their whole patent shall be equally divided and laid out to each freeholders of said towne, his just proporcon in all the common lands abovesaid, except those that have but an house and a home lott, which are only to have but half share of the lands aforesaid. And for the laying out of the said land, there are chosen and appointed by the freeholders abovesaid, Capt. Henry Filkin, Jacobus Vanderwater, Daniel Rapalje, Joris Hansen, John Darlant, and Cornelius Vanduyne. It is further ordered that no men within the township abovesaid, shall have privilege to sell his part of the undivided lands of Brookland not yet laid out, to any person living without the township abovesaid. It is likewise ordered, consented to, and agreed by the towne meeting aforesaid, that Capt. Henry Filkin shall have a full share with any or all the freeholders aforesaid, in all the common land or woods in the whole patent of the towne of Brookland aforesaid, beside a half share for his home lott; To have and to hold to him, his heirs and assigns forever. It is likewise ordered, that no person whatsoever within the common woods of the jurisdicon of Brookland aforesaid, shall cutt or fall any oake or chesnut saplings for firewood during the space of foure years from the date hereof upon any of the said common lands or woods within the jurisdicon of Brookland patent, upon the penalty of six shillings in money, for every wagon load of saplings abovesaid soe cutt, besides the forfeiture of the wood or timber soe cutt as abovesaid, the one-half thereof to the informer, and the other half for the use of the poor of the towne of Brookland aforesaid.

By order of the towne meeting aforesaid, and Justice Henry Ffilkin.

JACOBUS VANDERWATER, Towne Clerk."

ADVERTISEMENT.

The Compiler here closes his notes, and has only to remark, that throughout the whole of this little work, he has been less solicitous about his reputation as an author, than a correct compiler. Studies of this nature are but ill calculated to admit of a luxuriance of diction or sentiment, and to these he has in no place aspired. His business was to collect authentic information concerning subjects at once obscure and interesting, and in what degree he has effected this object he leaves his readers to determine, feeling conscious himself that however imperfectly he may have executed his design, his only aim was the public good.

BIBLIOGRAPHY OF LONG ISLAND.

By Henry Onderdonk, Jr.

Alvord, J. W. His Address in First Church, Stamford, Dec. 22, 1841. Pp. 40.

Andros, Thos. Captivity and Escape from Jersey Prison-ship. 1833. 24mo, pp. 80.

Armstrong, John J. Oration at Queens, July 4, 1861. 8vo, pp. 28.

Oration at Flushing, July 4, 1862. 8vo, pp. 24.

Oration at Jamaica, July 4, 1865. 8vo, pp. 31.

Ayres, J. A. The Legends of Montauk. A Poem. 1849. 8vo, pp. 127.

Ayres, Dr. Case of Membraneous Croup. 1852.

Contributions to Surgery. 1857.

Bailey, J. T. His. Sketch of Brooklyn and its Neighborhood. 1840. 12mo, pp. 72.

Barber, J. W. His. Coll. of N. Y. 1841. 8vo. Pict.

His. of the State of N. Y. 1846. 8vo, pp. 376.

Barclay, Sidney. See Post.

Bard, Dr. John. Malignant Pleurisy of L. I. in Winter of 1749.

Barroll, Wm. H. Oration at Hempstead, July 4, 1835.

Beecher, Lyman. Ser. on Duelling, at Aquebogue, April 16, 1806. 8vo, pp. 44.

Beecher, Ser. on Death of Mrs. F. M. Sands, E. Hampton, Oct. 12, 1806. 8vo, pp. 20.
Ser. on His. of E. Hampton, 1806. pp. 40, 8vo.
Ser. on Government of God Desirable (Matt. vi. 10). 1809.
Ser. on Reformation in Morals.

Beers, And. (of Danbury). L. I. Almanac and Register, 1823. 12mo.

Bedell, Rich., and others *vs.* Saml. Denton and others. Chancellor's Opinion, filed Dec. 27, 1824. A. Spooner, printer, Br. 8vo, pp. 12.
Case of (Respondent's Case), 1818. 8vo, pp. 584.

Bennett, Jas. A. (N. Utrecht). Bookkeeping (1846), and Arithmetic (1835): On Swimming.

Benson, Egbert. Dutch Names. Read before N. Y. His. Soc., Dec. 31, 1816. Reprint.

Bergen, Tunis G. Translator of De Sille's His. of New Utrecht.
Genealogy of the Bergen Family, 1866. 8vo, pp. 298.

Betts, Wm., LL.D. (Jamaica). Oration, July 4, 1838. 8vo, pp. 16.

Bishop, A. H. Ser. on Deaths of Abm. Remsen and A. R. Schenck. 8vo, 1849, pp. 35.

Bogart, David S. Ser. before a Religious Society, N. Y., Dec. 17, 1787. 12mo, pp. 14.
Thanksgiving Ser., Southampton, Nov. 22, 1804. 8vo, pp. 24.
Ser. at Clerical Bee, at the Parsonage, Hempstead Harbor, Ap. 6, 1814. 8vo, pp. 16.
Ser. on his Death, by Thos. DeWitt, D.D., N. Y., Aug. 4, 1839. 8vo, pp. 22.

Bogart, Miss Elizabeth. Fugitive Poems. 1866. 12mo, pp. 307.

Bokee, David A. (Br.). Oration, July 4, 1851. 8vo, pp. 11.

Bowden, Jas. His. of Friends in America (and on L. I.). 2 v. 8vo. London, 1850.

Bownas, Samuel (Quaker). Life and Travels (imprisoned at Jamaica). 1756. 8vo.

Brenton, Jas. J. (Jam.). Voices from the Press, 1850. 8vo, pp. 312.

Brinckerhoff, John N. (Jam.). Oration, July 4, 1838. 12mo, pp. 14.

Brood, Amos. Discourse to U. S. Army, at Brooklyn, Sept. 3, 1814. 12mo, pp. 18.

Brodhead, Jacob, D.D. His Ser. in Central Ref. D. Ch., Br., July 27, 1851. 8vo, pp. 25.

Jno. Romeyn. Hist. of N. Y., 1609–64. 8vo, 1853.

Brooklyn. All Procedings relative to South Ferry, from Dec., 1825, to Jan., 1835. 8vo, pp. 100.

Directories, 1797, and to date.

East New York and Rockaway Railroad Charter, 1864. 8vo, pp. 28.

Battle of. A Farce in 2 Acts, as played by the Rebels, Aug. 27, 1776. Rivington, printer, N. Y., 1776.

Act of Incorporation, 1816. 8vo, pp. 12.

Policy of the Nation respecting a Navy, 1814, 8vo. (Price 25 cts.).

Militiaman's Guide and His. of Gen. Stevens' Officers, Oct. 20, 1814. (Price 37½ cts.)

Height's "Patriotic Diggers." A Song. (Price 6 cts.) Aug. 23, 1814.

Brooklyn. Expenses and Receipts of Fire Department from 1784 to 1817.

Management of the Old or Fulton Ferry, 1822. 8vo, pp. 80.

Reply to Pamphlet on Steamboat Ferry, 1822. 8vo, pp. 46.

Law Papers relating to Fulton Ferry, 1822. 8vo, pp. 80.

Act to amend Act of Incorporation, passed Ap. 9, 1824. 8vo, pp. 8.

Act Incorporating the City as reported, Nov. 10, 1825. 8vo, pp. 32.

Memorial to Corporation of N. Y., 1825. 8vo, pp. 19.

Bible Society, 1825, pp. 7. Officers of Bible Society. 1847, pp. 4.

On Removal of Jail and Court-House of Kings Co., Feb. 1825. 8vo, pp. 8.

South Ferry Question, by a Freeman, 1826. 8vo, pp. 63.

Young Men's Miss. Soc. of Ref. Dutch Church. First Report, 1827. 12mo, pp. 11.

Lyceum By-Laws, 1833.

Conference on Incorporating N. Y. and Brooklyn, Jan., 1834. 8vo, pp. 14.

Wealthy Men and Women of. By Lomas & Pearce, 1847. 12mo, pp. 48.

Constitution of St. Nicholas Society of Long Island, 1848. 12mo, pp. 15.

Manual of Clinton Av. Cong'l Church, Jan., 1851. 18mo, pp. 32.

Report of Standing Com. on Water, Dec. 22, 1851. 8vo, pp. 24.

Brooklyn. By-Laws of Atheneum, May 2, 1853. First Ann. Report, Jan. 10, 1854.

Atheneum and Reading-Room Report (2d), 1855. 8vo.

City and Kings Co. Record, pub. by Wm. C. Smith, 1855. 12mo.

Heights Seminary. Cat. of 1854–5–6. 8vo.

Report of Water Commissioners, 1856. Proposals for Water Loan, 1857.

Debate on Water Question in Com. Council, 1853.

Manual of First Presb. Ch. (Van Dyck's). Members' Names. 18mo.

Young Men's Christian Association. Fourth and Fifth Reports, 1858–9. 8vo.

Cat. of Collegiate and Polytechnic Institute, 1858. 8vo.

Memorial to Legislature against Local Assessments, 1858. 8vo, pp. 12.

Atlantic St. Railroad Assessment, 1858. 8vo, pp. 12.

City Hospital, and Address by Dr. J. C. Hutchinson, 1859. 8vo, pp. 39.

Reports on the District that Supplies Br. with Water. By T. Weston, 1861. 8vo.

Dummy Engine from Bedford to Jamaica (plate), Jan. 1863. 8vo, pp. 15.

Manual of Com. Council from 1861 to date.

City Hospital Charter and Statistics for 1859. 8vo, pp. 38. Report for 1850. 8vo, pp. 11.

Buell, Sam'l, D.D. Ser. at Ord. of Benj. Tallmadge, Br. Haven, Oct. 23, 1754, pp. 62.

Ser. on Death of Mrs. Esther Darbe, Sept. 24, 1757, pp. 34.

Buell, Samuel, D.D. Ser. on Death of Mrs. Cath. Davis, April 11, 1759, pp. 38.

Ser. at Ord. of Mr. Occom, at E. Hampton, Aug. 29, 1759, pp. 38.

Account of the late Success of the Gospel in the Province of N. Y., contained in Letters from Messrs. Buell, Hazard & Prime. 1765. 8vo, pp. 16.

Letter to Rev. Mr. Barber, of Groton, Mar. 17, 1764. 16mo, pp. 8.

Ser. on death of Rev. Chas. Jeffery Smith, Aug. 10, 1770, pp. 42.

Ser. at Enfield on Spiritual Knowledge of God, 1771.

New Year's Ser. at E. Hampton, with Poem on "Youth's Triumphs," 1775, pp. 54.

Ser. on Death of his Daughter, Mrs. Jerusha Conklin, Feb. 24, 1782.

Ser. on Death of his only Son Samuel, 1787. 8vo, pp. 52.

Ser. at Ord. of Aaron Woolworth, Bridgehampton, Aug. 30, 1787, pp. 46.

Half-century Ser. at E. Hampton, 1792. 8vo, pp. 40.

Ser. on Death of Sam'l B. Woolworth, 1794.

Ser. at Ord. of Jos. Hazard, Southold, 1797. 8vo, pp. 30.

Correspondence with Gov. Tryon, 1776-80. (A MS. vol. in N. Y. State Library.)

Correspondence with Gov. Trumbull (in Library of Mass. Hist. Soc., Boston).

Buffet, Platt, Smithtown. Letter on Mr. Fletcher's Doctrine, 1794. 12mo, pp. 35.

Burnet, Matthias. Ser. at Jamaica, 1790. (In American Preacher.)

Burr, Aaron. Ser. at Ord. of David Bostwick, Jam., Oct. 9, 1745. 18mo, pp. 37.

Bushnell, Chas. J. Adventures of Christ. Hawkins (in Prison Ship), 1864. 8vo, pp. 316.

Busteed, Rich. (Jam.) Oration, July 4, 1861: at Huntington, July 4, 1862. 8vo, pp. 21.

Callicot, T. C. (Br.). Speech against Negro Suffrage, Feb. 10, 1860. 8vo, pp. 12.

Campbell, Wm. H., D.D. Ser. on Death of Thos. M. Strong, D.D., June 30, 1861. 8vo, pp. 12.

Carmichael, Wm. H., D.D. Rise and Progress of St. George's Ch., Hemp., 1841. 8vo, pp. 59.

Threefold Ministry of the Church. 1844. 12mo.

Carver, Dr. Jas., of Oyster Bay. The Veterinary Art. 1816. 8vo, pp. 32.

Chalkley, Thos. Journal, 1741. 12mo. (A travelling Quaker preacher on L. I.).

Chandos, Wm. A. Legends of L. I.

Cleaveland, N. Add. before New England Soc., Br., Dec. 21, 1849. 8vo.

Descriptive Notices in "Greenwood Illustrated."

Clowes, Tim., LL.D. (Hemp.). Sermons at St. Peter's Ch., Albany, 1816. 12mo, pp. 282.

Prospectus of Hemp'd Academy, April, 1818. 8vo.

The Tachymathist, Nos. 1 and 2. 1845. 8vo, pp. 32.

The Schoolmaster, folio. Started July 5, 1830.

Cobbet, Wm. A. A Year's Residence in U. S. (chiefly on L. I.). 3 parts. 1818–19. 8vo.

Congregational Church of L. I. His. of from 1791–1839. 12mo, pp. 36.

Crane, Elias W. (Jam.). Add. on Sacred Music. 1829. 8vo, pp. 8.

Cross, Robt. (Jam.). Ser. before Presbyterian Synod, Phil., 1735.

Currie, R. O., D.D. (N. Utrecht). Ser. at Death of Drs. Crane and Dubois. 1856. 12mo, pp. 15.

Memoirs of Rev. R. Sluyter, of Claverack, 1846. 18mo, pp. 132.

Ser. on Death of Rev. Geo. A. Shelton, Nov. 15, 1864. 8vo, pp. 21.

Curtenius, Antonius (Flatbush). His Eulogy in Dutch Pub. by H. Goelet, N. Y., price 3 coppers, 1756.

Cutler, B. C., D.D. (Br.). Ser. on Death of Mrs. Mary Augusta Greene, July 17, 1849. 8vo, pp. 24.

Ser. at Funeral of Rev. F. C. Clements, Jan. 23, 1853. 8vo, pp. 43.

Cypress Hills Cemetery, 1842. 12mo, pp. 14. Same, 1857. 8vo, pp. 72. (With names of lot owners.)

Daggert, Herman. Ser. on Death of Sam'l Buell, D.D., July 22, 1798. 8vo, pp. 23.

The American Reader for the use of Schools.

Davidson, Robt., D.D. Two Centuries of Presbyt. Ch., Huntington. 1866. 8vo, pp. 64.

Dawson, Henry B. Battle of L. I.

Degraw, J. W. Agricultural Address.

De Kay, Jas. E., M.D. (Oyster Bay). Indian Names on L. I. 1851. 12mo, pp. 12.

Demarest, Cor. T. Lamentation over Sol. Froeligh, D.D. 1827. 8vo, pp. 70. (Min. of Queens Co.)

Denton, Rev. Rich. (Hemp.). "Soliloquia Sacra."

Denton, Daniel. Brief Description of N. Y. (and of Queens Co.). London, 1701; N. Y., 1845. 8vo, pp. 57.

De Sille, Nicasius. His. of Settlements of N. Utrecht. Poems. (See Murphy's Anthologie.)

Devereux, Jno. C. Oration on Wm. Penn, July 4, 1852, at Jamaica. 8vo, pp. 16.

Dring, Capt. Thos. Recollections of the Jersey Prison Ship, 1829. 18mo, pp. 167.

Enlarged edition with notes and portraits, by H. B. Dawson. 8vo, 1865, pp. 201.

Drowne, T. Stafford. Ser. in the Holy Trinity, Br., July 24, 1853. 8vo, pp. 24.

Dunlop, Wm. His. of New Netherland and N. Y., 2 v. 8vo, 1839–40.

Dwight, Timothy, D.D. Travels in N. England (and on L. I.), 4 v. 8vo. 1821–22.

Dwight, Maurice W., D.D. Ser. on Death of Gen. Jer. Johnson, 1853. 8vo.

Ser. to Young Men in Ref. D. Ch., Brooklyn, May 21, 1837. 8vo, pp. 23.

Ser. on Death of Gen. Zach. Taylor, July 14, 1850. 8vo, pp. 19.

Eames, Theodore. Add. at opening of Class. Hall, Br., Mar. 24, 1831. 8vo, pp. 32.

Lect. before Brooklyn Lyceum, Nov. 7, 1833. 8vo.

East Hampton. Add. of, to Messrs. Tapping & Corwith. 18mo, pp. 14. *No date.*

Dialogue on Free Thinking, by Principal of the Academy. 1807.

East New York. Map of Lots, Aug., 1843.

Eclipse. His. and Pedigree of that noted Race-Horse. 1823. 8vo, pp. 37.

Edwards, Jas. C. Ser. on Death of Rev. Jno. Gile, of Setauket (drowned). 1850. 8vo, pp. 16.

Add. before Synod of Presby'n Church, 1848. 8vo, pp. 8.

Edwards, Jona, D.D. Ser. at Installation of S. Buell, Sept. 19, 1746. 8vo, pp. 16.

Embury, Emma C. Add. on Female Education, read by F. Tucker, at Br. Coll. Institute, 1831. 8vo, pp. 19.

Evergreens Cemetery. Rules, 1850. 12mo, pp. 22.

Faitoute, Geo. (Jam.). Ser. on Amer. Preacher.

Farley, Rev. F. A. Discourse Br. Lyceum, Ap. 9, 1843. 8vo.

Dangers of Business Life, Sept. 19, 1847. 8vo.

and S. H. Cox, D.D. Addresses on laying corner-stone of Br. City Hospital, June 11, 1851. pp. 20, 8vo.

Ferris, Isaac, D.D. Ser. on Death of Rev. Thos. M. Strong, D.D., Flatbush, July 17, 1861. 8vo, pp. 26.

Field, Thos. W. Editor of Garden's Anecdotes of Rev. 3 v. folio. 1865.

Fish, T. G. St. Ann's Church, Br., 1784–1845. 12mo, 1845.

Flatbush & Flatlands. First Report of Female Religious Tract Soc., Nov. 3, 1816.

Flushing. Celebration of Linnæus' Birthday, May, 1824. 8vo, pp. 16.

Utility of Turnpike across the Necks to Huntington. 1826. 18mo, pp. 11

Flushing. Journal of the Institute (vol. iii., No. 2). pp. 13–56, 8vo. 1834–5.

St. Paul's College, Fund to educate Teachers. 1838. 8vo.

Cat. of Wilcomb & King's Nursery (successors to Bloodgood), 1840. 8vo, pp. 47.

Gram. School of St. Paul's College, 1842. pp. 36, 12mo.

Circular of St. Thomas Hall, G. B. Docharty, LL.D., rector. 1844. pp. 11, 8vo.

Constitution and By-laws of Pacific Lodge, No. 85, I. O. of O. F. 1844. 18mo, pp. 24.

Cat. of Greenbrook Family School. 1846. 8vo, pp. 16.

First Ann. Report of Board of Education (Dis. No. 5). 1849. 8vo, pp. 47.

Annual Report of Bible Society to date.

Address of Trustees of School Dis. No. 1 to Parents and Guardians. 8vo, pp. 11. *No. date.*

Cat. of Officers and Students of the Institute. Dec., 1849. 8vo, pp. 16.

Force, Peter. American Archives, 1774–6, folio. (Revolutionary affairs on L. I.)

Foster, Nathaniel. Address to St. Alban's Lodge, Br., Dec. 27, 1797. 8vo, pp. 23.

Fowler, Jno. Oration, July 4, in Presby. Ch., Jam., 1850. 8vo, pp. 16.

Fox, Ebenr. (Roxbury). Rev. Adventures (in Prison Ships). 1838. 18mo, pp. 238.

Fox, George. Journal (Quaker preacher on L. I.) 1694. Folio.

Franklinville, 3d Ann. Report of Academy. 1859. 8vo, pp. 8.

Freeman, Bernardus. (Flatbush.) Balances of God's Grace (*in Dutch*). 1721. 12mo, pp. 583.

The Mirror of Self-knowledge. 1720. 18mo, 202. (*In Dutch.*)

The Defence against Complaints of Dutch Ch. in N. J. 1726. 18mo, pp. 126. (*In Dutch.*)

French, J. H. Gazetteer of N. Y. 1860. 8vo, pp. 739. (It has historical notes on Long Island.)

Freneau, Philip. Poem on the Prison Ships at N. Y., with Duyckink's notes. 1866.

Fulton, W. A. C. His. of Br. Newspapers. 1865.

Furman, Gabriel, LL.D. Notes Geographical and Hist. relative to Br. 1824. 12mo, pp. 116.

Gerrit-Maspeth. Poems. 1837. 18mo, pp. 128.

Long Island Miscellanies by Rusticus Gent. 1847. 18mo, pp. 185.

Gardiner, Jno. D. Ser. at Sag Harbor. Sept. 9, 1812. 18mo, pp. 20.

Jno. L. Notes on E. Hampton (in Doc. His. i., 683).

Mrs. Mary L. Prose and Poetical Writings. 1843. 12mo, pp. 359.

Garretson, G. J. Ser. on Death of Abm. Skidmore Rapelye. 1847. 8vo, pp. 16.

The Christian Citizen. 1842. 8vo, pp. 16.

(Newtown.) Quadragenian Ann. of Rev. J. Schoonmaker, D.D. 1842. 8vo, pp. 29.

Investigation of his Case. 1853. 8vo, pp. 76.

Giraud, J. P., Jr. Birds of L. I. 1844. 8vo.

Gleason, Luther (Smithtown). Duty of Parents to Children. 1803. 12mo, pp. 15.

Trial of, by Presbytery at Br. Haven, Ap. 13, 1808. 12mo, pp. 100.

Goetschius, J. H. Ser. at Newtown on "The Unknown God," Aug. 22, 1742. 18mo, pp. 57.

Goodenow, Sterling. Topog'l and Statis'l Manual of N. Y. State. 1822. 8vo, pp. 88.

Goodwin, F. J. (Flushing.) Farewell Ser. in St. George's Ch. 1844. 8vo, pp. 15.

Gordon, Thos. F. Gazetteer of State of N. Y. 1836. 8vo.

Wm. R., D.D. Rebuke of High Churchism. 1844. 8vo, pp. 32.

Gray, Rev. Horatio. Memoirs of B. C. Cutler, D.D., Br. 1865. 8vo, pp. 439.

Greenwood Cemetery. Report of Vice-Pres. J. A. Perry, Dec. 4, 1843. 12mo, pp. 12.

Rules, Names of Lot Owners, etc. 1852. 8vo, pp. 63 and pp. 65.

Griffing, Augustus, (Orient). First Settlers of Southold and Orient. 1857. 12mo, pp. 312.

Hall, Rev. Edwin. His. of Norwalk. 1847. 12mo. (It contains Jamaica names.)

Hammon, Jupiter. (Slave of Jos. Lloyd, Queen's Village.) Parable of 10 Virgins. Hartford, Dec., 1779.

Address to Negroes of State of N. Y. 1787. 8vo. Ditto, 1806. 18mo.

A Winter Piece, being a serious Exhortation, with a Call to the Unconverted. 1782. 8vo, pp. 24.

Halsey, Daniel (Southampton). Fourth of July Ode. 1831.

Hart, Rev. Joshua. Ser. at Huntington, July 4, 1813. 8vo, pp. 20.

Fast Ser. at Huntington (Luke xxii. 36). Jan. 12, 1815.

Seth. Ser. to Freemasons in St. George's Ch., Hemp'd. 1801. 12mo, pp. 23.

Ser. on 1st Sunday after Consecration of St. George's Ch. 1823. 8vo, pp. 14.

Hastings, H. P. On Selah B. Strong's management of a Law-suit, Oct. 27, 1851. 8vo, pp. 8.

Hawkins, Micah. Brookhaven. Composed music, songs and plays, about 1825.

Hawks, F. L. Flushing. The Church Record. 1840–2. 2 vols., 4to (weekly).

Hazard, Jos. Poems. 1814. 8vo, pp. 187. (A. Spooner, Br., printer.)

Hedges, Henry P. The 200th Ann. of Settlement of E. Hampton. 1850. 8vo, pp. 101.

Hegeman, Adrian, Esq. Oration in town of Oyster Bay. July 4, 1801. 8vo, pp. 15.

Hempstead. Case of Appeal from Court of Chancery. 1818. 8vo, pp. 504.

In error. Appellant's case. 1825. 8vo, (Suit for the Marshes.)

Annual Reports of Bible Society.

Hicks, Jno. J. Order of Lepidoptera, the White-winged Moth or Measurer. 1866. 8vo, pp. 10.

Hicks, Elias. (Quaker Preacher, Jericho.) On Slavery. 1811. 18mo, pp. 24.

Two discourses in N. Y., Dec. 17, 1824. 8vo, pp. 21.

Sermons in N. Y. taken in short hand, May, 1825. 8vo.

Hicks, Defence of the Christian Doctrine of Friends. 1825. 8vo.

Discourse at Rose St. Meeting-House, April 5, 1829. 8vo, pp. 20.

Six Queries and his Reply. 1830. 12mo, pp. 8.

Testimony of Jericho Monthly Meeting. 1830. 8vo, pp. 8.

Journal of his Life and Labors, by himself. 1832. 8vo, pp. 451.

Higgins, Daniel. Flushing. 2d Ann. Cat. of Fruit and Ornamental Trees. 1843. 12mo, pp. 20.

Hinman, R. R. Names of Puritan Settlers of Conn., 1635–65. 1846. 8vo, pp. 256. (It has L. I. names.)

Hoadly, Chas. J. Records of the Colony of N. Haven. 1638–65. 2 v., 8vo. 1857–58.

Horton, Azariah. Journal of. (He was Missionary to L. I. Indians, 1742–4.)

Howell, George R. Early His. of Southampton, with genealogies. 1866. 12mo, pp. 318.

Ireland, Rev. Jno. (Br.). Proceedings of Body of Clergy against. 1810. 8vo, pp. 23.

Second solemn Appeal to the Church. 1811. 8vo, pp. 74. (He was degraded.)

Jacobus, M. W., D.D. Fast Ser. at Brooklyn, 1841. 8vo, pp. 24.

Ser. on Death of Adrian Van Sinderen, Br., 1843. 8vo, pp. 16.

Jaggar, Wm. Address to People of Suffolk Co. on National Policy. 1836. 8vo, pp. 59.

Address to People of all Parties. 1838. 8vo, pp. 16.

Jamaica. Second Ann. Report of Soc. for Ameliorating Condition of Jews. 1824. 12mo, pp. 10.

Manual of 1st Presb. Church (names of members). 1840. 18mo, pp. 32.

Assembly Report on Union Hall Academy. 1846. 8vo, pp. 55.

Constitution and By-laws of Sons of Temperance. Feb. 13, 1844. 18mo, pp. 24. 1846.

By-laws of Protection Co., having charge of Engine No. 1, org'd May 14, 1849. 18mo, pp. 12.

Constitution of Jamaica Lodge, No. 81, I. O. of O. F., instituted Jan. 21, 1843. 18mo, pp. 43. 1849.

Rules and By-laws of Scott and Graham Club. 1852. 18mo, pp. 8.

First and Second Reports of Board of Education. pp. 12 and 18. 8vo. 1854–5.

Add. of Trustees to Parents, 1854. 8vo, pp. 16.

Const. of Order of U. A., and By-Laws of Woodhull Chap., No. 24. 1856. 18mo, pp. 67.

Const. and By-Laws of Neptune Fire Eng. Co. No. 2. (Org. April 9, 1849.) 1856. 18mo, pp. 24.

Bank of, Articles of Agreement. 1861. 18mo, pp. 13.

Johnson, Evan M., D.D. (Br.). Ser. on Church and Dissent, Dec. 6, 1846. 8vo, pp. 19.

Ser. on Church Union (Br.), Jan. 18, 1846. 8vo, pp. 25.

Ser. on Communion of Saints (Br.), March 26, 1848. 8vo, pp. 27.

Johnson, Mrs. Mary E. (Jam.). Christ's Fast and Temptation. 1848. 8vo, pp. 52.

Jeremiah. Three Articles on Rev. Incidents of Kings Co., in Nav. Mag. 1836. 8vo.

Rev. John B., Oration before Tammany Soc., N. Y., May 12, 1794. 8vo, pp. 24.

Sam'l R., D.D. Ser. in Grace Ch., Jamaica, Oct. 11, 1835. 8vo, pp. 15.

Samuel R., D.D. Ser. in Br., Nov. 25, 1847. 8vo, pp. 10.

Samuel R., D.D. Eulogy on Gen. Jeremiah Johnson, Oct. 20, 1853. 8vo, pp. 34.

Wm. Lupton, D.D. (Jamaica). National Blessings, Dec. 10, 1829. 8vo, pp. 22.

Wm. Lupton, D.D. Descent of the Holy Spirit. 1855. 8vo, pp. 40.

Wm. Lupton, D.D. Ser. on Death of Mrs. Eliza Poole, wife of Wm. S. Smith, May 7, 1855. 8vo, pp. 13.

Wm. Lupton, D.D. The Rector's Offering, annually. 1840–54. 8vo.

Wm. Lupton, D.D. Ser. before Annual Convention, N. Y., Sept. 27, 1848. 8vo, pp. 32.

Wm. Lupton, D.D. Ser. on Re-opening of Grace Church, Jam., Aug. 26, 1860. 8vo, pp. 31.

Jones, Dr. John (native of L. I.). On Wounds and Fractures. 1776.

Samuel (O. Bay). Notes on Smith's Hist. of N. Y., and Remarks on Spofford's New York Gazetteer, in Collections of N. Y. Hist. Soc., vol. iii., 350–65, and 328–40. 8vo.

Jones, Wm. Alfred (N. Y.). Memorial of Hon. D. S. Jones. 1849. 18mo, pp. 90.

Wm. Alfred (N. Y.). Life of Mount and of Walter R. Jones in Hunt's Magazine.

Keith, Geo. Journals of Travels, 1706. 4to. Reprinted 1851. (He preached on L. I., 1702–3.)

Keteltas, Rev. Abm. (Jam.). Charity Ser. in French Ch., N. Y., Dec. 27, 1773. 8vo, pp. 24.

Ser. at Elizabethtown to Canadian Soldiers, March 8, 1759.

Evening Lecture at Newburyport, Oct. 5, 1777.

Ser. on Extortion at Newburyport, Feb. 15, 1778.

King, Rufus (Jam.). Speech on American Naval Act. 1818. 8vo.

Speech on the Missouri Bill. 1819. 8vo.

John A., LL.D. Letter to his Constituents, April, 1851. 8vo, pp. 15.

John A., LL.D. Message while Gov. of the State.

Walter. Ser. at Ord. of Dan'l Hall, Sag Harbor, L. I., Sept. 21, 1797. 8vo, pp. 37.

Kings County. Annual Reports of Superintendents of Poor. 1851. 12mo, pp. 35.

Constitution of Agricultural Soc., adopted Aug. 17, 1819. 8vo, pp. 8.

Constitution of Med. Soc., adopted April 8, 1822. 8vo, pp. 32; and 1829, 12mo, pp. 32.

Lambert, E. R. Hist. and Description of Southold (in his Hist. of N. Haven). 1838. 12mo.

Lawrence, E. A. Flushing, Speech on Gov. Message, Jan. 20, 1860. 8vo, pp. 28.

Ledyard, Isaac. Oration at Jamaica, July 4, 1795.

Letter from L. I. Farmer, in a Pamphlet called Doctrines of the Church, or Methodism Displayed. (Printed by H. Gaine, price 6*d.*) by a member of Episcopal Church. Price, 1*s.* 6*d.* March, 1793.

Lewis, Amzi. Ser. at Ord. of Zach. Greene, June 28, 1787. 8vo, pp. 28.

L'Hommedieu, Ezra. On Manures (in vol. i. Trans. N. Y. Ag. Soc. 1795).

Livingston, Wm. (N. Jersey). Descrip. of Queens Village in his Poem on Philosophic Solitude. 1790.

Long Island Bible Society Reports from 1816 to date.

Bible and Common Prayer-Book Soc. Constitution. 1815. 8vo, pp. 6.

Bible and Common Prayer-Book Soc. First and Second Annual Reports. 1816–17. 8vo, pp. 12.

Presbytery. Circular Letter to the Churches, April 15, 1807. pp. 12.

Journal of Philosophy (monthly), Oct., 1825. 8vo, pp. 241–88, by S. Fleet, Huntington.

Railroad Engineers' Report. 1834. 12mo, pp. 24.

Railroad Report when completed to Greenport. 8vo.

Railroad Report. 1845. 8vo.

Report Uniting the South Bays by Canal from Coney Island to Br. Hampton. 1848. 8vo, pp. 22.

Documents Relative to Conveyance of Lands. 1850. 8vo, pp. 42. (Bell & Gould, printers.)

Long Island Railroad Special Committee's Report, and Opinion of Counsel, May 19, 1851, pp. 24.

North Side Railroad. Report of Engineer. 1854. 8vo, pp. 24.

North Shore Railroad. 1st Annual Report, Sept. 22, 1866. 8vo.

Fish, Guano and Oil Works at Southold. 1858. 12mo. (Printed at Wmsburg.)

Hist. Soc. 1863. 8vo, pp. 21. Constitution, By-Laws and Officers.

Hist. Soc. First, Second and Third Annual Reports. 8vo. 1864–5–6.

Lossing, B. J. Field-Book of Rev. 2 v. 8vo, 2d edition. 1855.

Diary of Washington on L. I. 1861. 12mo.

Lowe, Peter (Flatbush). Ser. at Org. of Classis of L. I., June 1, 1813. 8vo, pp. 24.

Lyman, Huntington. Add. to Temperance Soc. at Franklinville, Sept., 1830, pp. 55.

McCormick, R. C. Oration at Jam., July 4, 1864. 8vo, pp. 36.

Macdonald, Jas. M., D.D. Lecture on Credulity before Jamaica Lyceum. 18mo.

Sketch of Presby'n Church, Jamaica. 1847. 12mo, pp. 138.

Two Centuries of Presby'n Church, Jamaica. 1862. 12mo, pp. 329.

Makemie, Rev. Francis. Imprisonment and Trial of two Presb. Ministers. (Reprint.) 1755. pp. 52.

Mancur, John H. Christine, a Tale of the Rev. (Scene Flatbush.) 1843.

Mancur, John H. The Bride of Gowanus (in Arthur's Mag., March, 1846). 8vo, pp. 7.

Mandeville, Rev. G. H. Flushing, Past and Present. 18mo, plates, 1860, pp. 180.

Ser. on Death of Benj. R. Hoogland. 1858. 8vo.

Marcus, Moses. Val. Add. at Parsonage of Christ Ch., Manhasset, 1837. 8vo, pp. 38.

Marsh, Luther R. Gen. Woodhull and his Monuments. (Plates.) 1844. 8vo, pp. 33.

Martin, Jas. S. Adventures of a Rev. Soldier (in Battle of L. I.). Halliwell, Me., 1830. 12mo, pp. 213.

Massachusetts Records of Plymouth Col., 1628–86, 4to, 1851–61.

Mershon, St. L. Twelve Years' Ministry at E. Hampton, April 29, 1866. 8vo, pp. 27.

Minto, Walter, LL.D. (Principal of Acad., Flatbush). Theory of Planets, 1787. (Printed in N. Y.)

Meriam, E. (Br. Heights). Protection against Lightning, 1859. 4to, pp. 15.

Mitchell, S. L., LL.D. Picture of N. Y. (and L. I.), 1807.

Many essays in the Periodicals.

Moore, Thos. Lambert (Hempd.). Ser. in Convention, Nov. 3, 1789. 8vo, pp. 20.

Ser. on Religious Divisions, 1792. 8vo, pp. 14.

Mott, Robt. W. Report on North Hempstead Turnpike, June, 1845. 8vo, pp. 8.

Mulhenberg, Wm. A., D.D. (Flush.). Rebuke of the Lord. 1835. 8vo, pp. 16.

Murphy, H. C. (Br.). Translation of Jacob Steendam's Poems. 1861. 8vo, pp. 69.

Translation of De Vries' Journal. 4to.

Murphy, H. C. Speech in Senate on Ecclesiastical Tenures. 1863. 8vo, pp. 20.

Anthologia of New Netherland (Selyn's, Desille's and Steendam's Poems). 1865. 8vo, pp. 209.

Oration at Tammany Hall, July 4, 1863. 8vo, pp. 67.

Translation and Notes to "Journal of a Voyage to New Netherland, 1679–80." 8vo, 1867.

New Utrecht. Second and Third Reports of Female Bible and Miss. Soc., 1827–8. 12mo, pp. 11.

New York. Journal of the Council of the Colony. 2 vols. folio. 1691–1775–1861.

Journal and Correspondence of Provincial Congress. 2 vols. folio. 1775–7–1842.

Marriage Licenses to 1784. 8vo, 1860, pp. 480.

Nicholl, Henry. Early His. of Suf. Co., Nov. 16, 1865. pp. 18, 8vo. (Read before L. I. His. Soc.)

Nicholls, Walter (Hemp.). Essays and Miscellaneous Writings. 12mo, 1826, pp. 179.

North Hempstead, Catalogue of Library of.

Case of *vs.* Hempstead. Suit for Marshes, 1825. 8vo, pp. 400.

Case of Appellants. Same suit. 1825. 8vo, pp. 150.

Oakey, Rev., P. V. (Jamaica). The War, its Origin, Purpose and our Duty. 8vo, 1861, pp. 23.

O'Callaghan, Dr. E. B. (Albany). His. of New Netherland, 2 vol. 8vo, 1846–8.

O'Callaghan, Dr. E. B. (Albany). Documentary History of N. Y. 4 vols. 4to and 8vo. 1849–51.
Colonial History of N. Y. 13 vols. 4to, 1853–61.
Calendar of Land Papers, 1643–1803. 8vo, pp. 1087. 1864.
Register of New Netherland, 1626–74. 8vo. 1865.
Calendar of N. Y. His. MSS. (Dutch), 1630–64. 4to. 1865.
Calendar of N. Y. His. MSS. (English), 1664–1776. 4to. 1866.

Occum, Rev., Samson (Indian preacher). Religious notions of Montauk Indians (in Mass. His. Soc. Coll.).

Ogden, Dr. Jacob (Jam.) Malignant Sore Throat on L. I. (in N. Y. Mer., Oct. 28, 1769).
Jas. Depeyster. Add. at 50th Ann. of Union Hall Acad. 1842. 8vo, pp. 19.
James Depeyster. Lecture before Jamaica Lyceum on National Character, 1843. 8vo, pp. 32.

Onderdonk, Henry, Jr. Revolutionary Incidents of Queens County. 1846. 12mo, pp. 264.
Revolutionary Incidents of Suffolk and Kings Cos., Battle of L. I., Prison Ships. 1849. 12mo, pp. 268.
Capture and Death of Gen. Nath'l Woodhull. (Letters to J. F. Cooper.) 1848.
Long Island in Olden Times. 1851. 8vo. This was merged into
Queens County in Olden Times. 4to. 1865. pp. 122, and
Suffolk and Kings Cos. in Olden Times (with His. of Dutch churches). 4to. 1866.

Onderdonk, His. Notices of Agriculture of Queens Co. 1862. 8vo, pp. 6. (Reprinted in Trans. of State Ag. Soc.)

Names of Persons and Places, also Surnames and Nicknames, with Bibliography. 1863.

Bibliography of Long Island. 4to. 1866. (In MSS.)

Brief Notices of the Dutch Churches and Ministers in Queens and Kings Cos., published in the Christian Intelligencer, 1865–6–7.

Horatio Gates (Manhasset). Add. to the People of Queens Co., April, 1846. 8vo, pp. 16.

The Income Tax. What is "Income"? &c., &c., July, 1864. 4to, pp. 4.

Ordronnaux, Dr. Jno. (Roslyn). Eulogy on Rev. Zach. Greene, Feb. 10, 1859. 8vo, pp. 50.

Eulogy on Dr. Jno. D. Shelton, of Jamaica, 1863. 8vo.

Osborn, David. Ser. on Death of Jane Augusta Seabury (Jam.), Feb. 2, 1851. 8vo, pp. 22.

Oyster Bay. Statement of Yearly Accounts for 1845. 18mo, pp. 34.

Proceedings of Soc. for Suppressing Vice and Immorality, July 1, 1815.

Proceedings of Meeting opposed to Change of Name, June 22, 1848. 8vo, pp. 15.

Parsons, S. B. (Flush.). History and Culture of the Rose. 1847. 8vo.

Payne, Jno. Howard (East Hampton). Brutus and other Plays. On "E. Hampton" (in Dem. Rev., 1838).

Pemberton, Eben'r. Ser. at Ord. of Walter Wilmot (Jam.), 1738. 8vo, pp. 39.

Exhortation to Minister and People of Jamaica, Oct. 9, 1745. 18mo, pp. 54.

Penny, Joshua (Southold). Life and Adventures. 1815. 8vo, pp. 60 (carried off by the British).

Peterson, F. A. On Maj. Gen. McClellan from 1861 to 1862. 8vo, pp. 26.

Military Review of the Campaign in Virg. and Maryland in 1862. 8vo, pp. 55.

Phillips, Ebenr. (E. Hampton). Ser. on Death of Rev. Aaron Woolworth, D.D.

Pitkins, Jno. R. Price List and Guide Map of Woodhaven. 1854. 8vo, pp. 8.

Porter, E. S., D.D. Ser. at Williamsburg, 1850. 8vo, pp. 29. On Domestic Missions, 1851. 8vo, pp. 30 (at Albany).

Historical Discourse on leaving the old church, Nov. 4, 1866. 8vo, pp. 30. (At Williamsburg.)

Post, Mrs. Lydia Minturn. Personal Recollections of Amer. Revolution. 1859. 12mo, pp. 251.

Potter, Elam. Ser. at Southold on death of Mrs. Martha Horton, Dec. 18, 1792. 8vo, pp. 15.

Price, Nath'l (of Br.). Trial for Rape on Eunice Williamson, Aug. 29, 1797. 8vo, pp. 5.

Prime, Benj. Youngs. Columbia's Glory, 1791. 8vo, pp. 42.

Ebenr. Ser. at Ord. of Abner Brush (Br. Haven), Ju. 15, 1758. pp. 60.

Ebenr. Ser. at Funeral of Mrs. Freelove Wilmot (O. Bay), Feb. 27, 1744. 18mo, pp. 95.

Ebenr. Ser. at Ord. of Jonas Barber and Jno. Darbie, Nov. 10, 1757 (at Oyster Pond). 12mo, pp. 63.

Prime, Ebner. Ser. to Provincial Soldiers at Huntington, May 7, 1759.

Nathaniel S. Ser. on Intemperance, at Aquebogue, Nov. 5, 1811. 8vo, pp. 40.

Nathaniel S. His. of Long Island (in its Religious Aspects) to 1845. 12mo, pp. 420.

Prince, Wm. & Sons. Annual Catalogue of Fruit and Ornamental Trees, 1823. 18mo, and 1832. pp. 93.

Wm. R. Oration at Hempstead, July 4, 1831. 12mo, pp. 15.

Wm. R. Treatise on the Vine, 1830. 8vo.

Wm. R. Pomological Manual (2d ed.), 1832. 8vo.

Wm. R. Cat. of Fruit Trees (33d ed.), 1843. 8vo, pp. 60.

Wm. R. Select. Cat. of Trees (37th ed.), 1849–50. 8vo, pp. 22.

L. Bradford. Sketch of Agricultural His. of Queens Co., 1861. 8vo, pp. 15.

Queens Co. Lyceum By-Laws, 1832. 8vo, pp. 7.

Journal of Proceedings of Supervisors, from 1854 to date.

Constitution and Officers of Agricultural Society, 1819. 8vo, pp. 8.

Proceedings of Agricultural Society, 1862 (and other years). 8vo, pp. 8.

Twenty-fifth Ann. Report of Ag. Soc. (plate), by Jno. Harrold, 1866. 8vo, pp. 39.

Agricultural Society has had Addresses as follows:

Wm. T. McCoun, Hempstead, Oct. 13, 1842. 8vo, pp. 16.

Agricultural Society Addresses.—Continued.

Queens Co. D. S. Dickinson, Hempstead, Oct. 17, 1843. 8vo, pp. 28.

Gab. Furman, Jamaica, Oct. 10, 1844. 8vo, pp. 24.

John S. Skinner, Hempstead, Oct. 9, 1845. 8vo, pp. 18.

D. P. Gardner, Flushing, Oct. 9, 1846. 8vo, pp. 20.

John A. King, LL.D., Jamaica, Oct. 6, 1848. 8vo, pp. 24.

John A. Dix, Jamaica, Oct. 2, 1851. 8vo, pp. 20.

Chas. King, LL.D., Flushing, Sept. 29, 1852. 8vo, pp. 23.

James J. Mapes, Hempstead, Oct. 6, 1853. 8vo, pp. 18.

Caleb Lyon, Jamaica, Sept. 28, 1854. 8vo. pp. 11.

Geo. W. Clinton, Flushing, Sept. 20, 1855. 8vo, pp. 16.

D. R. F. Jones, Flushing, Sept. 22, 1858. 8vo, pp. 21.

Wm. H. Onderdonk, Hempstead, Sept. 15, 1859. 8vo, pp. 22.

Maj. M. R. Patrick, Jamaica, Sept. 19, 1860. 8vo, pp. 28.

R. C. McCormick, Flushing, Oct. 3, 1861. 8vo, pp. 21.

A. B. Conger, Jamaica, Oct. 5, 1864. 8vo, pp. 22.

Ralph, G. W. (Flush.) Add. to 1st Congressional District, July, 1852. 8vo, pp. 14.

Redfield. A Tale of Long Island. 1824.

Ref. D. Ch. on L. I. Const. and Add. of Education Soc. of. Instituted May 1, 1828. 12mo, pp. 18.

Renne, T. W. (Newtown). Add. to Young Men's Debating Society, Feb. 22, 1825. pp. 12.

Reynolds, Sam'l. His. of Williamsburg, 1852. 12mo, pp. 137 (reprint from Directory).

Rhode Island Colony Records, 1636–1776. 8vo, 9 v 1856–64.

Riker, Jas., Jr. Annals of Newton, 1852. 8vo, pp. 437.

Riverhead Temp. Soc. First Annual Report, Jan. 1, 1831. 8vo, pp. 10.

Rubel, J. C. (Minister, of Flatbush). On Unlawful Proceedings of Church Meetings in N.Y., 1784. 12mo, pp. 19.

Romeyn, Benj. (Review). "Tombs of the Martyrs" (plate), July 4, 1839. 8vo, pp. 7.

Sabine, Lorenzo. Lives of the Loyalists, 1847. 8vo, 2d ed., 2 v. 8vo, 1864. (L. I. Tories.)

Sag Harbor. Report of Bible Society, Nov. 1, 1857. 8vo, pp. 11.

Constitution of Literary Society, adopted Feb. 9, 1807. 18mo, pp. 11.

Sands, Joshua (Br.). On Filling up a Pond (Wallabout), 1826–7. 12mo, pp. 11.

Elisha (Jamaica). Ser. on the Ironsides, July 19, 1863.

Savage, Jas., LL.D. Genealogical Dict. of New England Settlers. 4 v. 8vo, 1860–2.

Sayres, Sam'l W. Ser. on Death of Mrs. Betsy Cunningham, Dec. 29, 1861. 8vo, pp. 14.

Schenck, Wm. Ser. on Death of Noah Wetmore, Mar. 10, 1796, Sag Harbor.

Schoonmaker, R. L. Ser. on Death of Mrs. Sarah J Treadwell, 1851. 8vo, pp. 9.

Schroeder, Rev. J. F. (Flushing). Oration at St. Paul's College, July 5, 1841. 8vo.

Schroeder, J. F. Circular of St. Ann's Hall, Flushing, 1840. 8vo.

Seabury, Samuel (Flush.). Study of the Classics, April 18, 1831. 12mo.

Seaman, Arden (Jerusalem). Genealogy of the Seaman Family. Folio, 1866.

Selyns, Henry (Minister at Br.). Poems. See Murphy's Anthologia.

Shelton, Rev. F. W. (Jam.). Two Lectures before Huntington Library Association. 1850. 12mo, pp. 36.

Kushow property; Tinnicum Papers; Trollopiad, 1837.

Rector of St. Bardolphs. 1852; Peeps from a Belfry. 1855.

Crystalline; Up the River; Salander and the Dragon. 1850.

Sherburn, And. Memoirs of a Pensioner of the Navy of Rev. 1828. 12mo, pp. 262.

Sleight, H. C. (Editor of L. I. Farmer). Cat. of his Cir. Library. Jam., 12mo, pp. 24. *No year*.

Smith, Wm. History of Province of N. Y. to 1762. 2 v. 8vo. 1829.

Egbert, Tangier. Speech in Assembly on Union Resolutions. 1851.

Rev. J. Carpenter (Flush.). Thanksgiving Ser., Nov. 28, 1861. 18mo, pp. 16.

Southampton, Notice of, in Literary World. Oct. 2, 1847. 4to.

Spafford, H. G. Gazetteer of State of N. Y. 1813. 8vo. 2d Ed. 1824. 8vo. Maps.

Spear, T., D.D. (Br.). Two Sermons for the Times. 1861. 8vo, pp. 56.

Spencer, Ichabod S., D.D. A Pastor's Sketches. 12mo. 1851. 2d Series, 1853. 12mo.

Sermons. 2 v. 12mo. 1855.

Elihu (Jam.). The Dissenting Interest in Middle Colonies: Origin and Growth of Episcopacy.

Spooner, Alden (Br.). Cat. of his Cir. Library. 12mo, pp. 24.

Br. Cir. Lib. 1821. 12mo, pp. 34.

Cultivation of the Vine, and Wine Making. 1846. 12mo; On taking a Newspaper.

Sprague, Wm. B., D.D. Add. at opening of Br. Female Academy, May 4, 1846. 8vo.

Annals of Amer. Pulpit. 7 v. 8vo. 1856–65. (It has Lives of L. I. Ministers.)

Spooner, Alden J. Memorial in relation to Ferries.

Wood's, L. I. With Memoirs of the Author. 4to, & folio, pp. 208. 1865.

Furman's Brooklyn, with Memoirs of the Author. 4to, pp. xxxiv. 117; xxxix. 1865.

Steendam, Jacob. Flatlands. Poems. See Murphy's Anthologia.

Stiles, Dr. H. R. Interment of Amer. Patriots who died in Prison Ships. 1865. 8vo, pp. 246.

Letters from Prison Ships and British Prisons of the Revolution. 1865. 8vo, pp. 49.

Storrs, R. S., Jr., D.D. Lectures before Brooklyn Institute. 8vo. 1857. pp. 338.

Miss. Ser. at Cleveland, Oct. 1, 1861. 8vo, pp. 45.

St. John, Peter. Poetic Relation of Capture of the Congregation of Middlesex, July 22, 1781. 18mo.

Strong, Thos. M., D. D. His. of Flatbush. Map & Plates. 12mo. 1842. pp. 178.

Thos. C. (Newtown). Ser. on Death of Dr. Stoothoff.

Stuart, Isaac W. Life of Nathan Hale. (Taken on L. I.) 1856. 12mo, pp. 230. 2d Ed.

Suffolk Co. Constitution of Bible Soc. Adopted Oct. 3, 1815. 12mo, pp. 5.

Qualification of a Dancing Master. 12mo, pp. 8. *No date.*

Com. School Arithmetic. Riverhead, 1850. 12mo, pp. 252.

Confession of Congregational Churches of L. I. 1823.

Sabbath School Association & Ann. Meeting. Ju. 14, 15, and 16, 1864. 8vo, pp. 16.

Talbot, Silas. Life (in Prison Ship). 1803. 18mo, pp. 147.

Talmadge, Benj. Memoir of, prepared by himself. 1858. 8vo, pp. 70.

Taylor, Geo. (Br.) Martyrs on Prison Ships. Map, 1855. 8vo, pp. 64.

Teale, Thos. P. Add. on bat. of Br. before Marion Chap. Aug. 29, 1848. (In L. I. Star.)

Thompson, A. G. Petition for L. I. Canal. With Map, May 25, 1825. 18mo, pp. 5.

Documents on L. I. Canal for Legislature. pp. ix.; 27 1826. 18mo.

Thompson, B. F. His. of L. I. 1839. 8vo, pp. 536. 2d Ed. 2 v. 8vo. 1843.

Titus, Rev. Jacob (negro). Oration before Af. Ben. Soc. Br. In L. I. Star, Feb. 18, 1818.

Townsend, Jas. C. (O. Bay). Memorial of Jno. Henry & Richard Townsend. 12mo. 1865.

Union Hall Gazette. Jamaica. Fortnightly.

Valentine, D. T. Manual of Corporation of N. Y. 1842, to date.

Valk, Dr. Wm. (Flush.) On the Non-organization of Congress. Feb. 21, 1856. 8vo, pp. 14.

Remarks on Diet for Convalescents. 1843. 8vo, pp. 49.

Van Cott, J. M. (Br.) Discourse on Jas. Madison, July 28, 1836. 8vo.

Van Doren, Rev. Isaac. Prospectus of School in Brooklyn. 12mo, pp. 12.

W. H. Ser. on Death of Rich. W. Redfield. 1847. 12mo, pp. 26.

Van Dyke, H. J. (Br.) Moses, servant of God. Ser. Aug. 15, 1858. 8vo, pp. 24.

Thanksgiving Ser., Nov. 29, 1860. 8vo, pp. 24.

Ser. on Abolitionism in 1st Pres. Ch., Dec. 9, 1860. 8vo, pp. 38.

Vanderbilt, Jno., Jr. Masonic Oration at Br., on presenting Vase, Dec. 28, 1807. 8vo, pp. 41.

Vanderbilt, Jno., Jr. Add. in N. Y. for 50 Orphans of Masons, Dec. 27, 1809. 8vo.

Van Pelt, Peter. Oration on Washington, Feb. 22, 1800. 8vo, pp. 24 (in Ch. at Flatbush).

Wallabout. Interment of Remains of 11,500 Martyrs. 1808. 12mo, pp. 96.

Ward, G. A. Battle of L. I., with Map, in Knickerbocker Mag., xiii., 297. 8vo.

Washington, Geo. Agricultural Tour on L. I., April 20-5, 1790. See Lossing.

Watson, Winslow C. The Plains of L. I. 1860. 8vo, pp. 23.

Webb, Edwin, M.D. (Hemp'd). Oration, July 4, 1830. 12mo, pp. 14.

Weeks, Refine. Wm. Penn and other Poems. 1824. 12mo, pp. 192.

West, N., Jr. (Br.). Ser. in 2d Presb. Ch., Nov. 28, 1861. 8vo, pp. 39.

Wetmore, Noah, of Setauket, Ser. on Death of. Sept. 13, 1797.

Whitaker, Epher (Southold). New Fruits from an Old Field. 1866. (Essays.)

Whitman, Walter. Leaves of Grass. 18mo, 1856; new edition, 1867, with additions, 12mo, $3.

Wickham, Martha. Sea Spray, a Long Island Village. 1857. 12mo, pp. 460.

Williams, Mrs. Cath. Life of Lt. Olney (in Bat. of Br.). 1839. 12mo, pp. 312.

Williamsburg. By-Laws of Farmers' and Citizens' Bank. 1852. 18mo, pp. 19.

Third Ann. Report of Bible Soc. (names). 1847, pp. 12.

Willis, Thos. (Jericho). Doctrine of Quakers, in Reply to Hibbard. 1812. 18mo, pp. 141.

Wilson, Hugh N. (S. Hampton). Manual of Church Membership. 1843.

Wilson, Hugh N. (S. Hampton). Ser. on Death of Rev. Amzi Francis (Br. Hampton). 1846. 8vo, pp. 16.
Sabbath-School Add. at Sag Harbor.
Ser. on Death of President Harrison.
Ser. on Death of Rev. Sam'l Huntting.
Thanksgiving Sermon.
Duty of the Church to her Poor Members.

Wilmot, Mrs. Freelove (Jam.). Journal. (See Prime.) 1744. 18mo.

Winter, Gale & Co.'s Catalogue of Trees in Flushing Nursery. 1843-4. 8vo, pp. 92.

Wood, Silas. Sketch of First Settlement of L. I. 1824. 8vo, pp. 66.
Enlarged edition. 1828. 8vo, pp. 184.
Sketch of Geography and Rev. Hist. of Huntington. 1824. 8vo, pp. 30. (Printed at Washington.)
Claims of Huntington to Islands in South Bay. 1816. 12mo, pp. 16.
Speech on Bill to amend Constitution of U. S. 1826. 8vo.
Speech on Panama Mission. 1826. 8vo.
Letter to 1st Electoral Dist. of N. Y. 1826. 8vo.

Woodbridge, Sylvester. Hist. of Presb. Ch., Hemp'd. 1840. 8vo, pp. 23.

Woodhaven, Plan of Lots in. Map No. 2. Amended April 10, 1855.

Woodward, A. B. On Executive Govt. of U. S. 1809. 8vo. (Printed at Flatbush.)

Woolworth, Rev. Aaron, D.D. Revival of Religion in E. Hampton, 1764, by Buell, his Life, his Sons, his Daughters, and Revival in East and Bridge Hampton in 1800. 12mo, pp. 144. 1808.

Woolworth, Rev. Aaron, D.D. Ser. at Ord. of Henry Fuller, Smithtown, Oct. 23, 1816.

Worthington, Wm. Catalogue of his Cir. Lib., Br. 1832. 12mo, pp. 20.

Youngs, Daniel K. (O. Bay). Culture of Onions. 1862. 8vo, pp. 6. Premium Essay.

INDEX.

THE END.

www.ingramcontent.com/pod-product-compliance
Lightning Source LLC
LaVergne TN
LVHW020930110826
845150LV00004B/812

* 9 7 8 1 4 2 5 5 5 2 9 6 1 *